WHITMAN, MELVILLE, CRANE, AND THE LABORS OF AMERICAN POETRY

Whitman, Melville, Crane, and the Labors of American Poetry

Against Vocation

PETER RILEY

OXFORD
UNIVERSITY PRESS

OXFORD
UNIVERSITY PRESS

Great Clarendon Street, Oxford, OX2 6DP,
United Kingdom

Oxford University Press is a department of the University of Oxford.
It furthers the University's objective of excellence in research, scholarship,
and education by publishing worldwide. Oxford is a registered trade mark of
Oxford University Press in the UK and in certain other countries

Published in the United States of America by Oxford University Press
198 Madison Avenue, New York, NY 10016, United States of America

British Library Cataloguing in Publication Data
Data available

Library of Congress Control Number: 2018964543

ISBN 978-0-19-883625-4

Printed and bound by
CPI Group (UK) Ltd, Croydon, CR0 4YY

For Alicia and Rosa

Acknowledgments

What follows was only made possible through the generous guidance of some very gifted and wonderful people. While the kinds of labor and thinking that went into this book altered across states of mind, economic circumstance, and political epoch, what remained constant was the willingness of others to engage with, and comment on, my work. If there's one thing I can say I've learned throughout the process of writing and researching this book, it's that ideas only get better in dialogue with colleagues and friends.

Thank you to my PhD supervisor Fiona Green, as well as to my teachers and examiners at the University of Cambridge: Anne Stillman, Sarah Meer, Tamara Follini, Becca Weir, Ian Patterson, and Lee Jenkins. Later, as Early Career Fellow in American Literature at the University of Oxford, I was lucky enough to receive the intellectual guidance and support of Lloyd Pratt, who was always able to show me the next thought along. I would also like to thank Laura Marcus, Patrick Hayes, Ed Sugden, Hannah Sullivan, Tara Stubbs, Tessa Roynon, Michèle Mendelssohn, Elleke Boehmer, and Kevin Brazil, for the many engaging and enjoyable conversations we had together.

Writing a speculative email to Wyn Kelley in the first year of my PhD was one of the best decisions I made. Her guidance has been a great source of inspiration, and my times staying with her family during research trips in Boston have been some of my happiest. For the friendship and counsel of Mark Storey I am truly grateful: being in the company of his intelligence and wit is one of my favourite pastimes. I also want to thank my mentor and friend Michael Jonik for reading my manuscript so carefully: his suggestions were instrumental in transforming this project into a book. I also owe a significant debt of gratitude to the intellect, friendship and all-round savvy of Tom F. Wright. For the many enriching moments of intellectual exchange we have shared together, I am also very thankful to Jay Grossman, Rodrigo Andrés, Éric Athenot, J. Michelle Coghlan, Cathryn Setz, Katie McGettigan, John Bryant, Mary K. Bercaw Edwards, Sam Otter, Tim Marr, Ed Folsom, Ken Price, Hilary Emmett, Elisa Tamarkin, Natalia Cecire, Michael J. Collins, and Cécile Roudeau.

Against Vocation became a book while I was working as Lecturer in American Literature at the University of Exeter, and I feel blessed to have so many brilliant and supportive colleagues. I have become a better Americanist scholar by being in the company of Sinéad Moynihan, Paul

Williams, Ellen McWilliams, Joanna Freer, and James Harding. Laura Salisbury has been, and continues to be, a key intellectual influence on my work. Laura's ability to see the shape of an idea so clearly (and be so generous as to then ask all the right questions) has been a gift. Karen Edwards, Regenia Gagnier, Jo Gill and Vike Plock, also all generously read and provided valuable feedback on various sections of the manuscript. And through their comradeship and friendship, the following people have all enriched this book by making my time at Exeter such a pleasure (in no particular order): Sam North, Daisy Hay, Andy Brown, Henry Power, Chris Campbell, Benedict Morrison, Florian Stadtler, Mark Steven, Treasa De Loughry, Felicity Gee, John Bolin, Ayesha Mukherjee, Helen Hanson, Simon Rennie, Jane Feaver, Debra Ramsay, Angelique Richardson, Andrew Rudd, Philip Schwyzer, Naomi Howell, Eric Lybeck, Beci Carver, Ranita Chatterjee, Abram Foley, Rob Turner, Paul Young, Jason Hall, and Adam Watt. Thank you all.

I also want to acknowledge the foundations and institutions that made much of this work possible, specifically the Arts and Humanities Research Council (AHRC); Clare College, Cambridge; the Rothermere American Institute; Linacre College, Oxford; and the Melville Society. And thank you to those at my current institution, the University of Exeter, for granting me the time and space to finish this project. Thanks also to the helpful and considerate staff of the David M. Rubenstein Rare Book & Manuscript Library at Duke University; the Special Collections & University Archives of the University of Iowa; the Rare Book & Manuscript Library at Columbia University; the Beinecke Rare Book & Manuscript Library at Yale University; the Manuscript Division of the Library of Congress; The Museum of Modern Art Archives; and in particular to Mark Gaipa at the Modernist Journals Project for his enthusiastic assistance and support. Portions of this book have appeared, in earlier versions, in the edited collections *The Cambridge History of American Working-Class History* (Cambridge University Press) and *Melville as Poet: The Art of 'Pulsed Life'* (Kent State University Press), as well as the journals *Leviathan: A Journal of Melville Studies* (Johns Hopkins University Press) and the *Walt Whitman Quarterly Review* (University of Iowa Press). I am thankful to the editors of these publications for their feedback and encouragement. I have tried to incorporate, as far as possible, the generous and helpful comments from my anonymous readers at Oxford University Press. I would also like to express my gratitude to the commissioning editor Jacqueline Norton for supporting this project from the outset, as well as to Aimee Wright, Markcus Sandanraj, and Howard Emmens for seeing it through to print.

For their care, love, and forgiveness, I am also heavily indebted to Ellie Stedall, Jim Blackstone, Merlin Sheldrake, Katya Herman, Stuart Sheppard, Patrick Kingsley, Sophie Crawford, Grace Jackson, Martin Dubois, Greg Seach, Alex Owen, Roisin Dunnett, Matilda Wnek, Alice Farren-Bradley, Tom Neenan, Nish Kumar, and Ed Gamble. This book, and a good deal besides, would also not have been possible without Tom Evans, who combines the deepest intelligence with the best sense of humour. And I am lucky to know Steve Graves, Mariangela Milioto, and their children, Leo (my godson), Frank, and Max: your long-standing friendship, generosity and wisdom has kept me going.

Thank you to my mum, Claudia Riley, for the encouragement, love, and support you have always shown me. You are an inspiration and guide to many people, and that goes for me too. Thank you also to my dad, Michael Riley, for his continuing love and support. Most of all, I want to express my admiration and gratitude to my wife and comrade Alicia Dell Williamson. In relation to this book, I have benefited from the clarity of her thinking, her patience and brilliance as a reader and editor, and the brightness with which she approaches everything. In relation to my life, it is thanks to her that I now know something of happiness and fulfillment. Our beautiful daughter Rosa has just learned to walk and is currently watching me write this from under the coffee table. You are both unspeakably wonderful, and this, for what it's worth, is for you.

Contents

List of Figures

Introduction

Whitman's Wallpaper and Poetry's Archives of Distraction

While searching through Duke University's "Walt Whitman Papers," I came upon this curious artifact (Fig. I.1). Labelled "1855 or before," it is a fragment (most likely a sample) of wallpaper dated to the year that Whitman published the first edition of *Leaves of Grass*. Turn it over, and you find a draft of what would become the final poem of that edition, later called "Great are the Myths." At first glance a seemingly innocuous find, and yet something in me could also not help but feel a degree of incongruity in this trace of the poet's early career. What was the Whitman of 1855 doing with a sample of wallpaper? Did he really have such questionable taste in interior design? No, it was easier to imagine that this rather ostentatious bit of decor was just something he randomly picked up in a moment of inspiration—an eminently dismissible item that just happened by chance to find its way into the archive of a celebrated American poet.

The question is, of course, why would such a seemingly insignificant scrap of ephemera come preloaded with certain discomforts? What unspoken assumptions quietly urged me to distance Whitman the poet from an unassuming piece of wallpaper? On reflection, it became increasingly apparent that my instinctive reaction constituted a problematic vestige of an oft-challenged yet enduring archival hermeneutic: the desire to dissociate poetry from the seemingly trivial contingencies that so often define its production. This cheap manufactured wallpaper, with its finials and foliage, hints at bourgeois affectation and trifling domestic preoccupation. And the iconic loafing poet of the 1855 *Leaves of Grass*, with defiant hand on hip, open top button, and cocked hat, didn't suffer from those, did he?

And yet, the pattern on the wallpaper—green leaves and other finials—also began to seem surprisingly consonant with the very patterns embossed

Fig. I.1. A sample of wallpaper with Whitman's draft of "Great are the Myths" on the back. "Materialism": manuscript notes from Volume 44 in Walt Whitman Papers, David M. Rubenstein Rare Book & Manuscript Library, Duke University.

on the front of the book Whitman was about to publish (Fig. I.2). This unexpected link then spurred a re-examination of the archives that eventually revealed the extent to which Whitman was diverted by other, apparently trivial extra-literary concerns while writing *Leaves*. In fact, his substitution of wallpaper for the traditional notebook was by no means random: in the rush to ready his house for the New York house-trading period, or "The Moving Season" in May (the deal that would actually raise the money to fund his prospective book of poems), it turns out that Whitman the Brooklyn real estate developer was decorating his houses *as* he decorated *Leaves of Grass*. What at first appeared to be a seemingly arbitrary archival fragment ultimately provided an alternative documentary perspective on a creative process that

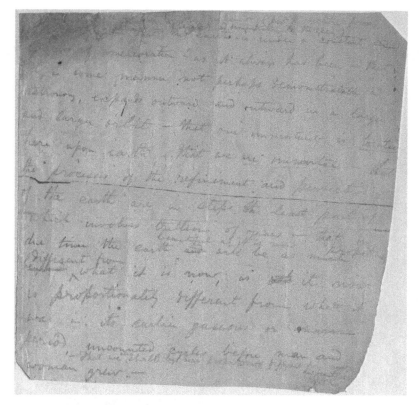

Fig. I.1. Continued

produced a book of poems while distracted by other, decidedly non-poetic forms of labor.[1]

This is not how poetry is supposed to work. As Robert Frost once neatly put it, the poet is meant to articulate "a momentary stay against confusion" (777); or, at the very least, maintain some kind of detachment from

[1] Throughout this book, and across a range of cultural and philosophical fields, I employ the terms "work" and "labor" interchangeably, as any strict conceptual distinction between the terms would be detrimental to the purposes of my discussion. Broadly speaking, however, I try to adopt the critical self-consciousness developed by post-Marxist philosophy (and particularly the work of Jacques Rancière), which is careful to display a historiographical awareness when deploying various familiar terms. So in Rancière's writing, "labor," "worker," "proletarian," and "people" always appear accompanied by a modifier so as to draw attention to their tendency to drift towards convenient theoretical abstraction. See his various usages in *Staging the People: The Proletarian and his Double* (2011).

Fig. I.2. The front cover of the first edition of *Leaves of Grass* (Brooklyn, NY, 1855). University of Iowa Libraries, Special Collections & University Archives.

quotidian concerns in order to effectively pursue their higher calling. In a widely shared 2013 comic strip (Fig. I.3), Grant Snider offers a familiar gloss on the supposedly divided nature of poetic careers.

Encoded into each of these biographical representations is an aspirational dynamic of competing priorities, one that implies a strict hierarchy

DAY JOBS OF THE POETS

GRANT SNIDER

Fig. I.3. Grant Snider, "Day Jobs of the Poets" (2013). Notice that Frost himself has been provided with a protective ring of bunnies to help shield him from that ultimately threatening incursion: the day job.

and division of labor. The charm and humor of the piece relies upon the implicit contrast of two apparently discrete forms of production that always makes the poet's non-poetic labors look variously disposable, pointless, alienating, unfulfilling, uncreative, and unexceptional—interruptions to the poet's "real" work, the work of poetry. This is why William Carlos Williams the paediatrician points a medical instrument at a baby in an almost semi-negligent fashion; why Neruda the diplomat half-heartedly meets no one in particular, slightly misjudging the tone with those over-eager flowers; why Eliot stares away from his paperwork and towards us; why Stevens looks out of his office window at his blackbird(s); and why

Angelou leans her microphone away from the paying public, towards the implied sanctuary of her own interiority. In other words, Snider's comic strip manifests a cultural logic that tends to automatically frame non-vocational—or what I want to think of in terms of "contingent" labor—as the necessary sacrifice that contaminates and frustrates the righteous progress of that apparently purest of callings: poet.

Something else is going on here too. While Snider's comic is ostensibly about the past careers of canonical poets, it is, of course, also about most of us. Working increasingly unsatisfying and precarious jobs—dreaming of those endlessly deferred creative aspirations—these poets simultaneously stand in as exemplary, vocationally frustrated subjects of late capitalism. Audrey Freedman coined the term "contingent labor" in the mid-1980s to describe the increasing presence of "conditional and transitory employment arrangements as initiated by a need for labor" (35). Depicted as always implicitly struggling against the economic necessity of having to engage with this kind of work, these representative poets provide the neoliberal "precariat" with some (much-needed) consolation.[2] The poet's own (successful) vocational struggle promises the very possibility of personal fulfilment and eventual overcoming: the fact that T. S. Eliot had to work as a bank clerk and still managed to write *The Waste Land* offers at least some solace that one or two of us might yet produce something meaningful; or become someone meaningful.

The problem is that this mollifying narrative often comes at a cost. According to social anthropologist Francesca Sidoti, employers in the post-2008 context tend to cast contingent work in precisely these reassuring terms: as a prerequisite and necessary "rite-of-passage" that will eventually lead to some kind of personal fulfilment (43). This is a narrative that says: essentially, it does not really matter if you find yourself working without basic rights, protections, and benefits because contingent labor is an integral part of the natural meritocratic struggle towards discovering and/or consummating one's true calling. After all, "we all had to struggle once."[3] Framed within the terms of a common-sense work ethic, the

---

[2] "Precariat" studies have gained momentum in the last few years in the wake of the several post-Occupy movements. See for example Guy Standing's *The Precariat: The New Dangerous Social Class* (London: Bloomsbury, 2011); or André Singer's "Rebellion in Brazil: Social and Political Complexion of the June Events," in *New Left Review* (85): 19–37. Singer uses Ruy Braga's definition of "precariat": "the mass formed by unskilled or semi-skilled workers who rapidly enter and leave the labor market." See Ruy Braga, "Sob a sombre do precariado," in Ermínia Maricato et al., *Cidades rebeldes* (2013): 82.

[3] See Francesca Sidoti's "Untangling the Narratives of Precarious Work: An Auto-Ethnography," in *Social Alternatives 34* (4): 43–9: "The narrative of waiter-makes-movie star is a popular one in contemporary society. The precarious work within this narrative is constituted as a rite-of-passage" (7).

neo-Calvinistic parable of the poet at work plays a key role in affirming the exploitative logic of the neoliberal job market. Broadcasting an exceptional vocational faith that your (usually) immaterial satisfaction will come in the (endlessly deferred) hereafter, the "Day Jobs of the Poets" topos stands in as both apology and alibi for the increasing insecurity of work, including the slide towards the casualization of contracts in an ever more "flexible" short-term "gig economy."[4] As a distraction to the mythic main event, contingent labor becomes a fait accompli, an inevitable nuisance that the heroic poet either struggles against or keeps at bay—but never manages to reclaim or reimagine.

Tellingly, the poet persists as a potent icon of vocation in the popular imaginary even as the popularity and marketability of poetry itself has continued to wane. Supposedly engaged in a discrete and exalted form of creative labor performed without reference to moneymaking, the poet epitomizes the value of immaterial rewards, providing a cultural coping mechanism for a society in which there is no correlation between material and spiritual satisfactions. In many ways, the American poet remains the representative of vocation par excellence, doing a kind of cultural work that merely reconfirms the Romantic myth of poetry as politically and economically exempt. Ralph Waldo Emerson set out the familiar oppositional terms as early as 1844:

> Doubt not, O poet, but persist. Say 'it is in me, and shall out' . . . God wills that thou abdicate a manifold and duplex life. Thou shalt lie close hid with nature, and canst not be afforded to the Capitol or the Exchange.
>
> ("The Poet," 283)

According to Emerson, the "manifold and duplex" distractions presented by other forms of activity fundamentally encumber the emergence of poetic vocation. Indeed, such a higher calling depends upon the abdication of social and economic responsibilities that are presented as arbitrary, man-made artifices. It is only in lying "close hid with nature" that the individual genius might inhabit that necessary space of repose and begin fulfilling his (because he is nearly always coded masculine) exceptional, God-given destiny. Of course, Emerson's provocation initially sounds like a challenge to the emerging capitalist order: a poetic soul rejecting reductive commercial valuations of his work, resisting corrupting influences, and locating true compensation in the spiritual gratifications of calling. Upon closer inspection, though, Emerson's ideas pose no threat to the status quo at all. Instead, as an icon of vocational fulfilment, the American

---

[4] See Mark Fisher's discussion of "no long term" in *Capitalist Realism: Is There No Alternative?* (2008), 32.

poet reinforces a persistent reactionary myth of competitive self-realization that says: the contingencies presented by your political and economic environment are an irrelevance—a trivial distraction—because the true poet, backed by a thoroughgoing Emersonian persistence and self-reliance, will always eventually out.

The proverbial poet thus provides a mechanism for implicitly disparaging anyone who finds themselves unable to rise above their immediate material circumstances, while simultaneously diminishing the contingent labors they perform. Such a propensity, I would suggest, encodes a very particular kind of politics. Dean Morse, in *The Peripheral Worker* (1969), identified what he viewed as a foundational distinction that had, since the early nineteenth century, characterized the division of labor in the United States. In what remains a fairly accurate portrait of the present, Morse argued that it was always representatives of difference who shouldered the burden of the most disposable, precarious, and contingent roles within the workforce:

> the basic drama has continued to be enacted, the only change being in cast [. . .] It always remained proper that irregular, casual, part-time, intermittent work should be performed by the 'outsider' who is by definition biologically inferior. (29)

Presented as fundamentally antithetical to contingent labor, the embattled career of the poet consequently stands in not only as a topos of exemption but also as a means of political and social stratification. As a case in point, notice the ways in which Snider's attempt to include diversity in his cartoon—two women (one African American), as well as a Chilean political dissident—goes ever so slightly astray. In each of these cases, the vignette becomes less apt, slightly less amusing: Emily Dickinson's affiliation with the domestic sphere has transformed her into a cat lady (a half-apologetic footnote confirms that there is no definite evidence that Dickinson kept cats);[5] Maya Angelou the nightclub crooner is not working a day job at all (she was at this moment in her working life, also involved in sex work and employed as a fry cook); and Pablo Neruda, emissary of the Chilean Communist Party, has the dubious honor of being the only one here who was exiled (and then possibly murdered) for being in his particular line of work. These representatives of difference (in contrast to the "unmarked" white men) are not quite able to epitomize the clean split that the exceptional discursive parameters of the comic require. That is—as black, female, or foreign—they already tautologically represent the contingent labor they are supposed to be rejecting, causing a malfunction in the comic's default oppositional dialectics. Put another

---

[5] See http://www.incidentalcomics.com/2013/04/day-jobs-of-poets.html.

way, they come pre-entangled with contingent labor they perform—bound to what Pierre Bourdieu would term the "extraordinary realism" of their already embodied difference (381). In a sense, they *are* the contingent work they do (and therefore unable to reject it); and this contrasts with the "universe of possibles" (381) represented by the privileged white male bourgeois poet who is automatically able to hold the incursive contingencies of the marketplace at bay.

This reading of the implicit politics of poetic labor casts rather a different light on the present critical consensus surrounding the vocational nature of the poetic career. In a recent book on the "first books" of modernist poets, Jesse Zuba "treat[s] the representation of career as the product of a diverse set of practices geared toward the affirmation of vocation and the construction of authority at every step of the way" (8). It is exactly this sense of an inexorable vocational determinism, defined unilaterally as being in competition with a "diverse set of practices" and funnelling towards a final "affirmation", that I want to be more politically cautious about. Indeed, I want to trouble the assumptions that undergird a statement that can claim:

> whether, like Jorie Graham, employed to teach creative writing in a university, or, like Wallace Stevens, to run a commercial company, all authors know that, ultimately, the poet's work is the poem.   (Crawford, 267)

Against Vocation historicizes, and presents an alternative account to, the exceptional poetic labor that underpins this kind of affirmatory thinking. Incorporating the always politically-freighted and most often overlooked workaday ephemera of three canonical U.S. Romantic poets—Walt Whitman, Herman Melville, and Hart Crane—this book offers a re-examination of celebrated literary careers that fundamentally challenges their enduring status as triumphant icons of vocation. The poetry of Whitman, Melville, and Crane, I argue, does not constitute the formal inscription of an implicitly antagonistic poetic labor struggling (against contingent work) towards the fulfilment of exceptional calling. Instead, their writing comes pre-entangled with a variety of apparently lesser labors, giving form to a distracted drift that is in fact irretrievable within confirmatory conceptions of personal calling. Ousting poetic production from its default sheltered habitat of exemption and repose, this book refigures the work of the poet as always equivocating at the emerging thresholds of divisions and hierarchies of labor. In so doing, I suggest, it also begins the work of unfastening the very logic upon which our seemingly inevitable capitalist future depends.

* * *

Christopher Wilson has described the figureheads of nineteenth-century U.S. Romanticism as all exhibiting a distinctive "vocational anxiety." "The problem for the Romantics," he writes, "had continued to be one of 'vocation'—not merely of 'jobs' but of occupational roles that American intellectuals could find socially potent and satisfying" (8). Reinforcing British Romantic antinomies between the inspired individual calling and "mere" industry—and increasingly apprehensive about what Ann Douglas has famously described as the "feminization" of contemporary American writing—these writers tended to gravitate towards particular incarnations of the transcendent intellectual (85). Variations on this theme include Emerson's poet "close hid with nature," Whitman's loafing persona in *Leaves of Grass*, and the "chamber in a fine old farmhouse—a mile from any other dwelling" that Melville imagines as the right place to write of "Hawthorne and his Mosses" (*Piazza*, 239).

As several scholars have pointed out, these vocational anxieties were compounded by a variety of legal, economic, and infrastructural uncertainties that defined the literary marketplace in the antebellum period. Chief among these difficulties was the lack of an international copyright law, which made it much cheaper to print pirated British works than those of American authors (this meant that Charles Dickens could become a celebrity while home-grown writers such as Poe and Hawthorne were often forced to publish anonymously). Added to this was the fact that at least until 1853, when according to Meredith McGill "literary markets became centralized and literary culture became stratified" (3), it was impossible to establish anything like a national literary reputation because of a basic lack of distribution networks. Given the nature of the medium, the situation for a would-be poet (even after 1853) was always going to be challenging. As William Charvat explains, "Longfellow and Whittier notwithstanding, poetry is and always has been primarily an avocation— an amateur activity rather than a professional one." Throughout the nineteenth century, poetry was predominantly "issued by the local printer, in pamphlet form, at the author's expense," and "continued to be, for the most part, something that was not marketed but inflicted on friends and libraries" (33).[6] Those who aligned with the U.S. Romantic or Transcendentalist tradition always had to contend with an inescapable political and

---

[6] Charvat points out that the "Fireside Poets" were the exception to this rule. According to John Timberman Newcomb, poets such as Longfellow, Bryant, and Whittier were so successful that they helped "establish a distinctive antimodern account of literary value, claiming independence from local and material contingencies and insisting on fidelity to established traditions, formal conventions, and universal moral laws." Such poets "paradoxically remained so dominant in the nation's literary culture that their great age registered as the obsolescence of the entire generation of poetry" (*Would*, 4).

economic inevitability: without patronage or personal means, the poet, by necessity, was compelled to reverse Emerson's injunction to abdicate the manifold and duplex life—and take a job. This particular political and economic reality was integral to determining the contours of the various "transcendent ideals" that emerged over the following decades (and well into the twentieth century); such ideals "compensated for the realities of the Custom House, the vagaries of the marginal life, the feeling that one was only a sojourner in civilization" (Wilson, 9). With reference to Hart Crane's later place in this history of U.S. Romanticism, Harold Bloom has suggested that "Crane's quest was for agonistic supremacy, against Eliot, in order to join Whitman, Dickinson, Melville in the American Pantheon" (xvi). This particular formulation—the Romantic search for "agonistic supremacy"—also seems to aptly characterize the challenge presented by wage labor. Whitman, Melville, and Crane stand out because, without secure personal finances, they all had to contend with the realities of work. The archives of their working lives consequently share a common trait: they refer to labors that have been, by default, cast as fundamentally incompatible with the work that canonical Romantic poets might be reasonably expected to perform. Whitman, Melville, and Crane were all employed, at one time or another, in contingent positions with uncomfortably direct ties to "the Capitol and the Exchange": Melville as a politically vulnerable deputy Customs inspector; Whitman as real estate dealer who was not quite an artisan and not quite an entrepreneur; and Crane as a junior copywriter who wrote variously about the merits of hot water heaters, lead paint, and cheese. What these mere moneymaking labors have in common is that they have always been impossible for critics to reconcile with these poets' exceptional callings. They are by default cast as compromises and encumbrances: the agonistic reinforcing dialectical counterparts to otherwise exemplary careers.

Primarily then, I am interested in uncovering and refiguring these poets' involvement in especially illegible and politically compromising forms of work. This is why I do not focus on Whitman's work as an editor, journalist, farmer, or teacher, or novelist; or delve into Melville's personal experiences with teaching or whaling; or seek to recuperate any inherent creative value in Crane's copywriting. Each of these scenarios has a tendency to enter into an all too cozy relationship with poetic calling—adjusting and aligning themselves with the related print cultural or educational sphere (teacher, journalist, editor, copywriter); benign pastoral scene (farmer); or the kind of work that is immediately relatable to subject matter (whaling, sailing). One of the most interesting aspects of Whitman's real estate dealings is just how often biographers and critics (and Whitman himself) rushed to transform this contingent, market-bound activity into the more legible and artisanal work of a Thoreauvian house-builder or carpenter."[7] And how frequently Melville's final years have been portrayed as a personal tragedy of frustrated calling; and how often Crane has been remembered for raging against "the quotidian mercantile forces that seemed bent on destroying his peace" (Mariani, 98). This book resists any such retrospective archival sorting towards more recognizable poetic careers. In doing so, it provides a corrective to the ongoing critical urge to implicitly dismiss contingent labor out of hand—as a trifling distraction to the main event.

Even archival approaches that explicitly seek to recuperate extra-literary labor tend to ascribe to this vocationally oriented perspective. Take Leslie Elizabeth Eckel's *Atlantic Citizens: Nineteenth-Century American Writers at Work in the World* (2013). Eckel "considers the records of [. . .] author's written statements and oral performances that have gone relatively unnoticed—and in some cases, unpublished—due to their extra-literary nature. Transcripts of speeches, newspaper articles, editorial columns, personal journals and letters, teaching notes, juvenile magazines, and critical reviews all can serve as clues to the missing pieces of these writers' multifaceted vocational personae" (14). She claims that "the critical enter-prise" of her book is therefore at once contextual, in the sense that it views the territory of American literary studies not as "terrestrial" but "trans-oceanic" in scope, and intertextual, in the way that it "brings other forms of knowledge and authority to bear on the imaginative work of literary production" (14). While Eckel meaningfully expands the scope of trad-itional archives, each of these extra-literary components, I would suggest, are still eminently compatible with any recognizable literary vocation. Furthermore, this "transoceanic" reorientation implies the default privil-eged cosmopolitan nature of these authors' work. Participating in the broader Transatlantic turn in American Studies, scholars such as Eckel have done much to challenge the politics of U.S. exceptionalism that underwrite myths of poetic vocation. However, these global perspectives can sometimes produce a different politics of exclusion. The understand-able critical move to turn away from a writer's agency, or immediate biographical setting, can wind up implicitly denigrating that which is static or located—those facets of modernity that are not in step with transnational circulation. As Arjun Appadurai suggests, the transnational considerations that have dominated for the last twenty years or so tend to privilege certain forms of cosmopolitan agency over others, overwriting

---

[7] See for example, the1886 *Brooklyn Eagle* interview with Whitman, entitled "A Visit to Walt Whitman: He Recalls the Years When He Lived in Brooklyn [. . .] Leaving the Carpenter's Work to Turn Poet."

the less glamorous experiences of modernity not immediately consonant with Marx's dynamic metaphor of solidity melting into air (*Modernity*, 178). Transnational perspectives, in fact, have frequently been in danger of operating within a binary value system when it comes to considerations of historical dynamism and stasis—with movement and circulation coded in terms of its imaginative possibility and progress, and locatedness in terms of its implicit insularity and inertia. This book, then, is particularly interested in recovering and thinking through the more ambiguously "bounded" and "terrestrial" aspects of a poet's career—those politically awkward forms of work we still don't quite know what to do with.

Though the critical epithet "modernity" speaks to a plethora of contradictory and often irreconcilable experiences associated with the accelerations and disorientations of industrial capitalism, I specifically employ the term here in relation to a persistent pattern that structures the broad historical scope of this study.[8] Despite being situated at distinct political and economic junctures, from the decade preceding the Civil War up until the crash of 1929, what allows the particular careers of these poets to speak to each other, as well as our neoliberal present, is their imbrication within the obstinate *longue durée* of what I want to term "vocational modernity." In the *Protestant Ethic and the Spirit of Capitalism* (1905), Max Weber examined what he saw as a binding temporal experience that continues to exert a shaping force on modern subjectivity, referring to the "duty in one's calling that prowl[s] about in our lives like the ghost of dead religious beliefs" (124). If this ethic initially served to reconcile religious belief with early capitalist accumulation, it also steadily continued (and continues) to discipline the workforce at large. In spite of its various specific iterations over the period I treat, it is the persistent gravitational draw of this Calvinistic and Puritanical legacy that I take as a diachronic historical constant of my readings.[9]

Vocational modernity, I want to suggest, comprises an ongoing dialectical struggle, whereby enfranchised subjects consistently strive to secure the parameters of calling against its perceived antithesis: a threat embodied by what Karl Marx describes as a disenfranchised "reserve" labor force.

[8] In her oft-quoted essay "Definitional Excursions", Susan Stanford Friedman goes some way towards capturing the knottiness of the term, writing that "modernity encompasses both centripetal and centrifugal forces in contradiction and constant interplay," posing it "neither as a concept of historical stages nor as a utopian dialectic." Rather, she insists upon "a meaning produced liminally in between, a dialogic that pits the contradictory processes of formation and deformation against each other, each as necessary to the other" (505).

[9] Weber also saw this in terms of diachronic continuity: "the Puritan wanted to work in a calling; we are forced to do so." See Weber, 123.

According to Marx, an increase in worker competition always results in a "submission to over-work and subjects workers to the dictates of capital" (*Capital*, 789). Capitalism thrives on the upward pressure produced by reserve labor because it enables employers to exploit the increasingly cheap, docile, and pliable work of those for whom the threat of being supplanted often overrides any progressive concerns regarding decent pay, regular hours, worker solidarity, or a shared humanity. To the enduring benefit of the bourgeoisie, anxieties surrounding personal expendability (of having to "deskill") intensify in relation to perceptions of a flooded labor supply, producing a variety of disciplinary and reactionary divisions and antagonisms throughout any given labor market. Vocational modernity, then, is one such reaction to "reserve anxiety." It describes a historical process whereby the exceptional sovereign individual is formed in relation to precariously embodied representations of difference, a relation that intensifies at those junctures when the promises of personal calling seem most at risk of unravelling.

Even from Walt Whitman's 1855 New York (ambiguously white and blue collar) perspective, his beloved population of "SAILORS, STEVEDORES, AND DRIVERS OF HORSES, PLOUGHMEN, WOOD CUTTERS, MARKETMEN, CARPENTERS, MASONS, AND LABORERS" (*Complete*, 1315) often seemed threatened by a reserve and increasingly unfamiliar workforce now largely based in disoriented urban centers.[10] Variations on this reactive stance inform each of the distinct political and economic environments inhabited by the poets I examine. Spanning the most dramatic and sustained period of industrialization, urbanization, and immigration in U.S. history, the instabilities of the market repeatedly manifested as a suspicion towards its least empowered actors: an ever more heterogeneous body of contingent labor. Women were visibly entering the paid workforce for the first time in mills, while the end of chattel slavery meant the emancipation of an enormous (potentially wage-undercutting) surplus body of labor.[11] An unprecedented influx of immigrants, no longer dominated by the traditional northern and western European countries of origin, brought

---

[10] The following numbers may be familiar, but are worth restating in the context of this discussion: between 1850 and 1930, the population of New York City (Five Boroughs) alone increased from five hundred thousand to almost 7 million. See "Population" by Jane Allen in *The Encyclopaedia of New York City*, ed. Kenneth T. Jackson (1995), 910–14.

[11] As women began entering the paid workforce, most visibly in the early New England textile mills, "unskilled" industrial production began relying on, and took on cultural associations of, women's work. Such feminizations of labor (not confined to the literary marketplace) helped articulate a labor hierarchy with increasingly paternalistic and infantilizing structures. See Thomas Dublin's *Transforming Woman's Work: New England Lives in the Industrial Revolution* (1995).

Fig. I.4. Frontispiece Portrait of *Leaves of Grass* (1855), from daguerreotype by Gabriel Harrison, copied by Samuel Hollyer onto a lithographic plate and reprinted opposite title page of the 1855 *Leaves of Grass*. University of Iowa Libraries, Special Collections & University Archives, FOLIO PS3201 1855, copy 1.

another demographic shift in the labor market.[12] As each of these new populations of "reserve" labor emerged—women, African Americans, "new" immigrants—so did a variety of racist, misogynistic, and classist projections of (white, male) sovereignty that successively undermined the potential for collective anti-capitalist resistance.

The unfolding reaction to this amorphous, intersectional threat has been central to a critical tradition of U.S. whiteness studies that gained momentum in the early 1990s with the work of Ruth Frankenberg, Theodore Allen, David Roediger, Alexander Saxton, and Dana Nelson.[13] Such critics read the historical emergence and maintenance of an unmarked standard of whiteness, throughout the nineteenth century and into the early twentieth century, as imbricated within the coextensive racial, gendered, and class-based antagonisms that defined the majority of responses to the injustices of accelerating mercantile and then industrial capitalism.[14] Like the myth of exceptional vocation, the myth of white superiority provided a form of spiritual compensation that offered both consolation and justification for exploitation. For Saxton and Roediger (as well as Eric Lott in his classic *Love and Theft: Blackface Minstrelsy and The American Working Class* [1992]), it was also a related consolidation of a nationalistic popular culture that aided in the construction of a remarkably cohesive politics of racial solidarity predicated on the sanctities of an always-threatened individual work ethic. Enduring stock characters such as the heroic Yankee, frontiersman, or Jeffersonian mechanic—all integral to Whitman's self-representation in 1855—emerged at this time, and spoke of a natural inheritance that required defending against the bewildering threat of reserve labor.[15] As various predatory industrialists accumulated their empires of capital by taking advantage of successive

[12] Ariane Chebe D'Appollonia explains that "hostility to foreigners accelerated in the late nineteenth and early twentieth century as a racial ideological component, and anti-Semitism became part of the Anglo-American ethno-nationalism." See *Frontiers of Fear: Immigration and Insecurity in the United States and Europe* (2012), 31.

[13] Theodore Allen, in *The Invention of the White Race* (1994), explored the creation of the "White Republic" and its various conflations between Irish, African American, and Native American communities in constructing the parameters of privilege and difference (a process through which particular immigrant demographics *became* white). Roediger and Saxton provide the most detailed accounts of the class dynamics that aided in the construction of various white commonalities. See *The Wages of Whiteness* (1991), and *The Rise and Fall of the White Republic* (1990).

[14] Ruth Frankenberg's foundational *White Women, Race Matters* (1993) defined whiteness as "a location of structural advantage" referring "to a set of cultural practices that are usually unmarked and unnamed" (1).

[15] Another important contribution to this debate was Dana Nelson's *National Manhood: Capitalist Citizenship and the Imagined Fraternity of White Men* (1998) that examined the cross-class allegiances that ultimately constructed a framework for an exclusionary white "national manhood" (3).

Fig. I.5. "Uncle Sam's Farm in Danger", *The San Francisco Wasp* by George F. Keller, 9 March 1878. Notice that figure standing next to Uncle Sam in this particular anti-immigration cartoon from 1878 (which identifies Chinese immigration as the latest invasive threat) is dressed exactly like the Walt Whitman of the 1855 frontispiece portrait. *The Wasp*, v. 2, Aug. 1877–July 1878 no. 84 [pages 504–5]. Courtesy of The Bancroft Library, University of California, Berkeley.

economic depressions that struck in roughly ten- to fifteen-year cycles—from the beginning of the Free Banking Era in 1836 through to the Crash of 1929—the politics of blue- and white-collar work remained resolutely protectionist and segregationist.[16]

This basic dialectical antagonism underpins each of the poetic production processes I discuss. Whitman, Melville, and Crane are all personally embedded within the political and economic fabric of this story. But here's the difference: far from exemplifying the reactionary assumptions

[16] According to Walter Benn Michaels, the "Johnson-Reed Immigration Act" (or "National Origins Act") of 1924, as well as the "Indian Citizenship Act" of the same year, marked a shift in U.S. rhetoric towards protectionist narratives of national sovereignty that resolutely began championing "the meaning of remaining—rather than becoming—American" (31). Michaels attributes the notion of "remaining American" to Calvin Coolidge's "Fourth of July" Speech of 1924, connecting this nativist moment with the emergence of explicitly racist texts such as Lothrop Stoddard's infamous *The Rising Tide of Color Against White World Supremacy* (1920), as well as more identifiably modernist texts such as Willa Cather's 1926 *The Professor's House*. See *Nativism*, 29–30.

of vocational modernity by confirming their transcendent state of exception as "poets," they all variously subvert their assumed antagonistic relation to contingent labor. Indeed, their poetry is not only at odds with the promise of exclusionary vocational fulfilment but also capable of envisioning renewed political possibilities in this context—possibilities that refuse incorporation within affirmatory vocational thinking. My readings consequently reframe these poets' formal characteristics not as so many affirmative inscriptions of a discrete labor corresponding to a particular mode of exalted creative production, but as a formalization of impatience with vocational modernity's existential fictions.[17] Broadly speaking (and in line with Fredric Jameson's conception of literary form), I interpret the "content" of particular literary forms as ultimately determined by political and economic horizons. But more locally, I understand poetic form in terms of a production process that is always irretrievably intermixed with the political and economic implications of other, apparently lesser labors.[18] The resulting agitating formal tendencies constitute the uneven crystallizations of coeval working lives. Poems in this instance are not the hallmarks of anything recognizably or implicitly "poetic" (the end results of the work that poets tautologically "do"), but uncooperative fusions that remain out of sync with any discrete or prior divisions of labor.

Moreover, if whiteness and masculinity delimit the privileged horizon of a poet's illusory vocational progression, then a recognition of their entanglement within alternative networks of contingent labor also convolutes the possibility of their being conscripted within what Anne Jamison has described as the successive displacements that tend to define exceptional literary periodicities.[19] These poets' careers do not struggle to

---

[17] Such a claim recalibrates, at a local level, Fredric Jameson's conception of the literary work "as a field of force in which the dynamics of sign systems of several distinct modes of production can be registered and apprehended" (*Political*, 84).

[18] "Literary form" in this context, already encompasses a discussion of "content." Such a distinction, Jameson suggests, cannot be thought of as discrete components of a particular literary work; instead a "dialectical reversal" has to take place whereby it becomes possible to grasp such formal processes as "sedimented content in their own right" and "as carrying ideological messages of their own, distinct from the ostensible of manifest content of the works" (*Political*, 84).

[19] See Anne Jamison's discussion of the problem of linear literary chronology in *Poetics En Passant: Redefining the Relationship between Victorian and Modern Poetry* (2009). Jamison considers the ways in which English poetry in the nineteenth century tends to split into two sequential periodizing strands: the "Victorian" followed by the "Modern," and how such ordering deleteriously sorts the careers of two near-contemporaneous poets: Christina Rossetti and Charles Baudelaire. Jamison argues that these writers in fact share overlapping aesthetic traits and political continuities that are occluded by literary histories that move from Victorian "restraint" to Modern "shock."

progress in affirmative stages towards any kind of personal or literary-historical consummation; rather, I take it as a given that "literary careers and forms materialize unevenly, proceeding by way of elliptical turns and untimely retrievals that are worlds apart from the finely delineated chronologies stipulated by modernization narratives" (Hagar and Marrs, 268).[20] These poems are the result of an assemblage of politically ambiguous activities, deviating from vocation's exceptional horizon and fused instead with labors that tend to gesture towards the byways of marginalization and disenfranchisement. To be clear: I am not referring to poets who were apparently unable to fulfil their inborn "promise"; rather, I am dispensing with this kind of vocational promise altogether.

Positioned at multiple occupational thresholds, Whitman, Melville, and Crane each discerned those permeable exchanges and continuities that drifting away from a particular vocational path paradoxically opens up.[21] The model of intersectionality I adopt here constitutes an alternative take on Kimberlé Crenshaw's foundational metaphorical roadmap of discrimination. "Intersectionality", she writes:

> is what occurs when a woman from a minority group tries to navigate the main crossing in the city [. . .] The main highway is Racism Road. One cross street can be Colonialism, then Patriarchy Street [. . .] She has to deal not only with one form of oppression but with all forms, those names as road signs, which link together to make a double, a triple, multiple, a many-layered blanket of oppression." (Quoted in Yuval-Davis, 196)

I conceive the traffic of such a roadmap in terms of the opportunities afforded by the transforming labor market, with Racism Road and Colonialism and Patriarchy Streets traversed most stridently and thoughtlessly by the most self-assured vocational subjects. Of course, the poets under discussion never inhabited the byways that define the multiply disenfranchised subject, but they were susceptible, in their own vocational uncertainties, to being partially waylaid, distracted into states of alternative

---

[20] Among the several path-breaking works that rearrange the politically problematic chronologies of "modernity," perhaps the stand-out version of the argument is still Paul Gilroy's *The Black Atlantic: Modernity and Double Consciousness* (1995). Fundamentally challenging any timescale that moves from modernity to the apparent hyper self-awareness of postmodernity, Gilroy reminds us, are the experiences of slave subjects during the middle passage. An African diasporic postmodernity emerged when the traditional narratives of modernity were only in their infancy. See also Lloyd Pratt's discussion in *Archives of American Time* (2009) of the competing temporalities that hindered the consolidation of a forward-looking, manifest "national" time signature.

[21] Jack Halberstam has written that "under certain circumstances failing, losing, forgetting, unmaking, undoing, unbecoming, not knowing in fact offer more creative, more cooperative, more surprising ways of being in the world." See *The Queer Art of Failure*, 2–3.

consciousness and apprehension. To have written poetry while negotiating the tangled intersections of the increasingly fraught labor market was also in some way to encode those unfolding conditions. *Against Vocation* locates its readings in the cross streets of Crenshaw's city grid, scanning for moments of resistant intensity that emerge when poetic careers do not proceed along straight white masculine lines, but linger somewhat askance of such exceptional trajectories.

This kind of perspective signals a decisive shift from thinking about authorship as a discrete labor commensurable with the logic of vocational security, to a newly malleable activity that becomes an integral resource for postcapitalist thinking. In his "Theses on Feuerbach," included in *The German Ideology* (1845), Marx envisioned a flexible laboring life under communism in which "society regulates the general production" (rather than general production regulated by individual capitalists who exploit the divisions of labor for accumulations' sake). Contra any innate or hierarchical divisions of labor, such flexibility would

> make it possible for me to do one thing today and another tomorrow, to hunt in the morning, fish in the afternoon, rear cattle in the evening, criticise after dinner, just as I have a mind, without ever becoming hunter, fisherman, shepherd or critic.　(53)

This famous formulation makes an important distinction between being and doing, envisioning the performance of labors that are not immediately conscripted within the stipulations of preordained social roles. In other words, Marx stresses the absolute necessity of having to resist the doctrine of vocation if capitalism is ever to be superseded. The generation of surplus value (profit) within the capitalist mode of production depends entirely upon the supposedly "natural" divisions that define wage labor, necessarily reducing all our multifarious, messy, inextricable doings into transcendent, predetermined being. Marx's flexible laboring life, in turn, replaces any "natural" state of being with a process of spontaneous and non-conscripted becoming, disturbing the necessary conditions that make primitive accumulation possible. To be clear, Marx's "flexibility" in no way resembles with neoliberalism's current demands for increasingly "flexible" or "zero-hour" work, that are themselves justified within narratives of progressive self-sacrifice that presage the promise of vocational fulfilment. Marx's flexibility interrupts the ontological division between bourgeois and proletariat, clearing the ground for a kind of thinking that extends beyond any capitalistic horizon that has mistaken itself as an historical inevitability.

Released from any prescriptive framework, poetic labor transforms into a far more capacious and unwieldy entity, approaching what Marx and

Engels describe in terms of a "living sensuous activity" that defines the peculiarities of laboring "practice" (*German*, 64). Kathi Weeks has suggested that by engaging with living sensuous activity, "materialism as Marx and Engels conceive it is a matter not merely of the social construction of subjects but of creative activity," pointing to its "capacity not only to make commodities but to remake the world" (19). Even while operating within the strictures of an output-driven regime, a personal laboring practice holds out the promise of alternative imaginative permutations that remain resiliently unmapped within the binary framework of productivity or unproductivity. Such activity has the potential to remake the world, according to Weeks, because it implies its own non-dialectical process of becoming. Pre-entangled within a contested matrix of classed, raced, and gendered labors, the production of certain poetry falls short of fulfilling the criteria of any normative capitalistic *dispositif* (in Deleuze's sense, the dominant material/social apparatuses that determine the production of subjectivity). *Against Vocation* therefore reimagines a poetic practice that exceeds specific consummations of ontological being (or any predetermined divisions of labor) and agitates "to become other" (36). The poems I engage with do not constitute the formal horizon at which poetic labor begins or ends; rather, they represent a nexus of production that signals the potentiality of non-capitalist worlds to come.

It is in this world-making or at least world-glimpsing sense that I am adopting the term "archives of distraction," an epithet that does not really do justice to the German equivalent "Zerstreuung." The latter was a concept that the young Walter Benjamin was drawn towards because of its quality of approximating coterminous and fruitfully overlapping connotations of diaspora, dispersal, and distraction. While Benjamin uses the term in relation to the reception of the artwork, in the context of this discussion I want to think about its implications for the artwork's, and specifically poetry's production. For Benjamin, distraction's revolutionary potential refers to the specific sensory shocks of a new form of media: cinema. The visual stimulus of the cinematic medium relays the world with such shocking intensity that the audience (the "masses") are stunned into internalizing (at hitherto unprecedented speeds) new temporalities and potentially new patterns of behavior. According to Benjamin, such "reception in distraction" [Die Rezeption in der Zerstreuung] agitates against capitalistic individuation towards the coalescing potential of alternative political kinships and states of becoming.

In the second version of his 1936 "The Work of Art in the Age of Its Technical Reproducibility," Benjamin clarifies this process when he distinguishes between two different ways of receiving an artwork: the first as practiced by the "masses," and the second by the "art lover." On the one hand, he writes, "the masses are criticized for seeking distraction [Zerstreuung] in the work of art," and on the other, "the art lover supposedly approaches it with concentration and devotion" (119). For Benjamin, "distraction and concentration" form a class-based antithesis, with the distraction of the masses usually regarded as frivolous and fickle, and the attention of the art lover or critic imbued with a depth and permanence. Benjamin makes it clear, though, which of these modes he is most interested in. In terms of receiving—by which Benjamin also implies producing—non-capitalist alternatives, the devoted attention of the art lover or critic is actually quite limiting. Because of their individual concentration, the art lover remains largely impervious to that which is beyond the immediate focus of their finite perceptions, intellectually insulated from anything that might challenge their sovereign calling. The distracted masses, by contrast, receive the world in a far less focused and identifiable way, making them more susceptible to the forces of historical transformation. If the former's approach is "optical" and perception-based, for the most part constrained to a conscious level, the latter's is "tactile" and use-based, a fundamentally embodied experience. The masses' contact with increasingly disorienting sensory data overwhelms the capacity for conscious resistance to this data's determining force. The analogy Benjamin draws on to illustrate these distinct modes is the reception of buildings (with "art" now taken in its broadest sense): "Tactile reception comes about not so much by way of attention as by way of habit. The latter largely determined even the optical reception of architecture, which spontaneously takes the form of casual noticing, rather than attentive observation" (120). The negotiation of a cityscape, the reception of moving images on a screen—but also, I want to suggest, the distracted coterminous activity that defines any participation in a rapidly transforming labor market—necessitates an analogous mutation in the parameters of the subject. Attention at such junctures either redoubles its effort to remain attentive, in the case of the art lover (and transcendent poet), or potentially becomes distractedly receptive to the parameters and possibilities of an alternative political and economic futurity.

With regard to my own strategy of close textual analysis, I seek to incorporate Benjamin's class-based (as well as concomitantly gendered and raced) critique of the limitations of critical focus. In turning my attention to particular poems and their specific contexts of production, I aim to produce what Bruno Latour might describe as a "thick description" of my object (136); that is, I attentively read until I come into a sense of a poem as something like the political antagonist of critical attention. Jonathan Crary reminds us that "attention and distraction cannot be thought outside of a continuum in which the two ceaselessly flow into one another, as part of a social field in which the same imperatives and forces incite one and the other" (51). This book explores the viability of a mode of close reading that paradoxically reveals the episodic sensuous dissipations, provisional fixations, suspensions, vacillations, extensions, transitions, and tactile Benjaminian receptions that certain poets tend to give expression to in their writing. Moving away from any conception of these poets as either attentive or distracted—away from related familiar oppositions concerning either authorial intention or unconscious transcription— what follows instead reveals these poets to be vacillating subversively at the divisive thresholds of apparently discrete labors: emphatically not conforming to any straightforward vocational roadmap.

While this all sounds promising, a potential problem for a scholar wishing to integrate a consideration of a particular poet's contingent labor into their argument is the question of where to find it. How, methodologically speaking, do you begin the imprecise process of assembling enough pieces of documentary evidence to illuminate specific moments in a poet's quotidian working life? Presumably, such ephemera are usually either lost or discarded amid the distracted hustle they represent. Aspects of a working life, however, often do get recorded, in the contracts, receipts, and paycheques that clutter every household. These constitute my archives of distraction—those neglected boxes of files usually labelled "miscellaneous," since they do not fit neatly or legibly within the traditional categories suggested by established narratives of poetic careers. The Walt Whitman Collection at the Library of Congress, for instance, is a treasure trove of work-related material, containing scores of house plans, dockets, inventories and building contracts, all dated from around 1848–56. Whitman, the poet known for "leaning and loafing at his ease observing a spear of grass," was also apparently scrupulously organized, ably managing the financial affairs of his entire family (*LG*, 1855, 1). Although comparatively little of this type of material exists in connection with Herman Melville, there is a collection of his personal ephemera kept in the Berkshire Athenaeum in Pittsfield, Massachusetts. The room is reputedly arranged in a similar fashion to the study in which he wrote his last works. Displayed in the corner of the room is a small jacket pin in the shape of a star; it is the official badge he wore on his daily rounds as customs inspector—not thrown away triumphantly after Melville retired, but kept because it meant something to him. The Hart Crane papers at Columbia and Yale also contain a range of work-related documents: Crane would often dash off a note to a friend on company stationery and spend long sections of his correspondence, which were subsequently expunged by editors from the published collections of his letters, complaining about the frustrations of his various jobs (see Fig. I.6). Recovering such marginalized materials yields new insights into Crane's career: for instance, the extent to which he was financially comfortable, organized, or under pressure at any given time. They also reveal the lengths to which his editors went to posthumously release him even from the documents that represented the shackles of non-poetic labor.[22]

The approach here draws on Jacques Rancière's archival practices as outlined in *Proletarian Nights* (1981). In this study of nineteenth-century French labor history, Rancière set out to question the received tenets of structural (and particularly Althusserian) Marxism, which he suspected of having become an alibi for political inertia rather than a genuine means for revolution. I take my cue from Rancière's re-attuned receptivity to archival "babble," listening to the asides of a "suspect population of deserters" who always seemed to not be conforming to any historical preconceptions

Fig. I.6. J. Walter Thompson stationery, Hart Crane to Grace Hart Crane and Elizabeth Belden Hart, New York City, August 18, 1923. Hart Crane Papers, Rare Book & Manuscript Library, Columbia University in the City of New York.

[22] See for example Brom Weber's selections in *The Letters of Hart Crane 1916–1932* (1952). These problematic archival omissions speak to Virginia Jackson's conception of the "lyricization of poetry" in *Dickinson's Misery: A Theory of Lyric Reading* (2005), a process whereby the print and pedagogical practices associated with modernism collapsed the variety of poetic genres into "lyric" as a synonym for a once socially and materially embedded poetry. Dickinson's "lyrics" were consequently mined from the variety of letters and other textual ephemera in which they were originally situated. Modernism, according to Jackson, didn't invent the lyric-persona but rather instantiated it as the default epistemological starting point for critical enquiry, foreclosing on the alternative socialities, networks, and archival scope of a once far more expansive and capacious cultural phenomenon.

concerning what constituted a revolutionary worker (13).[23] In searching for the "deserters" of their distinctive poetic calling, I engage with the shadowy margins of literary historiography so as to formulate a conception of poets who continually wrote askance of their retrospectively sanctioned vocations. If current conceptions of poetic labor are implicitly founded upon exceptional progression, then what follows comprises an attempt to tarnish its historical plausibility, reimagining the distracted permeable contours of a precarious labor that has little to do with any vocational self-confirmation.

This volume divides into three parts, dedicated to the careers of Whitman, Melville, and Crane respectively and each containing two chapters. Chapter 1, "*Leaves of Grass* and Real Estate" focuses on the period leading up to the publication of the first *Leaves of Grass* in 1855, revealing how Whitman financed his poetic output by successfully negotiating the notoriously unstable Brooklyn real estate market between 1848 and 1855. Throughout this time (while also working as an editor, and on his novel *Jack Engel*), he bought and sold several properties, moving from house to house, project to project as he went along. The adaptations of a provisional, transacting self in response to this destabilizing context provided a prototype for the fugitive Whitmanic self. In the years leading up to 1855, Whitman forged an adaptable marketplace persona—"Walter Whitman Jnr."—deploying it repeatedly while composing receipts, contracts, and house-plans. Whitman's experiences of moneymaking inextricably inform his familiar narratives of transcendence and organic wholeness. In the attempt to transcend the particularities of his urban activity, he ends up building his poetic vision out of the rhythms and inflections of the real-estate market. This has significant implications, I claim, for the way we read his later works: for the rest of his career, Whitman concentrated on tearing down, annexing, and building over again his subsequent poetic projects, aligning his imaginative undertaking with the restless rhythms of the city from which it emerged.

"Whitman and the Transformations of Labor," my second chapter, examines Whitman's entanglement within the broader politics and reserve anxieties of labor relations in the mid-nineteenth century. Reading his unpublished manifesto of 1856 "The Eighteenth Presidency" as a prose poem, and in relation to the shifting currencies of the labor market, I see

---

[23] For every blacksmith on the verge of organizing dissent, Rancière suggests, there were ten who were not doing that, who seemed to be betraying their own innate political credo: "when one proceed[s] to scrape the varnish off those too civilized savages and those too bourgeois proletarian laborers, there comes a moment when one asks oneself: is it possible that the quest for the true word compels us to shush so many people?" (*Proletarian*, 11).

Whitman as thinking through an alternative figuration of Marx's labor theory of value, with the various corporeal metaphors and formal experiments in his poetry serving as an affirmative counterpart to Marx's gothic dystopian depictions of alienated labor. While Marx saw the body as "mortifying" in the context of industrialized production, Whitman reimagined these accelerating forces as an opportunity to experiment with new forms of intimacy (Marx, *1844*, 71). The laboring body becomes a conceptual balm in Whitman's hands—a generative "coagulation" (Marx's analogous term is "Gallerte") that informs the dimensions of his alternative social vision. Whitman's sensitivity to the fluctuating dynamics of his laboring environment, embodied chiefly by the rising tensions between slavery and the expanding free market, rescued his poetic vision from restating the reactionary vocational essentialisms that defined the popular labor movements of the 1850s. In spite of his stated allegiance to the burgeoning Free Soil party, which viewed the geographic spread of American slavery as a potential threat to the promise of the white Jeffersonian inheritance, he articulated a poetics that resisted contemporary fictions of racial purity, and along with it any mythic notion of free exchange.

Turning to Melville in Part II, I investigate how his diverse writings consistently display a preoccupation with undermining the teleology of artistic, and specifically poetic, calling. Though Melville has more or less served as the archetype of frustrated vocation in American Letters, he actually remained intensely self-conscious and skeptical of vocational thinking throughout his varied career. Chapter 3, "*Moby-Dick* and the Shadows of The Poet" initially engages with the phantom supporting cast included in the prefatory materials at the beginning of Melville's career-defining novel. Reading the "Sub-Sub librarian" and "consumptive usher" as experiments in "virtual biography," I examine how the author-narrator uses these contingent figures to explore the various possibilities that may have otherwise defined his working life. Rather than impose any implicit hierarchy on these virtual biographical threads, Melville draws attention to their necessary dialectical interrelation, exposing an exceptional politics of sovereign authorial labor whose maintenance depends upon occlusion and deselection. This scepticism towards vocational thinking can also be seen in the narrative's implicit juxtaposition of Ishmael and Ahab. Focusing on "The Grand Armada," I read the traumatic whale hunt depicted in this chapter as the dramatization of an existential retreat from industrial violence towards the security of a "lyric center." Ahab's formal turn to blank-verse soliloquizing in this context, I argue, functions as a critique of the Emersonian poet, who cannot but be in thrall to the certainty of his own inexorable calling. Ishmael, by contrast, resists the Emersonian abdication of the "manifold and duplex life" and proceeds to apprehend alternative sympathies and continuities in a scene of otherwise violently consolidating divisions. In a coda to this chapter, I think through Melville's decision to write an 18,000-line epic poem set in Jerusalem while holding down a six-day-a-week job as a deputy customs inspector on the New York docks. While this phase of Melville's career typically has been characterized as one of creative decline or poetic retreat, I offer a reconsideration of *Clarel* (1876), arguing that its form embodies a sustained engagement with the contingencies of his working context rather than an attempt to escape them.

In Chapter 4, "*Billy Budd* and Melville's Retirement," I reassess common biographical and critical accounts of Melville's exit from the workforce in 1885, examining the vocational vacillations that produced *Billy Budd*. Contrary to any perceived professional disappointments, Melville the retiree continued to experiment across a variety of formal approaches, personas, and settings. Melville's final writings did not simply signal a release from the quotidian world of work into one last affirmative creative garret, but another opportunity to practice his ongoing commitment to "becoming-other": in fact, "Billy in the Darbies," the ballad that accompanies *Billy Budd,* consciously sets up and then undermines the Romantic topos of the isolated solitary singer, finally "set free." "Late Melville" approached literary composition and revision as an extension of (rather than a release from) other forms of work, probing a variety formal continuities that ultimately refuse the consummation of any particular authorial destiny.

Chapter 5 then examines the instantiation of "The Ideology of Modernism," a cultural logic that continues to inform the vocational framing of standard poetic biographies. Emerging in tandem with the nativist discourses of the 1910s and 1920s, as well as various consolidating nationalist politics, it was a group of transatlantic literary modernists that extended the logic of vocational modernity by embodying, or better, "disembodying," an influential figuration of innate poetic calling in their careers choices. They achieved this by aligning an anti-Romantic patrician "classicism" with the affirmative discourses of Progressive-era literary professionalism. In disseminating and participating in a privileged cult of "impersonality," such "classical modernists" (poets and New Critical pedagogues alike) secured the parameters of an exceptional poetic labor that now defined itself strictly in opposition to quotidian work. An important and overlooked legacy of classical modernism, I suggest, is the way it promoted a series of Manichean icons—T. S. Eliot, Bank Clerk; Wallace Stevens, Insurance Salesman among them—which had the effect of reinforcing a dialectical relationship between distinct (though mutually defining) spheres of labor. These poets, updating and reinforcing Emerson's vision, perversely came to encapsulate a parable of threatened vocational integrity, drawing on the broader reserve anxieties of the era while in fact capitalizing on stable and well-paid employment. We still tend to read poetic careers, and conceive of poetic labor, I claim, through this particular cultural lens, retrospectively assimilating any anomalous continuities within this politically troubling modernist bifurcation.

My final chapter, "Making Ends Meet: Hart Crane's Job" examines the continually waylaid career of one of Eliot's and Stevens' contemporaries, Hart Crane. Crane worked contra the vocational example set by his modernist colleagues (and almost always in spite of himself), consistently producing work that undermined the very possibility of any privileged conception of poetic labor. His erratic career represents an important alternative to the modernist binary vocational model exactly because this model always eluded him. He provides an insight into what happens when a modernist poet lacks the necessary privilege, infrastructural trappings, and personal consistencies possessed by an Eliot or a Stevens. Crane's poetry contorts his own shortfalls into some fabulous poetic dividends, catapulting his ideas into manifold, discordant directions and then working to tirelessly to fix these impulses into some kind of provisional formal accord. His manuscripts at Columbia University testify to this; it took him scores of false starts and revisions to contort a poem like "Atlantis" or "Voyages II" into their published forms. Looking over the continual crossings out, you see the drafts working themselves up into such a state that, perhaps inevitably, they start speaking in symptomatic shaking suspension bridges and apocalyptic vortices: a symbolic register that gestures beyond any inevitable divisions of labor towards a reimagined world beyond.

Finally, a coda, "Why I am not talking about Frank O'Hara" speculates on the recent corporatized adoptions of "distraction" such as Linda Stone's "continuous partial attention." In an examination of O'Hara's time at the "Museum of Modern Art" in New York (that once again engages various ephemeral archival materials), I read this career as finally dissolving the political threat posed by poetic distraction. Marking a shift towards postmodernity, this is a moment when the subversive potential of distraction was refolded back into the logic of vocational modernity—ultimately becoming refigured as a new hyper-self-conscious mode of depoliticized productivity (O'Hara's preoccupied persona on the page fell well within the remit of his cosmopolitan profession). The coda ends with a discussion of the ways in which "continuous partial attention" and the new "flexibility" might be resisted (particularly within the academy), and reflects on how the implications of Marx's living sensuous activity could be reaffirmed in the present.

PART I

WALT WHITMAN, BROOKLYN PROPERTY SPECULATOR

1

Leaves of Grass and Real Estate

A year before the publication of *Leaves of Grass* in 1855, Walt Whitman was considering the designs both of houses and of front covers, sketching down ideas on the back of wallpaper samples as he readied his house and book for their respective markets (see again Figs. 1 and 2). Contra the various (often self-perpetuated) "loafing" depictions of this iconic American poet, a more preoccupied Whitman has started to come to light in recent years. Ed Folsom, the most influential Whitman scholar of the last three decades, has shown most clearly the ways in which many of the distinctive features of the 1855 book came about by chance and experiment in response to pressing material circumstances rather than via any preconceived artistic intent. He suggests, for example, that the unusual formatting of *Leaves* was the result of the Rome Brothers printing house only having legal paper to hand at the time of going to press. Since most of their commissions were contractual documents, this was the only paper size they had in stock when Whitman approached them with his manuscript. He was consequently forced to rethink the entire layout of his book ("Learning," 15). Folsom also contends that, potentially, every single copy of that first print run is unique. While detailing one difference between the various copies, he envisions "Whitman [stopping] the press, [rewriting] the line, and [resetting] it about a third of the way through the pressrun" (19).[1] Short of cash, Whitman also directed his printers to bind together pages that he knew included typos, aiming for an approximate mean average of mistakes bound in each copy. Then, too, recent critical reflections on the book's packaging provide insight into how *Leaves* bears the marks of Whitman the opportunistic "self-promoter," the man who, for publicity purposes, was so enthusiastic to stamp Emerson's words of (private) praise on the spine of his 1856 edition, as well as appropriate many of Fanny Fern's popular book designs from the early 1850s

---

[1] See also Gary Schmidgall's "1855: A Stop-Press Revision", *Walt Whitman Quarterly Review*, 18 (Summer/Fall 2000); 74–6, in which he discusses Whitman's stopping the print run of the 1855 edition in order to make a substantial change.

(Dowling, 84).[2] Perhaps most startlingly, Ted Genoways has shown that Whitman instructed the engraver of the famous frontispiece portrait to alter the image so as to increase the bulk of his crotch and better illustrate his exceptional "goodshaped and wellhung man" (87–123). *Leaves of Grass*, from these points of view, is a set of heterogeneous books comprised of quick fixes, improvisations, and experiments, rather than any successfully implemented distinctive vision.

What follows extends these scholarly explorations of the production of *Leaves* in an extra-literary direction by examining Whitman's involvement in New York's burgeoning real estate market. For, if he kept watch over the movements of the literary marketplace in the run-up to his first book of poems, then he also had a keen eye on the fluctuations of the notoriously unstable housing market—the market in which he had invested most of his family's money, and on which their financial fortunes and security, as well as the publication of his first book of poetry, depended. This chapter suggests that *Leaves of Grass* was in important ways shaped by Whitman's speculation in Brooklyn real estate between 1848 and 1855, and that the complications, transactions, and bureaucracy involved in getting these structures off the ground are inextricable from the book's conception and formal makeup. It goes on to claim that the notoriously unstable market, and formulations of a transacting self in response to this context, provided a formal prototype for the recognizable Whitmanic "self"; a self that went on to negotiate the utopian amalgamations and bodily coagulations that underpin the experimental scope of Whitman's poetic achievement.

In the years leading up to 1855, he traded under the name "Walter Whitman Jr," a persona that established him at the time as a legitimate business man in the family line but which has not sat particularly easily with many of the subsequent political estimations of his poetry. This entrepreneurial version of himself represented the activities of an urban speculator in a state of perpetual negotiation—buying land, hiring labor, organizing construction and selling for profit. The fluctuating currencies of this transacting self (its buying power, reputation, credibility, and security) were contingent on canny interactions with a mercantile capitalistic marketplace. Walter Whitman Jr, in fact, managed to successfully sidestep and even profit from a real estate crash in the spring of 1854, which could easily have eradicated his bargaining potential altogether by

---

[2] For a discussion of his adoption of various aspects of Fanny Fern's popular *Fern Leaves from Fanny's Portfolio* (1853), and *Fern Leaves, Second Series* (1854), see Matt Miller's "The Cover of the First Edition of *Leaves of Grass*," *Walt Whitman Quarterly Review* 24 (Fall 2006): 85–97.

bankrupting both himself and his family. Indeed, there was no doubt a real urgency to these dealings; his stock was not so high as to enable him to direct his affairs from a secure family home. When Whitman bought and sold his various houses, he was forced to move the entire family along with him. With two aging parents and a severely disabled brother to care for, the three years leading up to the publication of *Leaves* in 1855 was laden with a weight of personal responsibility and financial risk.[3]

This reassessment builds on the work of two important Whitman scholars who have focused on the economic contexts and implications of his oeuvre: M. Wynn Thomas's study *The Lunar Light of Whitman's Poetry* (1987) and Andrew Lawson's *Walt Whitman and the Class Struggle* (2006). Thomas makes the valuable connection between the invigorating force of the antebellum mercantile capitalist economy and Whitman's notion of the "Kosmos." He states that: "[Whitman] transform[s] the capitalist spirit by which his society was in fact animated into the indwelling spirit of the living universe" (80). He goes on to suggest that Whitman's poetry manages to resolve his conflicting feelings about "the uncompromising competitive origins of [capitalism's] exciting energy", by "desocialising and 'naturalising' this energy" within the idealized realms of an organicist system (79). Thomas pinpoints one of the central tensions in Whitman's work—the idea of the poet as being caught in an ambiguous post-artisanal phase of production. *Leaves of Grass* expresses the conflict between the nostalgia Whitman felt for the disappearing artisan class and the new possibilities inherent in the rise and promise of the early laissez-faire marketplace. Thomas suggests "that the conception and genesis of Whitman's Self should be sought not only in his efforts to avoid becoming a possessive self, but also in his determination to avoid being appropriated by others" (51). I want to rearrange this line of argument and suggest that Whitman avoided being "appropriated by others" exactly by appropriating for himself and his family enough property, and that his successful entrepreneurial efforts forge the formal dynamics of *Leaves*. This is, of course, rather troubling given his radical political credentials.

Expanding on Thomas's work, Andrew Lawson reads the first *Leaves of Grass* as a product of Whitman's uneasy relationship to evolving questions

---

[3] Matt Miller has argued that Whitman's "nomadic" lifestyle in the years leading up to 1855 left its mark on many of the stylistic elements of the first book: "the manuscript evidence suggests that the process of packing and unpacking text was crucial to his writing process, and the idea of mobile units of language powerfully informs most of the first edition." See Matt Miller, *Collage of Myself: Walt Whitman and the Making of "Leaves of Grass"* (2010), Chapter 2: "Packing and Unpacking the First *Leaves of Grass*," 51.

of class. The poet is figured as both "artisan and autodidact" (xix), a member of an expanding lower middle class population:

> Whitman's first poetic production is marked by a mixture of self-assertion and anxiety, which can be traced to the uncertain position of the lower middle class as it moves from agrarian folkways to the urban marketplace.   (4)

Lawson goes on to say that "Whitman catches [...] the energy of the marketplace, that space of assembled particularity where differences of value are established and resolved [...] the speaker of 'Song of Myself' plunges into this space of motion and exchange, identifying himself with it" (14). A trenchant analysis—however, Lawson slightly obscures the angle from which Whitman "catches" the energy of the marketplace, depicting him as "plunging" in instead of already enmeshed in its rhythms: Whitman's exemption from the market in this formulation is always prior.

What needs pointing out here is that both Thomas's and Lawson's accounts are premised on a chronological inaccuracy that has significant ramifications for understanding the political and economic contexts for *Leaves'* production. Whitman biographer Joseph Jay Ruben set the scene for the appearance of the first edition by honing in on a contemporary economic crisis: "in the spring of 1854 the full force of the depression struck the entire metropolitan area. Banks dissolved, private credit vanished, failures came daily to Wall Street, 'to let' signs filled windows on Broadway and in Brooklyn" (298). This gives the impression that Whitman's real estate speculations suffered in a similar way and that he was forced out of the market prematurely. Thomas's subsequent account of the effects of this crash on Whitman's poetry is even more explicit, and assumes he is among those forced out of the capitalistic realm:

> [I]n the spring of 1854, came the slump that put [Whitman's] family, like thousands of others, out of work. Carpenters and printers, along with longshoreman, laborers, and the rest of the New York work force, flocked in such numbers to the soup kitchens that charitable food supplies were quickly exhausted. And it was during this period of enforced, but in his case welcome, idleness that Whitman, personally protected against the worst consequences of the depression, probably first seriously turned his attention to poetry.   (34)

Similarly, Lawson has Whitman "unemployed in 1854 ... work[ing] on his poems" (85), diminishing the poet's active involvement in the sphere of moneymaking during the crucial period of creativity in 1854 and 1855. No doubt the market collapse of spring 1854 had serious repercussions for many workers in the metropolitan area, but Whitman was not forced into the state of idleness that enabled him to turn exclusively to the work of writing.[4] In fact, the market uncertainty made property a more pressing preoccupation.

A close inspection of the little-considered everyday ephemera archived in Whitman's personal papers at the Feinberg Collection suggests a messier, preoccupied narrative of poetic production. These banal commercial documents associated with his early career have hitherto gone largely unnoticed. As numerous receipts and building plans in this archive of distraction reveal, Whitman was not in fact a victim of the economic crash that immediately preceded the first publication of *Leaves*; far from being unemployed, he carried on speculating, developing, and profiting well into 1855.

The perpetuation of this biographical inaccuracy reflects the tendency in Whitman studies in general to distance the more politically problematic real estate developer from Whitman the poet, instead recasting the entire narrative of his career in accordance with his existentially pristine poetic vocation. This trend, symptomatic of the way non-exceptional, politically questionable labor is so often forcibly occluded within poetic biography, subtly detached Whitman from the problematic (but enabling) economic sphere to retrospectively realign him with his supposedly artisan background. Thomas describes Whitman's real estate involvement as the activity of "his recent artisanal self" (35). In an important sense, this is not quite accurate. The documents associated with Whitman's real estate ventures show that he was also a hirer of labor, an overseer of production. Because Thomas dissociates Whitman from this working context, he is able to describe him as a detached and disaffected artistic observer, able to consciously subvert and transform the energies of free market capitalism in his discretely poetic activities. The poet is seen as an "alchemist" (78), consciously undermining and redirecting economic and social forces into his transcendent fictions, rather than someone directly caught up and distracted by the systems he attempts to transform. As a result, the claim that Whitman "catches . . . the energy of the marketplace" becomes somewhat opaque (as though Whitman had temporarily caught a cold).[5]

---

[4] Andrew Lawson, quoting Ruben, writes that "in the winter of 1851 the banks collapsed, and there followed a 'veritable carnival of beggary by the unemployed'." In the winter of 1852 the journeymen carpenters were on strike for seventeen shillings a day. In the spring, Whitman set up as a builder and seller of small houses—a period of prosperity swiftly ended by the depression of the following spring, when banks and businesses once again failed and "gangs of destitute young girls, filthy and obscene" roamed the streets. Unemployed in 1854, Whitman worked on his poems while mechanics marched with banners reading "if work be not given we will help ourselves to bread"' (*Class Struggle*, 84–5).

[5] Lawson details how the "multifaceted language" of Whitman's poetry reflects and absorbs "the bewilderingly rich and complex range of texts circulating within the print

Lawson's reading, in turn, positions the poet in a succession of "liminal" spaces—stuck between classes, out of work, and in a state of "social and political isolation" (104): from this detached and alienated position he observes and converts the tensions of his society into his poetry. What such an account downplays is the extent to which Whitman was distracted at this time by the need to make money; a need that that was no doubt exacerbated by the economic disappointment of his most recent novelistic endeavor *Life and Adventures of Jack Engle: An Auto-Biography* (1852).[6]

Both Thomas and Lawson establish that Whitman somehow channels the energy of the marketplace into his poetic fictions, and that the restive Whitmanic self is in various ways linked to the perpetual motion of exchange, but, in the process, they lose a sense of Whitman's prior imbrication within coextensive processes of production. I want to re-examine the period in the immediate run-up to publication in 1855 to offer an analysis that takes into account the complicated coeval labors that produced it. Whitman the property speculator and Whitman the poet are integrated contemporaries: he is not set apart from the economic and social context he embodies and transfigures. Instead, his own, difficult to assimilate, market-bound activities mold the dynamic framework for his fictions. It is because Whitman was simultaneously an entrepreneur and a disaffected artisan poet, or unemployed, lower-middle-class poet loafer, that he is able to formulate a provisional, continually transacting self capable of negotiating the shifting contours of his kosmos-marketplace. And it is because he was personally tied to the multivalent stresses of the market that his poetry produces such an abundance of restless forms. Viewed in this way, Whitman becomes a member of Jacques Rancière's historically awkward population of defectors: those who are illegible according to any preconceived notion of identity, who "travel the road in the opposite direction, deserting what was said to be their culture and their truth to go toward our shadows" (*Proletarian*, 13). Such difficult-to-assimilate shadows force us to reconceive the parameters and political potential of those precarious labors that are liable to complicate the exceptional unfolding of an apparently innate poetic nature.

Besides troubling traditional biographical accounts of Whitman as artisan-poet, this reconsideration of his preoccupied working life also

---

culture of the antebellum period". See *Walt Whitman and the Class Struggle*, xxi. Lawson argues that Whitman is part of the lower middle class—caught between social strata—and yet he confines his exploration almost exclusively to the realm of published textual sources.

[6] See Zachary Turpin's "Introduction to Walt Whitman's *Life and Adventures of Jack Engle*", *Walt Whitman Quarterly Review* 34 (Winter/Spring 2017): 225–61. Whitman had previously published *Franklin Evans; or The Inebriate* in 1842.

illuminates the ways in which Whitman's extra-literary labor has implications for the formal composition of his writing. John Hollander has described Whitman's contribution in terms of a new "metrical contract." His "commitment is made not to convention, but to the poetic self." In other words, the poet claimed to have created a prosody emerging from the unique and organic rhythms of personal expression, instead of the inherited structuring devices of the past. Whitman's poetry appears as though it has taken on the "natural form from the self that releases it," though in fact, as Hollander continues, "the actual constituents of his metrical style are syntactic; his invariably end-stopped lines are connected by parallelism, expansions of sentence matrices, types of catalogue, and so forth" (*Vision*, 204). Whitman's "free" verse does not constitute a liberation, but rather the arrangement of an alternative set of structuring devices. Hollander's "new metrical *contract*" has a real potency here, because in writing *Leaves of Grass*, Whitman scored his poetry with the structuring contractual patterns of an urban speculator. As we shall see, Whitman's apparently organicist prosody is rooted—no—*founded* upon contingent adaptations to (as well as embellishments and truncations of) the synthetic world of antebellum real estate economics.

* * *

In November 1845, Whitman published an article in *The American Review* entitled "Tear Down and Build Over Again." This was a treatment of what he saw as the "restless" activities of property speculators who were radically transforming the urban geography of Brooklyn and New York City. Whitman called attention to a "feverish itching for change" and "dissatisfaction with proper things as they are" that characterized the urban developments of his city: "Let us level to the earth all the houses that were not built within the last ten years; let us raise the devil and break things!" ("Tear," 536). On one hand, Whitman articulates a sense of loss at the destruction of many of the city's historically consecrated places; on the other, he is sure to point out that he is "by no means desirous of retaining what is old, merely because it is old" ("Tear," 538). He adds: "we would have all dilapidated buildings, as well as all ruinous laws and customs, carefully levelled to the ground, forthwith and better ones put in their places." He concludes by warning that "the blindness which would peril all in the vague chance of a remotely possible improvement, has something of the same mischief of the soul... [as] that father of restlessness, the Devil" ("Tear," 538).

By 1848, Whitman was not practicing what he preached, taking an active part in the restless redevelopment of his city. As of 1846, the Brooklyn housing market was enjoying an unprecedented boom.

Williamsburg, a village of just 3,000 people in 1835, had become a large town of 40,000 people by 1855, the year it was absorbed by Brooklyn. Manhattan was becoming increasingly expensive, filthy, and overcrowded, and people were escaping in droves across the water (Spann, 84).[7] New transport links meant that the metropolis could be reached by cheap ferry crossings so people were actually losing very little by moving out. This was the speculative bandwagon Whitman jumped on. And he was competent at his job; by 1855, thanks to the sale of his house on Skillman Street, he was able to buy an unmortgaged property for his family and, on top of that, take the time to organize and finance the run of 795 copies of *Leaves of Grass*. It is a curious irony to consider that Whitman, the champion of "Mannahatta"—"The beautiful city! the city of hurried and sparkling waters! the city of spires and masts! | The city nested in bays! my city!"[8]—was able to pay for his initial poetic output because Manhattan, for many people, was becoming an impossible and undesirable place to inhabit.

In the following page from his notebook, Whitman details the number of houses he both inhabited and flipped between the years of 1846 and 1859:

Moved into house in Prince st. in Dec. 1846

I built the place 106 Myrtle av. in winter of 1848–9, and moved in, latter part of April '49

I Sold the Myrtle av. house in May, "52, and built in Cumberland street where we moved Sept. 1ˢᵗ, 52."

Sold the two three story houses in Cumberland st. March 1853. moved into the little 2 story house Cumberland st. April 21st, '53 (lived there just one year exactly)

Built in Skillman st. and moved there May, 1854

Moved in Ryerson st, May 1855. – Lived in Classon from may 1st '56,'7,'8, '9 . . .[9]

---

[7] See also James E. Bunce and Richard P. Harmond's account in *Long Island as America: A Documentary History to 1896* (1977), 104–8.

[8] Walt Whitman, *Leaves of Grass* (Boston: Thayer and Eldridge, 1860), 405. http://whitmanarchive.org/published/LG/1860/whole.html [accessed February 3, 2016].

[9] Walt Whitman, *Notebooks and Unpublished Prose Manuscripts*, Vol. 1: *Family Notes and Autobiography, Brooklyn and New York*, ed. Edward F. Grier (New York: New York University Press, 1984), 11. Hereafter *NUPM*. Whitman started keeping this record in about 1850 and added to it as events changed. Grier notes that the dates at the end have been added to gradually over time in different inks; Whitman clearly enjoyed tracking his own progressions and developments.

Fig. 1.1. "May Day in New York," *Harper's New Monthly Magazine* (May 1856), 861. This cartoon illustrates the experience of being shunted between properties, and notice that the young man (wearing Whitman's favorite style of hat in 1855) transports his chest of belongings while struggling to hang on to his fiddle. Such was the precarious balance that Whitman struck at this time, caught somewhere between coextensive artistic ambitions and the personal difficulties of surviving in a city.

Notice that most of the transactions occur around a specific date—May 1. As a real estate developer, Whitman's year revolved around one highly stressful period of trading. On "May Day" or "Moving Day", leases expired across the city (see Fig. 1.1). This forced thousands of New Yorkers and Brooklynites to move house simultaneously. Families and their belongings were temporarily stacked up on the sidewalks as people scrambled to find a new place to live. The sudden increase in demand enabled landlords to hike up rent, and it was not uncommon to see open brawls erupt over the ensuing negotiations.[10] On March 5, 1854, as Whitman prepared for the sale of his two newly built houses on Cumberland Street, a *Brooklyn Eagle* article entitled "The Moving Season"

---

[10] See Elizabeth Blackmar, *Manhattan for Rent 1785–1850* (1989) for a detailed description of this calamitous annual event: "As moving day brought all other trade to a halt and focused the commercial city's attention on the single commodity of shelter, the tensions of competing needs frequently erupted in the streets. Freely flowing liquor fuelled and rewarded movers' exertions through the inevitable traffic jams and moving day brawls. Refusing to give up their homes, old tenants sometimes fought with new leaseholders, each side drawing support from crowds of relatives and acquaintances" (214).

complained of "the harassing and absurd custom that a great number of people have fallen into of changing their place of residence about the 1st of May." This was "so troublesome, expensive and destructive of property that the cause or motives which could have led to its origin must ever remain beyond conjecture" (np). The upheaval of "Moving Day" was something that Whitman had to deal with. This was the time of year when people did real estate—it presented the best (and really only) opportunity for buying and selling—so he had to adapt his movements and plans accordingly.

It was in tandem with this highly volatile housing cycle—in tune with the new growth associated with spring—that Whitman began, in 1848, by selling the family home and building a three-story house on a plot of land he had recently bought on Myrtle Avenue, Brooklyn. In 1852, he sold this property for a good profit and immediately set about buying other plots of land on Cumberland Street. He contracted building firms to erect three further houses during 1852–3. He sold two of these properties and moved into the other. From this address, he ran a shop with the (somewhat misleading) sign "Carpenter and Builder" above the door. The sale of the Cumberland Street properties allowed him to build the house on Skillman Street (1854–5). The family moved into this address in May 1854 and one year later, just before the book's publication in June, Whitman sold the property, his last and seemingly quite profitable transaction. With the money raised, he bought a house outright in his mother's name on Ryerson Street and the family moved in (Rodgers, 63–9). Whitman was jumping from house to house, project to project, becoming complicit in the urban restlessness of which he had previously complained. The driving force behind this restlessness, Whitman writes lines like:

My ties and ballasts leave me . . . . I travel . . . . I sail . . . . my elbows
    rest in the sea-gaps,
I skirt the sierras. . . . my palms cover continents,
I am afoot with my vision.

By the city's quadrangular houses. . . . in log huts, or camping with lumbermen,
    along the ruts of the turnpike. . . . along the dry gulch and rivulet bed, . . .

                                                                    (*LG* ,1855, 35)

These are the movements of the restive Whitmanic self, drawing on the commotions of a distinctive urban praxis. The speaker casts the "I" as a ship cut adrift, bereft of "ties" and "ballasts." Any rest the poet finds is only tangential, his elbows provisionally placed in sea-gaps, his palms stretching over continents. The poet starts his journey "By the city's quadrangular houses," leaping to "log huts" and then a lumbermen's encampment, before transforming into an elemental liquid that runs along the ruts of the turnpike and rivulet bed. With the liquidity of a new economic force, the speaker courses from setting to setting: the poetic vision is "afoot" with the impermanence of Whitman's own activities, tracing the pattern of an itinerant self that cannot help but be urged along by the fluctuating tide.[11]

As already noted, Walter Whitman Jr's involvement in Brooklyn real estate development and the influence this had on the production method and formal makeup of his subsequent book of poems has been largely passed over in favor of more palatable accounts of the emergence of his artistic calling.[12] However, there is compelling evidence in his archives that demonstrates how Whitman the real estate developer and Whitman the poet remained amalgamated, undertaking integrated production processes very different from an artist who could now "seriously turn his attention to poetry" (Thomas, 34). A notebook dating from around 1853–5 contains entries that are written in Whitman's distinctive poetic voice: "The poet is a recruiter | He goes forth beating the drum.—O, who will not join his troop?" On the verso two pages later you find:

Front windows on first floor—lights 13x17—Windows five lights high—

A sash of two lights across top—the other eight lights made in two door-sides, hung each with hinges.   (*NUPM*, 116–17)

Whitman sketched out his ideas for *Leaves of Grass* whilst thinking about the design of his houses. This dashed-off plan, with its improvised and fleeting feel, echoes the bustling, draft-like, often itemized quality of his 1855 lines, moving fluidly and elliptically from task to task: windows to sashes to doors to hinges. In the year leading up to the spring and summer of 1855, Whitman had two convergent ambitions: to sell a house come the moving season and to publish a book in June with some of the proceeds. In November 1854, as Whitman shaped and reshaped the lines that would be incorporated into *Leaves of Grass*, he was also organizing substantial improvements to the Skillman Street property, turning parts of the then family home into a building site. As he revised his poems,

---

[11] This "homeless self" coexists with another American type of the period, the newly emerging, street-smart cosmopolitan, recognizable as Melville's "Confidence Man" of course, but also as the traveling American. See Herman Melville's *The Confidence Man; his Masquerade*, ed. Harrison Hayford, G. Thomas Tanselle, and Hershel Parker (1984), and also Gary H. Lindberg's *The Confidence Man in American Literature* (1982).

[12] Of the few critics who refer to this context, Ed Folsom has said that "Whitman's experience as a house builder may be relevant to the way he imagined book objects: when you needed more space for a new resident, you added an annex." See Ed Folsom, *Whitman Making Books/Books Making Whitman: A Catalog and Commentary* (2005), 37.

he was simultaneously revising an agreement with his builder—his poetic and building projects curiously syncopated. The following plan, apart from the signature at the bottom, is in Whitman's hand:

> Transposing front door to wall between rooms and back window to place of door, weatherboarding under it, removing stoop in front, finishing and setting door in their places, complete in every respect – Building an 12 × 11 shed in rear with sealing boards one side planed, roof well battened, with one good sized batten door – Making fence across rear of yard – setting joist partitions in 2nd story, two doors, battens, windows and doors cased, base around rooms, furring overhead as agreed upon, and all furring &c, including everything necessary for the mason's to commence work – black latches and bolts to the three doors – everything complete and done in a workmanlike manner – Work and materials forty five dollars. –
>
> Received Brooklyn Nov. 14th 1854 of Walter Whitman twelve and a half dollars in advance on acc't of the above job to purchase materials – the job to be done by the 1st of December, unless prevented by bad weather or sickness
>
> [Charles Burton][13]

As this document shows, Whitman was not quite the artisanal figure he has sometimes been mistaken for. Rather than contributing manually to these projects, he took a predominantly administrative role in the construction process—hiring builders, sketching designs, writing receipts.[14] Here and there, we get traces of an artisan's knowledge, requesting that the roof be "well battened, with one good sized batten door" and that things are in order for the mason to start work, but this document is governed predominantly by the voice of a "recruiter" giving orders to his workforce. This is Whitman as taskmaster concerned with the quality of the work he commissioned and for good reason. A general lack of building regulation led to the frequent collapse of newly erected structures in New York and Brooklyn at this time.[15] Aside from the financial risk of engaging with a

---

[13] Papers of Walt Whitman in the Charles E. Feinberg Collection, "Miscellany, 1834–1918," Manuscript Division, Library of Congress, Washington, D.C.

[14] See Justin Kaplan's account of this in *Walt Whitman: A Life* (New York: Simon and Schuster, 1980): "It was Walt who patiently docketed the payment receipts for surveying and interest, lumber and paint, doors and window glass, brackets and mouldings, sashes and blinds, tin and tinning, and it was Walt who drew up specifications for flooring, partitions, casings, shed roofs, stair rails, and masonry work, including 'Stone wall for cellar, chimneys and fireplaces, Plastering, Cistern, Privy, Cess Pool, Flagging in front,' and so on" (160).

[15] The Feinberg Collection contains similar documents relating to the construction of the houses on Cumberland Street in 1852–3. Again we get the textured voice of the artisan-cum-manager of labor. Structures were "to be framed complete, according to plan, with

volatile market, Whitman was also preoccupied with making sure that his buildings were properly secure: there is a certain anxiety implied in his request that the roof be "well battened." Various major accidents occurred whilst Whitman was active in the housing market: on November 24, 1851, the *Brooklyn Eagle* reported the caving in of a new two story building on Fulton Avenue;[16] on March 29, 1852, two three-story houses also came down in Manhattan, killing four laborers;[17] and on July 1, 1852, a four-story building on Carleton Avenue gave way and killed several passers-by.[18] If such an accident had befallen Whitman, he and his family would have been ruined. Inadequate protection against fires also put whole neighborhoods of Brooklyn and Manhattan at risk. Whitman's article "How to Avoid Dangerous Fires" (October 10, 1845) drew attention to the worrying fact that up to three quarters of Brooklyn's houses were constructed out of wood.[19] This turned out to be a prophetic warning: the great fire of 1848 destroyed vast sections of Brooklyn including the headquarters of Whitman's own newly established *Brooklyn Freeman*—a publication that only managed to put out one edition before it was burnt to the ground. Whitman knew what kind of gamble he was taking with real estate and made sure that those he employed did their jobs.

What also needs amplifying in these contractual documents is the vibrantly new social and economic stance implied by Whitman's managerial voice; it is a voice that straddles the increasing divide between artisan builder and capitalist opportunist. M. Wynn Thomas has provided the fullest account of this tension:

> in the post-artisanal phase the function (and with it the whole status) of the producer is fundamentally altered. He now produces for a middleman who deals in a complex, increasingly remote, and demanding market. In the first instance this intermediary may be only the distributor of the product, but even then he soon comes to dictate the terms of production . . . Under this

good stuff" and Mr Hedges was also "to seal up the stairs with good sealing boards, so as to enclose the same tight up to the front door."

[16] "Yesterday morning the new building, intended for a market and situated on the corner of Fulton Avenue and Bond Street recently commenced by Messrs. Stone & Sother and which had nearly been completed, fell to the ground, the whole building coming down." Anon., "Fall of a Building," *Brooklyn Eagle*, November 24, 1851.

[17] "About 11–12 o'clock on Saturday afternoon, two three story buildings in progress of erection [. . .] fell with a tremendous crash, burying in their ruins four out of seven laborers who were employed on them [. . .] They were recovered from the rubbish and taken to the hospital, where they soon died." Anon., "Fall of Building and Loss of Life," *Brooklyn Eagle*, March 29, 1852.

[18] Anon., "Fall of a Building—Serious Accident," *Brooklyn Eagle*, July 1, 1852.

[19] Walt Whitman, "How to Avoid Dangerous Fires," *Brooklyn Eagle*, October 10, 1845.

arrangement the former artisan, now effectively a supplier or hirer of labor in return for money, finds himself deeply implicated in a system of relations which alter his whole conception of himself and his work [...] He lives by the competitive accumulation of capital, rather than by virtue of what he produces through the exercise and public demonstration of patiently acquired skills.   (69–70)[20]

So, for example, Whitman built to sell, but was forced to move his family from newly built house to newly built house in order to cut down on living costs; he was also not so detached from the production process that he was saved from having to fix the various problems that always emerge when overseeing any construction project, especially when getting everything in order for the rush in May. His article "Tear Down and Build Over Again" is a manifestation of the conflict he struggled with throughout these years—an acute sense of vanishing tradition pushing against his own complicity in the rise of the volatile marketplace. A similar working relationship can be pieced together between Whitman and the Rome Brothers printing firm—with Whitman ordering renovations and alterations for others to execute whilst simultaneously chipping in with the advice of someone who was knowledgeable about the printing process.[21] One might ask why Whitman gave the job to the Rome Brothers when he had extensive knowledge of the printing trade and could probably have hired the necessary equipment and completed the project himself. The answer may lie in the fact that Whitman now had experience of an alternative mode of production, enabling him to mingle his experiences of real estate speculation with a printer's expertise, and flexibly combine a managerial perspective with an artisanal knowledge.

The Whitman, then, that emerges here is a much more politically ambiguous figure. Whitman's experiences of house building provided a new way of directing a workforce from the simultaneously detached and involved perspectives of the printer/artisan-cum-manager. This conflation is very much apparent in the experimental changes that were made to the second 1856 edition of *Leaves*. The book had 394 pages and contained 32 titled poems. Twenty of them were new, including "Broad-Axe Poem," "Sun-Down Poem," and "Poem of the Road." Whitman's long lines were refitted into a limited space, causing

[20] Lawson sees this tension embodied in the rise of the lower middle class, a demographic in which he convincingly places Whitman (4–8). His focus however is on how these tensions manifested themselves in print culture specifically.

[21] See David S. Reynolds's discussion of Whitman's knowledge of the printing trade in *Walt Whitman's America: A Cultural Biography* (1996), 44.

the lines to spill over into much more homogenous-looking blocks of language.[22] Whitman magnified the original frontispiece portrait so that it filled its page almost entirely. There was also a "Leaves-Droppings" section "annexed" (Whitman's word) to the back of the book that contained Emerson's complimentary letter and Whitman's open response.[23] It also included eight reviews of varying degrees of praise, bafflement, and outrage (one by Whitman himself), and the results of Whitman's own phrenological report. Whitman was tacking things on—adding extensions to a structure that had just undergone a major refurbishment with the idea of making it more saleable.

The material confines of the second book format became a further structuring, and by extension formal device that governed the visual aspects of the text as well as the rhythmic potential of words. This is a passage from the second poem of the 1855 edition, later entitled "A Song for Occupations":

> Grains and manures . . marl, clay, loam . . the subsoil plough . . the
>   shovel and pick and rake and hoe . . irrigation and draining;
> The currycomb . . the horse-cloth . . the halter and bridle and bits . . the
>   very wisps of straw,
> The barn and barn-yard . . the bins and mangers . . the mows and racks:
> Manufactures . . commerce . . engineering . . the building of cities, and
>   every trade carried on there . . and the implements of every trade,
> The anvil and tongs and hammer . . the axe and wedge . . the square and
>   mitre and jointer and smoothingplane;
> The plumbob and trowel and level . . the wall-scaffold, and the work of
>   walls and ceilings . . or any mason-work: [. . . .]   (*LG*,1855, 61–62)

This is the same passage in 1856:

> Grains, manures, marl, clay, loam, the subsoil
>   plough, the shovel, pick, rake, hoe, irrigation,
>   draining,
> The curry-comb, the horse-cloth, the halter, bridle,
>   bits, the very wisps of straw,
> The barn and barn-yard, the bins, mangers, mows,
>   racks,

---

[22] All quotations from the 1856 edition of *Leaves of Grass* are reprinted here with the line segments exactly as they originally appeared in *Leaves of Grass* (Brooklyn: Fowler and Wells, 1856): http://whitmanarchive.org/published/LG/1856/whole.html.

[23] Whitman includes two "annexes" in his final 1891 edition of *Leaves*—"Sands at Seventy . . . *1st Annex*" and "Good-Bye My Fancy . . . 2d Annex"—explicitly comparing his book to a building. See *Leaves of Grass* (Philadelphia: David McKay, 1891), 1: http://whitmanarchive.org/published/LG/1891/whole.html.

> Manufactures, commerce, engineering, the build-
>   ing of cities, every trade carried on there,
>   the implements of every trade,
> The anvil, tongs, hammer, the axe and wedge,
>   the square, mitre, jointer, smoothing-plane,
> The plumbob, trowel, level, the wall-scaffold, the
>   work of walls and ceilings, any mason-
>   work, [. . . .]   (*LG*, 1856, 131)

Aside from the narrowing of the page space, notice the cull of conjunctions and dotted ellipses, which moves the poem away from the more
paced metrical arrangement of interspersed rising duple and triple meters
of 1855: "the shovel and pick and rake and hoe" is now pared down in
1856 to "the shovel, pick, rake, hoe, irrigation, draining."[24] These revisions experiment with new ways of joining and battening words (metaphors that take on a material potency in this instance). Furthermore, the
removal of conjunctions condenses the stresses within the line and more
explicitly recasts it as an inventory. Henry David Thoreau, having been
given a copy of this edition by the author, stated that: "by [Whitman's]
heartiness and broad generalities he puts me into a liberal frame of mind
prepared to see wonders . . . and then—throws in a thousand of brick."[25]
Thoreau's metaphor aptly figures Whitman's second book as a new arrangement of raw materials, a trial of how best to arrange and join poetic building
blocks. Whitman's blanket application of the comma in 1856 provides a
new architecture to the content that is ultimately an experiment in rhythm.
The narrower material format serves as a pacing device that changes the way
we read the lines, endowing them with a modified temporality. In the future
editions of *Leaves*, all of these aspects would shift again, but for now, this
particular arrangement served as the provisional solution.

Some lines from *Leaves of Grass* appear in three different forms between
1855 and 1856. These are lines from 1855:

Pasturelife, foddering, milking and herding, and all the personnel and usages;
The plum-orchard and apple-orchard . . . .gardening . . seedlings, cuttings, flowers
    and vines, (*LG*, 1855, 61)

---

[24] Ezra Greenspan details Whitman's extensive use of the participle form: "he saw the
poetic act basically as one of physical and intellectual mobility, which required of him the
verbal necessity of pushing off immediately participally, as though from a springboard."
Although this notion of mobility is useful, Greenspan confines himself to a description
rather than an explanation. Ezra Greenspan, "Some Remarks on the Poetics of 'Participle-
Loving Whitman'" in Ezra Greenspan (ed.), *The Cambridge Companion to Walt Whitman*
(Cambridge: Cambridge University Press, 1995), 94.
[25] Henry David Thoreau to Harrison Blake, December 7, 1865, *The Writings of Henry
David Thoreau*, Vol. 11 (1894), 347.

1856 reads:

> Pasture-life, foddering, milking, herding, all the
>   personnel and usages,
> The plum-orchard, apple-orchard, gardening,
>   seedlings, cuttings, flowers, vines,   (*LG*, 1856, 131)

And "Leaves-Droppings", the annex at the back of the 1856 book reserved for reviews of the first edition, reads:

> Pasture-life, foddering, milking and herding, and all the personnel and
>   usages;
> The plum-orchard and apple-orchard, gardening, seedlings, cuttings,
>   flowers and vines, [...]   (*LG*, 1856, 380)

The London *Examiner*'s review quoted this last version, supposedly transcribing the 1855 text.[26] However, either the extract shows the reviewer altering Whitman's punctuation by leaving out the dotted ellipses, or it shows Whitman's work as it looked during the transition between volumes—more probably the latter, because every review included in "Leaves-Droppings" removed all traces of Whitman's ellipses. So it seems that the poet has let the reviews stand, but not the poems they quote. Whitman also fastidiously corrects "Pasturelife" to "Pasture-life," which updates the word to its 1856 appearance even though it is quoted as the 1855 text. Taken together, these three cross-sections show the poet impatiently revising or better administering to his writing, unable to settle on a permanent solution, and clearly drawn towards to the pleasures of overseeing production and reproduction.

And yet in spite of this predilection, Whitman, tended to simplify the complexity of his production processes and the narrative of his own career, choosing to align himself with the various artisanal and spiritual mythologies that were steadily being perpetuated by his ever-expanding circle of friends and admirers.[27] It was as the "Good

---

[26] See Matt Cohen's discussion of the London Examiner review in his "Martin Tupper, Walt Whitman, and the Early Reviews of Leaves of Grass," *Walt Whitman Quarterly Review* 16.1 (1998): 23–31.

[27] In 1868, Whitman's friend and admirer William Douglas O'Connor published "The Carpenter: A Christmas Story" in *Putnam's Monthly Magazine* (January 1867): 55–90. Although Whitman's name was not mentioned explicitly, it is made quite clear that the mysterious stranger who arrives and makes everyone's Christmas better is meant to be a cross between Christ and the poet. This story followed O'Connor's other work *The Good Gray Poet: A Vindication* (New York: Bunce and Huntington, 1866), a highly sentimentalized portrayal of Whitman that, along with "The Carpenter," was to significantly influence later perceptions of him as a neglected, bearded, benevolent prophet replete with Christ-like carpentry skills and the ability to make (fake) butterflies perch on his extended finger. See Michael Robertson's discussion in *Worshipping Walt: The Whitman Disciples* (2010), 33.

Grey Poet" or the Christ-like "Poet Carpenter" that Whitman speaks in
the following 1886 *Brooklyn Eagle* article, (lengthily) entitled "A Visit to
Walt Whitman: He Recalls the Years When He Lived in Brooklyn [. . .]
Leaving the Carpenter's Work to Turn Poet. What Might Have Been
Had He Continued to Build Houses—Where 'Leaves of Grass' First Saw
the Light":

> My father was a carpenter and came into that trade by inheritance. So I set to
> work at it after I gave up editing newspapers. I built the building which is at
> 100 Myrtle avenue. Afterward I added an extension to it in the rear yard,
> where I did job printing in connection with my building enterprises. Before
> long, however, I got the chance to sell this place at quite a good penny and let
> it go. I had begun to think of making my fortune as a builder. I bought
> several lots on Cumberland Street, between Fulton street and Atlantic
> avenues, where I put up five houses, all of which I soon sold at a good
> penny. I now had quite a little sum of money in hand. But I got a bee in my
> bonnet and took to the pen. I soon published *Leaves of Grass*. I ought to have
> stuck to the building of houses and buying real estate. If I had I should be a
> man of means now. As it is I am only the author of "Leaves of Grass."
>
> > (*Brooklyn Eagle*, July 11, 1886)

This reflection makes an implicit distinction between his real estate
and writerly work, presenting the former as a moneymaking activity
and the latter as the vocational identity to which he was called.
However, by casting himself as either a carpenter or, as with some
instances in the notebooks and poems, a builder/architect—"I see
them building churches to God . . . | If I build a church it shall be a
church to men and women" (*NUPM* 146)—Whitman aligned the
development of the 1855 *Leaves of Grass* within the organic narratives
of the skilled artisan, a figure who more properly "learns their trade by
inheritance"—who gains a spirit or knowledge passed down from
generation to generation. Whitman's early biographers John Burroughs and Richard Bucke, whose biographies were the product of
interviews with the poet and included Whitman's own amendments,
both relay the putting together of *Leaves* in more politically palatable
artisanal metaphors:

> In 1855, then, after many manuscript doings and undoings, and much
> matter destroyed, and two or three complete re-writings, the essential
> foundation of Leaves of Grass was laid and the superstructure raised.
>
> > (Burroughs, 83)

> By the spring of 1855, Walt Whitman had found or made a style in which he
> could express himself, and in that style he had (after, as he has told me,
> elaborately building up the structure, and then utterly demolishing it, five

different times) written twelve poems, and a long prose preface which was simply another poem.   (Bucke, 137)

As I have suggested, it is only partly accurate to speak of his poetry's development in the terms of a restless process of building up and demolishing, of reshaping and remodeling. What obscures the potency and material implications of these critical metaphors is the caricature of Whitman as himself a builder or carpenter, a form of work that all too easily aligns with an innate poetic calling. He was, however, neither of these things: instead he was implicated in the rise of a new post-artisanal bourgeoisie, a group of middlemen that had started floating away from the traditional coordinates of labor and production. It was Whitman's active exposure to, and skillful negotiation of, this new predicament that finds form in his writing.

When he wrote out the receipts for labor costs, title deeds, and housing contracts, Whitman adopted a specific marketplace persona, "Walter Whitman Jr." Here are three examples drawn from the scores of receipts collected in the "miscellaneous" boxes of the Feinberg Collection:

> Brooklyn, October 23rd 1852. Received of Walter Whitman, jr, Fifteen Dollars, in part payment of work done by me, by contract, on houses in Cumberland Avenue   [Signed Scofield]

> Brooklyn, June 14th 1853, Received of Walter Whitman, Jr. Sixty Five Dollars, being payment in full of all demands on my contract for carpenter work and materials on two story house in Cumberland St.   [Signed Hedges]

> Brooklyn, June 3rd 1854 Received of Walter Whitman Jr. One Hundred Dollars, as first payment On Work in Skillman St.   [signed Smith & Selleck][28]

As with the building contract, Whitman wrote the majority of his receipts himself and then handed them over to be signed by the workers he had employed. "Received of Walter Whitman Jr." is the insistently repeated refrain that Whitman formulated in these dockets. In such moments, Whitman inscribed an ephemeral self that floated above the tactile domain of labor in the realm of economic exchange. These are the inscriptions of what might be thought of in terms of Whitman's "homo economicus," a transacting self validated in the moment of a specific exchange and structured within a particular set of market conditions.[29] But far from

[28] Papers of Walt Whitman in the Charles E. Feinberg Collection, "Miscellany, 1834–1918," Manuscript Division, Library of Congress, Washington, DC.

[29] The OED defines "homo economicus" as "a hypothetical person who manages his or her private income and expenditure strictly in accordance with rational self-interest, with no regard to the welfare of others." In relation to industrial modernity, this abstract model of man is usually seen as having dominated and surpassed constructions such as "homo empathicus"

functioning as an existential given, the survival of this economic self
was dependent on the market forces that produced it in the first
place; this was a self that only materialized in a specific economic
context. Now imagine that another preoccupation momentarily
diverted this manifestation of economic self-interest away from its
original animating environment: in such moments, homo economicus
becomes partially waylaid, no longer the exclusive conduit of the forces
that had originally summoned its existence. Up for repossession, the
economic patterns of Walter Whitman Jr transformed into a series
of structuring poetic devices; linguistic husks that were now capable
of conveying or channeling other, stranger freight. It was into these
repossessed circuits of exchange that the "I" of "Song of Myself" took
up residence; Whitman's formal universe not "exist[ing] in opposition to the marketplace but produced by and contained within it"
(Michaels, 112).[30]

The first edition of *Leaves of Grass* is strewn with the linguistic
remnants of this economic world, removed from their initial context
and redeployed as vehicles that transmit Whitman's seemingly escapist
narratives of the Kosmic self. In fact, the unmistakable traces of this
realm are so structurally integral to Whitman's textual fabric so as to
even find inflection in the very title of his most famous poem "Song of
Myself." What does the "of" do in the repeated formulation "Received
of Walter Whitman Jnr"? As when Portia in *The Merchant of Venice* asks:
"What ring gave you, my lord? | Not that, I hope, which you received of
me" (5.1, 183–4, 478), "of" takes on the function of "from" in these
exchanges, which conveys a sense of transaction: Bassanio has received *of*

---

and "homo ethicus." See for example Martha Fineman and Terence Dougherty (eds),
Feminism Confronts Homo Economicus: Gender, Law, and Society (2005), or Daniel Cohen,
Homo Economicus: The (Lost) Prophet of Modern Times (2014). In this chapter, I try to
complicate any combative or bipartite model; not to suggest that homo economicus was in
any way prior but rather that all three figures are coextensive and integrated.

[30] This claim extends an argument put forward by Walter Benn Michaels in his well-
known essay "Romance and Real Estate." Michaels reads Nathaniel Hawthorne's apparent
affirmations of the "inalienable right in the self" in *The House of the Seven Gables* as
reproducing the very logic of property speculation that it attempts to reject. "Property,"
Michaels reminds us, "to be property, must be alienable," and in framing self-worth in
terms of a kind of property deed that ought to be possessed by the self, Hawthorne's
conceptions of "independence and integrity (artistic or otherwise) did not exist in opposition to the marketplace but are produced by and contained within it" (112). See Walter
Benn Michaels, *The Gold Standard and the Logic of Naturalism: American Literature at the
Turn of the Century* (1987), 110. Michaels' approach can be broadly associated with the rise
of the "New Economic Criticism" in the 1980s: Marc Shell, Jean-Joseph Goux, and
Michael Germana developed similar homologies between economic and language systems.
See for example, Marc Shell, *Money, Language, and Thought: Literary and Philosophical
Economies from the Medieval to the Modern Era* (1982).

Portia a ring; contractors have received *of* Whitman payment. John
Hollander, discussing the "multivalent service" provided by the preposition *of* in "Song of Myself" says that "a 'Song of Y' could be about Y,
composed by Y, composed of Y, from (the land of) Y, etc" (Hollander,
Work, 102).[31] This last option can be extended—a "Song of Y" is not
only a "Song from the land of Y" but also crucially a "song received from
Y." This implied transaction from poet to reader is formulated more
explicitly at the beginning of what would later become "A Song for
Occupations":

COME closer to me,
Push close my lovers and take the best I possess,
Yield closer and closer and give me the best you possess.

This is unfinished business with me . . . . how is it with you?
I was chilled with the cold types and cylinder and wet paper between us.

I pass so poorly with paper and types . . . . I must pass with the contact
    of bodies and souls.

I do not thank you for liking me as I am, and liking the touch of
    me . . . . I know that it is good for you to do so.   (*LG*, 1855, 57)

Whitman scores his poetry with the subverted imperatives of give and
take, as well as the repurposed dynamics of economic risk and trust. The
voice asks that we "*yield* closer and closer"; this is always "unfinished
business." The "touch *of me*" is both the touch from the "I" and the touch
of "you," a point of momentary contact and exchange as the dynamic "I"
passes through. He "passes poorly" and "is chilled" with the "cold types,"
"cylinder," and "wet paper between us," as though displeased by the
material processes that hinder the ease of exchange. He desires the
momentary consummation of the deal and "knows that it is good for
you to do so," attempting to convince us that we should enter into the new
complicities of his peculiar contract.

The song continues:

Were all educations practical and ornamental well displayed out
    of me, what would it amount to?
Were I as the head teacher or charitable proprietor or wise statesman,
    what would it amount to?
Were I to you as the boss employing and paying you, would that
    satisfy you? The learned and virtuous and benevolent, and the usual terms;
A man like me, and never the usual terms.

---

[31] Whitman occasionally writes "from" instead of "of": "Received from Walter Whitman
Jr." But he stuck to the more archaic usage for the majority of his dockets.

Neither a servant nor a master am I,
I take no sooner a large price than a small price . . . . I will have
    my own whoever enjoys me,
I will be even with you, and you shall be even with me.   (*LG*, 1855, 57)

The prepositional function of "of"—"well displayed out of me"—explicitly articulates a contractual transfer *from* "me" to "you." This is immediately followed up with a question of price: "what would it amount to?" The "I" adopts an attitude of perpetual and fluid negotiation in a form of sales pitch designed to shore up confidence in a deal. Virtue and authority—"learned", "benevolent"—merely reproduce the quotidian: "the usual terms". The dynamic, new man "like me", however, will go beyond what is customary and established and give you something extra: "never the usual terms." The "I" sells us the possibilities inherent in his shifting middle ground, transforming the strange, problematic lines from his notebook—"I am the poet of slaves and of the master of slaves" (*NUPM*, 67)—into "Neither a servant nor master am I". These contractual forms allows him to negotiate a new kind of agreement, not based on prefabricated decorum and fixed price but on the momentary and promiscuous satisfactions of a specific transaction: "I will have my own whoever enjoys me, | I will be even with you and you shall be even with me."

J. K. Gibson-Graham might describe Whitman's technique here in terms of "liberating a space of economic difference, one in which a noncapitalist politics of economic invasion might take root and flourish" (5). But such subversion is never guaranteed: the Whitmanic self simultaneously repossesses, reappropriates, but also so often seems to capitulate to the logic of primitive accumulation:

> I fly the flight of the fluid and swallowing soul,
> My course runs below the soundings of plummets.
>
> I help myself to material and immaterial,
> No guard can shut me off, no law can prevent me.
>
> I anchor my ship for a little while only,
> My messengers continually cruise away or bring their returns to me.
>   (*LG*,1855, 38)

At this juncture the "I" is figured as an all-engulfing elemental liquid, capable of swallowing up the cosmos; the overwhelming force of economic liquidity subsumes any earthly plummet that attempts to sound the depths of a universe only it can fathom. It is the embodiment of universality, capable of baptizing everything, both material and immaterial, in its infinite range. And yet again, sustaining this all-encompassing self is the language of production and consumption.[32] The "fluid and swallowing soul" is an insatiable scavenger; the "I" is a phantom mouth that helps itself indiscriminately to everything. The course of such an "I" runs beneath the sounding of plummets, divorced from the tactile world of human production, and comes into being only at the provisional moment of transaction, the moment when it manifests its consumptive power on the page: "I help myself to." It anchors itself to enable the transacting messengers to bring back their "returns." The movement of this self is attuned to Whitman's promiscuous urban activities; he stays still only in the moment of a particular exchange and then moves on.

When the speaker finds himself praising the animal kingdom, he does so because:

> Not one is dissatisfied . . . . not one is demented with the mania of
>   owning things,
> Not one kneels to another nor to his kind that lived thousands
>   of years ago,
> Not one is respectable or industrious over the whole earth.
>
> So they show their relations to me and I accept them;
> They bring me tokens of myself . . . . they evince them plainly in their
>   possession.
>
> I do not know where they got those tokens,
> I must have passed that way untold times ago and negligently
>   dropt them, [. . .]   (*LG*, 1855, 34)

After differentiating animals from the realm of human social and economic relations—they are not dissatisfied, they do not own, they are neither industrious nor respectable—Whitman initiates them into an alternative system of universal "tokens," which is floated on a transparent interspecies stock market: "They bring me tokens of myself." This carries the market connotation "from myself"—tokens from himself that he negligently dropped "untold times ago" that have now been brought back to him. Once again, in transmitting this vision, when the transcendent "I" materializes on the page, it is bound by market vocabulary. The animals exist in a world where "Not one kneels to another nor to his kind that lived thousands of years ago" and yet it is they that subserviently bring

---

[32] Richard Pascal has argued that "by overturning the standard meanings of terms associated with finance and commerce, Whitman attempts to twist capitalist discourse to his own purposes and subvert some of its basic assumptions without directly rejecting them." Richard Pascal, ' "Dimes on the Eyes": Walt Whitman and the Pursuit of Wealth in America', *Nineteenth Century Literature* 44.2 (September 1989): 141–72 (149).

tokens back to the poet who "passed that way untold times ago." This is shaded in terms of deference towards a supervisor; the animals show their relations and are "accepted," as if making a sales pitch to a possible client. The passage attempts to undermine the human world of ownership with a vision of a new transcendent natural order, and yet it does this by seemingly transposing the very patterns it seeks to repudiate. This is a language that pushes against the discursive parameters that makes it possible.

It is also a detached, commanding market persona that asserts itself again with the introduction of Whitman's name:

> Walt Whitman, an American, one of the roughs, a kosmos,
> Disorderly fleshy and sensual. . . . eating drinking and breeding,
> No sentimentalist. . . . no stander above men and women or
>   apart from them. . . . no
> more modest than immodest.
> Unscrew the locks from the doors!
> Unscrew the doors themselves from their jambs.   (*LG*, 1855, 29)

As the "I" announces itself triumphantly in the third person, we are presented with a persona seemingly distinct from the Walter Whitman of the book's title page who registered his book at the clerk's office in 1855. But the administrative "Walter" and the poet "Walt" are not so easily separated. Unlike Walter Whitman Jr who employs a workforce to build his houses, this Walt claims not to stand "above men or women or apart from them," and yet in the two subsequent lines we hear a remnant of an administrative voice ordering an invisible workforce to "unscrew the locks from the doors! | Unscrew the doors themselves from their jambs." It is also difficult not to be reminded of a similar order given by Walter Whitman Jr six months earlier in November 1854: "Transposing front door to wall between rooms and back window to place of door, weatherboarding under it, removing stoop in front, finishing and setting door in their places, complete in every respect."[33]

Those crucial couple of years before he published *Leaves* have been restructured according to certain political logics and priorities as a period in which Whitman concentrated solely on poetry—fostering the myth that the poet works best when isolated in his creative garret. Thomas described the later Whitman, now established as a poet, "grasping at air" and "building cloud castles" (79), producing verse that was disconnected from the chaotic energies that had shaped his early efforts. His monument

---

[33] Papers of Walt Whitman in the Charles E. Feinberg Collection, "Miscellany, 1834–1918," Manuscript Division, Library of Congress, Washington, DC.

in Harleigh Cemetery, Camden, most acutely demonstrates this uncoupling; a poetry shaped by house building ended with the construction of a granite tomb. Huge blocks, weighing several tons each, made up "the rudest most undress'd structure (with an idea)—since Egypt, perhaps the cave dwellers."[34] Friends and admirers could not believe that Whitman the "Good Gray Poet" was prepared to spend so much money ($4,000) on such an extravagant, self-aggrandizing monument. The structures he built on either side of *Leaves of Grass*—the houses that bookend his career—are an important gauge of his development from hustling entrepreneur of real estate to hustling promoter of his own inflated poetic mythos.

In providing these readings, I have offered only a fragment of the preoccupied creative confluence that forged *Leaves of Grass* in 1855. There are of course other aspects to this story, with Whitman's novelistic and journalistic ambitions also no doubt informing the contours of this book. But again, I have chosen to focus on Whitman's real estate dealings because of this particular labor's ideological ungainliness; because even Whitman himself seemed subsequently at pains to downplay and then sculpt his artisan-carpenter persona in relation to these market-bound activities. And this in spite of the fact that the 1855 *Leaves of Grass* would not exist if Whitman had been shielded from the economic energies that defined his precarious milieu. His strange conflation of production methods, the mixture of quick-fixes, amendments, and accidents, the half-glimpsed desire to transform and reroute the stresses of his situation: all of these elements filter and fiber the living sensuous activity that constituted this poet's work. The resulting political and poetical discord, with the writing caught somewhere between affirmation, assimilation, rejection, and reappropriation of market dynamics, unfolds a process of production that cannot be reduced or assigned to any division of labor or corresponding preconception of vocational identity.

---

[34] Walt Whitman to Richard Maurice Bucke, June 4, 1891, *The Correspondence*, Vol. V: *1890–1892*, edited by Edwin Haviland Miller (1969), 196.

2

Whitman and the Transformations of Labor

Up to this point, I have focused on how Whitman's real estate dealings informed the production of his early poetry. In claiming that his involvement with the marketplace can be seen in the transactional self registered in *Leaves*, though, I want to make it clear that I am in no way attempting to portray Whitman as some kind of inadvertent champion of liberal capitalism. Rather, I want to suggest that it is actually because of Whitman's compromised position, writing from within rather than outside of such relations, that his writing maintains a radical potential (though not necessarily in the sense traditionally ascribed to him by the Left). In order to develop this claim, I turn now to a less analyzed and likely unconscious characteristic of Whitman's verse: his consistent representation of coagulation, or elemental, metamorphic stickiness. With a tendency of tempering the sense of economic liquidity that often defines his work, Whitman's stickiness offers a counterbalance to his own (often troubling) attitudes towards the broader economic and social transformations that occurred in the mid-nineteenth century. Structuring his lines via the patterns of the marketplace, Whitman seized upon the idea of exchange, not in terms of its frictionless, exploitative potential, but as an opportunity to begin reimagining forms of bodily contact. In doing so, his poetry thinks through—or better reaches towards—an alternative labor theory of value, with his extended corporeal representations serving as an affirmative counterpart to Marx's more fully theorized and gothically dystopian depictions of alienated labor. While Marx saw the laboring body as "deforming" and "mortifying" in the context of industrial production, Whitman reimagined these accelerating promethean forces as an opportunity to recast the possibilities of intimacy (Marx, 1844, 71). In Whitman's hands, the production process issues forth a generative by-product; a newly malleable emollient that governs and glues together the dimensions of a new social contract.[1]

---

[1] Whitman's fascination with such malleable fluid-like substances—a means by which he pushes past the limitations of literary representation—has been most convincingly

Another way of saying this is that Whitman's participation in the fluctuating dynamics of his economic and social environment—exemplified chiefly by the rising tensions between slavery and the accelerations of capitalism—rescued his poetic vision from restating the reactionary essentialisms that defined the popular labor movements of the 1850s. In spite of his attraction and allegiance to the Free Soil lobby, which viewed the geographic spread of American slavery as a potential threat to the promise of white sovereign labor, he formulated a poetics that resisted contemporary fictions of racial and social purity and with it any abstractly conceived notion of free exchange. Whitman's poetry refused the allure of a racially inflected organicism while simultaneously avoiding any clear-cut affirmation of the supposedly inevitable march of U.S. laissez-faire capitalism. His is a poetry that spills away from such abstractions towards something more politically contaminated and suggestive.

Here again, is the opening of what Whitman, a year later, would entitle "Poem of The Daily Work of The Workmen and Workwomen of these States" (eventually "A Song for Occupations"):

> COME closer to me,
> Push close my lovers and take the best I possess,
> Yield closer and closer and give me the best you possess.
>
> This is unfinished business with me. . . . how is it with you?
> I was chilled with the cold types and cylinder and wet paper between us.
> I pass so poorly with paper and types. . . . I must pass with the contact
>   of bodies and souls.   (*LG*, 1855, 57)

Acutely aware and discomfited by the inanimate material qualities of the printed page, Whitman's speaker imagines yet one more way a familiarity might be established between the "lovers" (his readers) and himself. Modifying his initial personal overtures with some fair-dealing straight-talk that suggests an incomplete transaction—"this is unfinished business with me. . . . how is it with you?"—he simultaneously (and without consent) begins pushing or hatching through the paper. And having apparently emerged at the reader's side, justifies his actions by claiming (now in the past tense) that he "was chilled with the cold types and cylinder and wet paper" of the previous material arrangement. This maneuver fulfils two functions: first it goes some way in consummating an impossible

explored by Michael Moon in *Disseminating Whitman*. Moon suggests that Whitman "sets himself the problem of attempting to project actual physical presence in a literary text": "At the heart of this problem was the impossibility of doing so literally, of successfully disseminating the author's literal bodily presence through the medium of the book." See *Disseminating Whitman: Revision and Corporeality in* Leaves of Grass (1991), 5.

fantasy—literally emerging from the page in order to establish a further bodily contact with his lover-readers—and second, it draws attention to the semi-corporeal, semi-mechanistic arrangement of labor and paper-maché that has apparently defined the speaker–reader relation up to this point.

In Alan Trachtenberg's view, this fantasy remediation of body into book enacts the poet's ideal of exchange: "Whitman reimagines America as a space in which the encounter between poet and reader occurs on the surface of the page whose very thingness excites the desire and need for a closeness attainable only by tallying this for that, the thing or object for the price paid for it in living labor" ("Politics," 129). Whitman's revisioning of the proximity between poet and reader (as well as reader to the printed page) aims at an ideal correspondence, "a tallying of America with an economy of aesthetic exchange, a bartering of being for being" (129), as exemplified by the later lines, "I will be even with you, and you shall be even with me" (*LG*, 1855, 57).

Yet there is also, it seems to me, another impulse here, something that continually counteracts this supposedly utopian desire for equivalence and stalls the reification necessary for any such free exchange to occur. As with so much of Whitman's poetry—and this is what makes his early efforts so compelling—the passage partially forecloses on its implicit promise; neither body nor book ever fully settles into a final form or "thingness." Whitman muddles his transfer—"I pass so poorly with paper and types. . . . I must pass with the contact of bodies and souls"—writing the simple-present verb form as though it were semantically clear-cut: "pass." Is that "pass," "move past," "get by," "resemble," "hand over," "decline," or what? In spite of the imperative "must" and seeming rejection of the inanimate "cold types and cylinder and wet paper between us," the speaker lingers mid-production with that wetness. While affirming the ideal of free exchange, the speaker also undermines its very possibility by foregrounding a fantasy print shop assemblage of bodies, cylinders, and ink—a curiously sticky compound of wet sheets and chilling types, which only serves to further highlight the warmth and moistness of the bodies present. Contemporaries of Whitman's with any rudimentary knowledge of the printing process would have picked up on the erotic sensory implications of this passage. Having worked as a printer's apprentice or "printer's devil" himself, Whitman imbues these lines with an intimate knowledge of the physical labors (and bodily fluids) that went into producing any particular printed sheet. Bill Kovarik, a historian of nineteenth-century printing techniques, has detailed the ways in which young apprentices were assigned chores such as greasing the press with animal fat, and making sure the ink was sticky enough for the pressmen or "beater" to apply onto the types. The beater did this using two soft leather inking balls, which apprentices made from animal hides soaked in vats of their own urine.[2] Whitman's supposed impulse towards utopic exchange momentarily checks itself in such a context: just as this "ideal bartering" seems consummated through an escape from the confines of the book, the poem simultaneously draws attention to the alternative erotic arrangement of lingering between sticky wet sheets. We are left suspended somewhere in the production process in which transactions (poet to reader, labor into book, book into commodity) always remain "unfinished business."

A second staging of such intimacy in the 1855 *Leaves*, in what would later become "I Sing the Body Electric", also involves a curious sense of suspension:

> This is the female form,
> A divine nimbus exhales from it from head to foot,
> It attracts with fierce undeniable attraction,
> I am drawn by its breath as if I were no more than a helpless vapor . . . all falls
>   aside but myself and it,
> Books, art, religion, time . . the visible and solid earth . . the atmosphere
>   and the fringed clouds . . what was expected of heaven or feared of hell are
>   now consumed,
> Mad filaments, ungovernable shoots play out of it . . the response
>   likewise ungovernable,
> Hair, bosom, hips, bend of legs, negligent falling hands —all diffused . . mine
>   too diffused,
> Ebb stung by the flow, and flow stung by the ebb. . . . loveflesh swelling and
>   deliciously aching,
> Limitless limpid jets of love hot and enormous. . . . quivering jelly of love . . .
>   white- blow and delirious juice,
> Bridegroom-night of love working surely and softly into the prostrate dawn,
> Undulating into the willing and yielding day,
> Lost in the cleave of the clasping and sweetfleshed day.   (*LG*, 1855, 79)

Beginning with an increasingly diffuse "female," the passage ends with something like its enmeshed opposite. The female form "attracts with fierce undeniable attraction"—not the most convincing line in Whitman's oeuvre—as the speaker gently proceeds to coax this transforming (gender-neutral) "it" upwards into a cloud-like state of "helpless vapor." As this nimbus exhales and ascends with the "I," the poet once again prepares for a moment of ideal exchange as "all falls aside but myself and it." At this

---

[2] See Bill Kovarik's description of this process in *Revolutions in Communication: Media History from Gutenberg to the Digital Age* (2015), 44–5.

very point though, the speaker is waylaid, distracted even, by the thing being left in his wake. The exclusive union of "myself and it" has set in motion all other oppositions (material, temporal, celestial), and it is this consuming by-product that now commands the attention. Whitman's persona abandons the ethereal female at the altar of a transcendent realm and becomes fascinated by the tangled "shoots" that start emerging from this increasingly amorphous "it" (does "it" now refer back to the "female form," the "consummation," or some embryonic maternal nebula?). The "shoots" and "filaments" then materialize as body parts, a cauldron of half-articulated limbs and tendrils into which the speaker now plunges: "mine too diffused" (never mind the quietly abandoned "female form" who has floated off into the ether). Whitman then writes the most erotically confrontational lines of his career, a moment of surrogacy in which Whitman's self stands in (or better lies in) for a bride on her wedding night. The release of the next few lines, consonant with fantasies of inky paper and production, constitutes a further half-articulated merger of limbs, labor, book making, and seminal fluid. The scene floods with the "delirious juice" of a bridegroom, who works surely and softly throughout the night; this labor is then incorporated or "Lost in the cleave of the clasping and sweetfleshed day": lost among tangled folds of human flesh, but also between the folds of stained sheets "clasped" in book form. Viewed in this light, the passage becomes another eroticized representation of production, with the speaker once again refusing the clarity of any abstract or clear-cut exchange in favor of something far more enmeshed and embodied, an ambiguous coagulation in which ambiguously gendered bodies and the products of their labor mix in more unguent form.

*   *   *

Whitman's engagement with the emerging world of work in the mid-nineteenth century was more or less Janus-faced; and while this double-ness convoluted any prescriptive political or social agenda he might have offered, it also facilitated the startling experimentation that provoked his more molten poetic figurations. As we have already seen, Whitman was attuned to the stutterings of the accelerating New York housing market, formulating his malleable poetic persona in relation to the necessities of making a living in a turbulent social and economic environment. On the other hand, and in spite of such adaptations, it was a recognizable artisan-ideal that exemplified for Whitman the most desirable relation of the American people to the promise of its sovereign territories. This figure, coded white and defined in opposition to the encroaching threat posed by slavery, is the Romantic fiction that organizes so many of Whitman's recognizable literary traits—from the frontispiece portrait in which he

presents himself as a cock-sure laborer, to the loitering "self" that leans
and loafs at his ease in "Song of Myself." One of Whitman's primary
ideological commitments was to the Jeffersonian ideal that served as the
principal rallying promise of the Free Soil and then Republican movements of the 1850s.[3] It is this embodiment of the popular "dream of
labor" that informs the defiant depiction of white male sovereignty in the
1855 frontispiece portrait. The tilted hat, hands-on-hip "where do you
think you're going" attitude stares out as the representative bouncer of a
nation of free working men; this gatekeeper character, costumed in
solidarity with housebuilders, mechanics, and farmers looks in defiance
and contempt on those who would compromise this embodiment of
pastoralism and self-reliance. Slavery was to be opposed, not in terms of
human injustice but in so far as it threatened America's small holding
pledge to "each Young Man in the Nation, North, South, East, and West"
(*Complete*, 1856, 1312). The increasingly sectional differences and
polarizing geographies of the decade are not easily mapped onto the
partitions of Whitman's complicated political and poetical vision. The
ideal "Workmen and Workwomen of these States" stand in opposition
to a conflated threat presented by a combination of slaveholders, slaves,
politicians, and a rising population of middlemen; Whitman divides the
antebellum nation not so much along clearly delineated north–south/
east–west geopolitical axes but via the rather more diffuse corporeal, and
I want to suggest racially coded, polarities of wholesomeness and
contamination. Whitman's allegiance is to the utopic union; the threat
to this union stems from a sickness within that exceeds any specific
locality or agency.

Whitman's thinking about race never managed to completely untangle
itself from its role in delineating the dimensions of his free white national
imaginary (Trachtenberg, "Politics," 122). There is really no getting away
from the crudeness of his stance; in a biography of Whitman's Civil War
years Roy Morris, Jr is unflinching in his presentation of Whitman's
racial attitudes, including this from a *Brooklyn Daily Times* editorial of
1858: "Who believes that Whites and Blacks can ever amalgamate in
America? Or who wishes it to happen? Nature has set an impassable seal
against it. Besides, is not America for the Whites? And is it not better so?"
(qtd. Morris, 80). Then there's a remark to Horace Traubel thirty years

---

[3] Whitman joined the Free Soil Party in 1848 and was then elected a delegate to its
convention in Buffalo, New York. "Free Soil, free speech, free labor, and free men" was the
campaign slogan that secured Martin van Buren's nomination for president. See Eric
Foner's introduction to *Free Soil, Free Labor, Free Men: The Ideology of the Republican
Party Before the Civil War* (1995), 1–10.

later: "that is one reason why I never went full on the nigger question [...] The nigger would not turn—would not do anything for himself— he would only act when prompted to act. No! no! I should not like to see the nigger in the saddle—it seems unnatural" (qtd. Morris, 80). Underpinning these deeply troubling pronouncements was Whitman's consistent failure to separate the black body from its association with bondage and subjection. Contra to the concerns of his increasingly embarrassed followers, he continued to think of this body as a fundamental constituent of an imminent invasive threat to the promise of free labor. In "The Eighteenth Presidency!", an unpublished polemic and thought experiment of 1856, Whitman attempted to sketch his deeply conflicted stance:[4]

> As the broad fat States of The West, the largest and best parts of the inheritance of the American farmers and mechanics, were ordained to common people and workingmen long in advance by Jefferson, Washington, and the earlier Congresses, now a far ampler west is to be ordained. Is it to be ordained to workmen, or to the masters of workmen? Shall the future mechanics of America be serfs? Shall labor be degraded, and women whipt in the fields for not performing their tasks? If slaves are not prohibited from all national American territory by law, as prohibited in the beginning, as the organic compacts authorize and require, and if, on the contrary, the entrance and establishment of slave labor through the continent is secured, there will steadily wheel into this Union, for centuries to come, slave state after slave state, the entire surface of the land owned by great proprietors, in plantations of thousands of acres, showing no more sight for free races of farmers and work-people than there is now in any European despotism or aristocracy.   (*Complete*, 1856, 1312)

The key concern: "Shall labor be degraded?" Notice the intuitive conflation of slave-masters with the more general "masters of workmen"; is America to be ordained to the "masters of workmen" or "great proprietors" whose threat to the promise of labor is continuous with the potential contagion of plantation slavery? Whitman also performs a troubling elision here in which the subjected and implicitly raced body stands in as a synecdoche for the institution as a whole: "If slaves are not prohibited from all national American territory by law, as prohibited in the beginning, as the organic compacts authorise and require." Whitman defines his organic workingmen in opposition to a descending, tarnishing scale of

---

[4] In this he aligns himself squarely with the typical racial attitudes of the era. See for example Frederick Douglass's account of the racism he suffered in Baltimore: "All at once, the white carpenters knocked off, and said they not work with free colored workmen... they broke off, swearing they would work no longer, unless he would discharge his black carpenters" (Douglass, 1845, 95).

debased and debasing forms of labor, a scale that finds its nadir in this instance in the nightmare figure of a woman whipped on a plantation as a slave: "Shall labor be degraded, and women whipt in the fields for not performing their tasks?" What sounds like class-based commentary actually labors under both raced and gendered assumptions. Whitman's unmarked "women" (as well as his unmarked "labor") refers to an essential preconception of whiteness. Consequently, these "Plantation owners" menace the borders of "nature's impassable seal" by potentially forcing this pristine female into performing the contaminating or blackening work of slaves (who of course, male or female, are already indiscriminately whipped in the fields). Present then is an intersectional and compounded threat to an essential white masculinity; Whitman introduces his audience to the terrible possibility that, with the spread of slavery, their wives will not only cross over the domestic threshold by being forced into the field, but also become implicitly tarnished by performing the work of black slaves. To him, at this moment, slavery represents an unthinkable admixture of bondage, emasculation, and miscegenation.

Whitman's polemic then extends its reach to include an attendant population of other affiliated degenerates who are all placed somewhere on that scale of descending national sickness that threatens the promise and inheritance of the ideal workingman. In counterpoint to the organic compact between America and its "BUTCHERS, SAILORS, STEVEDORES, AND DRIVERS OF HORSES, PLOUGHMEN, WOOD CUTTERS, MARKETMEN, CARPENTERS, MASONS, AND LABORERS" (1315), Whitman gives us:

> Office-holders, office-seekers, robbers, pimps, exclusives, malignants, conspirators, murderers, fancy-men, post-masters, custom-house clerks, contractors, kept-editors, spaniels well-trained to carry and fetch, jobbers, infidels, disunionists, terrorists, mail-riflers, slave-catchers, pushers of slavery, creatures of the President, creatures of would-be Presidents, spies, blowers, electioneers, body-snatchers, bawlers, bribers, compromisers, runaways, lobbyers, sponges, ruined sports, expelled gamblers, policy backers, monte-dealers, duelists, carriers of concealed weapons, blind men, deaf men, pimpled men, scarred inside with vile disorder, gaudy outside with gold chains made from the people's money and harlot's money twisted together; crawling, serpentine men, the lousy combings and born freedom sellers of the earth. (1313)

One of the great Whitmanic lists, and what is so interesting is that it brings together, under a banner of unwholesome off-white mischief, such a diverse and malleable crowd: from "runaways" to "pushers of slavery" to "contractors."[5] These are all parasites on the social body—people throw a wrench in the ideal process of production as well as of transparent and reciprocal exchange. It is clearly lovingly done, and Whitman must have also recognized and counted something of himself in this catalogue, with the reactionary tone signalling an uneasiness (as well as fascination) at finding himself placed among this castigated contingent (certainly as contractor, jobber, and lobbyist by day, and perhaps even fancy-man by night). The enumeration of this half-repellent, half-delicious collection of fancy-men, blowers, and body-snatchers troubles the essentialist partitions of Whitman's organic political compact. When contrasted to this riotous, irredeemably contaminated population of social migrants, Whitman's representative "free race" of workingmen is imbued with an increasing vapidity. The binary he tries to impose between the wholesome artisan and opportunistic jobber breaks down, both socially and personally. The mobility and inclusivity of Whitman's "I" could never be quite satisfied with the ontological stasis of a CARPENTER.

"The Eighteenth Presidency!", while outlining a political vision, also constitutes a poetical manifesto, expressed in the shifting currencies of a steadily transforming vocational paradigm. It bespeaks the fundamental tension that saves Whitman's poetic vision from capitulating to the platitudes of his organicist Free Soil credo. Written in a call and response pattern "to each Young Man in the Nation," Whitman's prose fidgets with a tacit recognition that he is in danger of addressing a nebulous ahistorical void, populated by increasingly fictional (and capitalized) stock laborer-phantoms—men who have already been swept away by the new political and economic tide.

It is at this point in the "The Eighteenth Presidency!" that Whitman, in both senses of this word, articulates a (semi-)solution:

> You Americans who travel with such men [infidels, disunionists, terrorists et al.] you also understand not the present age, the fibre of it, the countless currents it brings of American young men, a different superior race. All this effervescence is not for nothing; the friendlier, vaster, more vital modern spirit, hardly yet arrived at definite proportions, or to the knowledge of itself, will have the mastery. The like turmoil prevails in the expressions of literature, manners, trade, and other departments.   (1314)

---

[5] Graham Thompson has explored an analogous conception of off-whiteness in Melville's short fiction. By probing both the class and racial affiliations and antagonisms, Melville "represents the vacuum that exists outside the language of race upon which the language of affiliation relies." Melville ultimately "registers a distance and sense of non-affiliation" to the political and social consolidations of the "white republic". See " 'Through consumptive pallors of this blank, raggy life': Melville's Not Quite White Working Bodies," *Leviathan: A Journal of Melville Studies* 14.2 (2012): 25–43.

Despite the obstinate affirmation of a qualitatively "different superior race," Whitman shifts, via a series of negatives, towards a cauldron of "fibre," "currents," and "effervescence"—a newly anatomized and coagulating body electric that froths and sparks as it shape-shifts to incorporate a "vaster, more modern spirit." "I loosen and pass freely," the speaker claims in "I Sing the Body Electric", only to immediately transform into a not-quite liquid "quivering jelly" and "white-blow" of a surrogate marital consummation. Visible here is the recognizable Whitmanic speaker who at once celebrates and yet simultaneously refuses the "definite proportions" of the national body. "The like turmoil," the voice confirms, will find its expression in literature, or in a poetry that might somehow incorporate the semi-soluble (rather than wholly liquid) opportunities of the present social disorientations.

*   *   *

So as to flesh these ideas out a little further, I want to return again to Whitman's actual book-making process in 1855 and 1856, a process that embodied the tensions of upholding the dream of labor while fully participating in the fluctuating opportunities afforded by the literary (as well as non-literary) marketplace. The principal creative experiment that Whitman undertakes at this time concerns the possibility of the self literally reforming into the material and formal properties of a book. And Whitman's desired emergence from the page at the beginning of "A Song for Occupations" did (at least in some sense) realize itself in many of the physical qualities of his various editions, perhaps most successfully in the 1855 first edition. Whitman attempted to encrypt his own distracted labors as bookmaker, printer, real estate dealer, journalist, poet, and collaborator into his texts, continually affirming a corporeal transference from "I" to "you" in body-book form: "For every atom belonging to me as good belongs to you." He conceived of *Leaves of Grass* in other words as a kinetic manifestation of his own coextensive production processes, thrilling at the laboring body's effort as it converted into a commodity:

> If I worship any particular thing it shall be some of the spread of my body;
> Translucent mould of me it shall be you,
> Shaded ledges and rests, firm masculine coulter, it shall be you,
> Whatever goes to the tilth of me it shall be you,
> You my rich blood, your milky stream pale strippings of my life;
> Breast that presses against other breasts it shall be you.   (*LG*, 1855, 30)

Here again Whitman defers to elemental substances that resolve into one more fantasy of a disembodied breast pressing against breasts, a semi-soluble articulation of bodies, machines, and books (the spread of the body across the translucent mould of the page, and the "tilth of me" as it is worked into something fertile). At this point I want to glance sideways to a metaphor being near-contemporaneously deployed by Marx, which shares some surprising traits with Whitman's formulation. Marx famously envisioned in the capitalist product, in contradistinction to the reified commodity form, an "undifferentiated congealed mass of human work"— "eine blosse Gallerte unterschiedsloser menschlicher Arbeit" (1872, 13). This, for Marx, was the human sacrifice that the consumer needed to be confronted with and disgusted by in order to undermine the free circulation of commodities. Keston Sutherland has offered a more idiomatically sensitive (and now iconic) translation of that crucial word "Gallerte". Questioning the static, frozen connotation of the standard translation "congealed," Sutherland identifies the more troubling analogy Marx was aiming for: "Gallerte," it turns out, was a glue-like, nineteenth-century foodstuff made up of boiled animal matter: "the image of human labor reduced to *Gallerte* is disgusting. *Gallerte* is not ice, the natural and primordial, solid and cold mass that can be transformed back into its original condition by application of (e.g. human) warmth; it is a 'halbfeste, zitternde,' that is, a 'semisolid, tremulous' comestible mass, inconvertible back into the 'meat, bone [and] connective tissue' of the various animals used indifferently to produce it" (Sutherland, 2008). In other words, Marx attempts to make his readers as uncomfortable as possible; the comparison of converted human labor to a jellied mass of undifferentiated non-human tissue draws attention to the product as irrevocably compounded. Another term of Marx's to focus in on here is "blosse," which brings with it connotations of exposure to further emphasize the presence of vulnerable human flesh. There is no way to reconstruct the individual human sacrifices embodied in this anonymous, processed comestible. For Marx, the consumption of the capitalist commodity is analogous to an act of cannibalism, a gothic Eucharist in which the consumer feeds on the naked and indistinguishable bodies of human laborers.

Refusing to align itself with any such diagnosis of violent alienation, Whitman's poetry figures an analogously tremulous compound ("quivering jelly") as a topos of opportunity, rather than as an irretrievable consequence of commodification. His kinetic, seminal version of "blosse Gallerte," which thrills at the transformative potential of the body at work, excites a variety of continually reforming intimacies and material combinations on the page: "You will hardly know who I am or what I mean | But I shall be good health to you nevertheless | And filter and fibre your blood." Whitman rewrites Marx's monstrous, irrevocably compounded bodies as an erotic, irrevocably coagulated poetics that refuses the possibility of commodification's immaculate consummation. By this reading,

Whitman's numerous miscues and incoherencies are integral to the effect, enumerating a body of work that continually falls short of any definitive form. The poet-producer's book extends contra to his stated reactionary politics, with his conflicted vision slackening the ideological partitions of any idealized "organic compact" in the search for adhesive contact and recombination. The preoccupied and thoroughly complicit Whitman partially unfastens his dream of labor from its reactionary ideological moorings, and is consequently able to envision the contours of an irretrievably contaminated inclusivity.

In providing this reading, I want to again stress that I am in no way seeking to affirm any "benefits" (aesthetic or otherwise) associated with being attuned to vaguely defined marketplace "energies." On the contrary, and as a challenge to a neoliberal narrative that would seek to claim Whitman as an ally, the poet's impulse was to transfigure capitalism's shocks away from any illusory notion of laissez faire towards something more laterally encompassing. His subversive—though always confused—stagings of labor allowed him to articulate what Peter Coviello might describe as a "future that would not come to be" (20). Whitman allows us to glimpse the outline of a subverted process of commodification that point towards alternative states of becoming rather than any static, exchangeable end. In Whitman's hands, it is not the accumulation of capital that entices, but the possibilities of the human form as it undergoes conversion to exchangeable commodity form. That moment in which effort transmutes itself into an increasingly alien object—in Whitman's case the process of manufacturing a book in 1855—is the promethean opportunity he seizes to climb in between perpetually damp sheets. Refusing any exemplary tallying of this for that, Whitman both arrests and then inhabits the instance of transference, plunging, come what may, into what he conceives of as a space of molten opportunity.

Returning a final time to that moment at the beginning of "A Song for Occupations":

> COME closer to me,
> Push close my lovers and take the best I possess,
> Yield closer and closer and give me the best you possess.
>
> This is unfinished business with me. . . . how is it with you?
> I was chilled with the cold types and cylinder and wet paper between us.
>
> I pass so poorly with paper and types. . . . I must pass with the contact
>   of bodies and souls.

One of the more surprising aspects of this mid-production arrest of cold types, cylinder, and wet paper is that the ink (mixed with urine, grease, and sweat) has not yet dried on the page. The "us" here, in damp embrace, is also potentially in the process of being smeared in black. This introduces a curious possibility; namely Whitman's narrator speaking this great paean of labor with a stained complexion, as if in partial, accidental blackface. And while such clumsiness does not point to any coherent sense of political solidarity, it does gesture to the sheer array of poetic anomalies that arise from Whitman's conflicted stagings of labor.

As is hopefully evident by now, Whitman was in no way a programmatic political or social thinker; on the contrary, his transgressive literary experiments bespeak a largely muddled and really quite troubling relationship to the urgent questions of his age. Follower after follower—Horace Traubel, William O'Connor, Sidney Morse—all appealed to Whitman for endorsement of their own progressive political visions, having credited the poet with energizing and shaping their variously progressive stances. Each came away disappointed by a man who could somehow write *Leaves of Grass* and hold such disorganized and retrograde views.[6] And yet this very disjunction also accounts for his enduring status as the poet laureate of the left. In spite of himself, he materializes a body of work, an elemental corpus, that always partially refuses the coordinates or paraphrase of any particular time or space, but is somehow tangible enough to have inspired a host of radical causes. By way of an ending, I want to let the ongoing and vivid critical work on Whitman's various political legacies speak for itself and instead focus on an alternative reception history that takes a certain degree of pleasure in observing the political tremors that Whitman caused for the succeeding generation of literary, and particularly modernist, icons.[7] Whitman's relentless attempt to embody himself in poetry is the foil against which key figures later constructed the mythic impersonality of their exceptional authorial personae. The curious feature of each of these responses is that they also conceived of Whitman's poetry (negatively) in terms of a Gallerte-like coagulation—and one that explicitly represented a threat to the social order. This is Henry James reviewing Whitman's *Drum-Taps* in 1865:

> It has been a melancholy task to read this book; and it is a still more melancholy one to write about it ... It exhibits the effort of an essentially prosaic mind to lift itself, by a prolonged muscular strain, into poetry [...]

---

[6] See for example Thomas ("Dreams," 149–50), and Morris (288–9).

[7] See the work of Bryan K. Garman, "'Heroic Spiritual Grandfather': Whitman, Sexuality, and the American Left, 1890–1940." *American Quarterly* 52 (2000): 90–126; Matt Cohen, "'To reach the workman direct': Horace Traubel and the Work of the 1855 Edition of *Leaves of Grass*" in *The Sesquicentennial Essays*, 299–320; and K. A. Harris, "The 'Labor Prophet?': Representations of Walt Whitman in the British Nineteenth-Century Socialist Press". *Walt Whitman Quarterly Review* 30 (2013): 115–37.

To become adopted as a national poet, it is not enough to discard everything in particular and to accept everything in general, to amass crudity upon crudity, to discharge the undigested contents of your blotting-book into the lap of the public. (James, 410)

In this fantasy Whitmanic deadlift, James imagines the brain-as-muscle straining to hoist itself into what he considers an exclusively non-corporeal realm: the realm of poetry. It is a surprisingly unmeasured response; his more familiar equivocal critical poise turned to an abrupt polemic by the perceived threat and allure of the Whitmanic corpus. Whitman, according to James, has obviously made a category mistake; his prosaic mind has strained to lift something into a territory that necessarily rejects such effort. Yet in articulating his stance, James defers to the very material morphology that Whitman advances: *Drum-Taps* constitutes the "discharge" of a substance that remains undigested; or rather, a substance that has not been properly sorted according to the strictures of aesthetic (by which James also means social) exclusivity. Whitman's poetry achieves two things here; the first is to force (through his expanding literary reputation) someone of James's social standing into actually reading his book; and the second is to provoke this proto-modernist sensibility into imagining (perhaps accurately) a monstrous book-gut vomiting its contents into the lap of the genteel public.

Even sixty years later (though far more sympathetically), D. H. Lawrence deferred to a surprisingly similar series of metaphors: "But what of Walt Whitman? | The 'good grey poet'. | Was he a ghost, with all his physicality?...A certain horrible pottage of human parts" (163). Lawrence expresses his apocalyptic sense of allure and recoil at the invasive potential of the amorphous en masse body: "Walt's great poems are really huge fat tomb-plants, great rank graveyard growths" (163). Published in 1923, the same year that the UK Labour Party formed its first (very short-lived) minority government, Lawrence's prose seethes with homoerotic fascination surrounding burgeoning union movements and the quickly mutating legacies of the 1917 Bolshevik Revolution. Against this backdrop he speaks of a proletarian fantasy, another half-digested and Gallerte-like "pottage" or compounded necromantic bodily invasion liable to overwhelm and upend the social order.

Whitman's achievement was to sing of bodies and worlds that have yet to find form. His poetry serves, and will continue to serve, as a confrontational, insurrectionary foil; a provocatively incoherent vision (a vision at least as incoherent as democracy itself) from which the right will continue to reactively shrink, and from which the left will continue to draw inspiration. His is a poetic labor that cannot be conceived of as either a retreat from, or a wholesale adoption of, the various market energies that surrounded him. Instead Whitman gestured towards the possibilities of a living sensuous activity that spreads out across competing priorities. Always more fascinated with the peculiarities of production rather than the final comestible product, Whitman emerges as a figure that cannot be recuperated within any conventional circuits of exchange or divisions of labor (and certainly not within any preconceptions regarding a discrete poetic labor). Little surprise that one of his creative experiments was to draft a poem on the back of a scrap of wallpaper: his words literally standing in as a surrogate adhesive paste liable to stick to, combine, and enable other stranger intimacies and combinations to come (see again Fig. 1).

PART II

HERMAN MELVILLE, DEPUTY CUSTOMS INSPECTOR

3

Moby-Dick and the Shadows of "The Poet"

The photograph on the cover of this book, included in László Krasznahorkai's *The Manhattan Project* (2017), is one of the latest efforts to eulogize the second half of Melville's life as a sad case of thwarted vocation. Apparently evoking his desolate office-cum-prison window vista of the Hudson River, the image quietly alludes to the melancholy lines of "Billy in the Darbies," the ballad that is often positioned as a kind of epitaph to Melville's last work, *Billy Budd*: "But, look: | Through the port comes the moonshine astray! | It tips the guard's cutlass and silvers this nook; | But 'twill die in the dawning of Billy's last day" (132). As Krasznahorkai (a celebrated novelist himself) disconsolately puts it: "I find out all I can about Melville's life in New York, including the location of the customs office where this destitute and completely forgotten author would go daily to work as customs inspector for four dollars a day, six days a week, for nearly 20 years" (40).

Since his revival in the 1920s, Melville has often stood in as the ultimate parable of frustrated vocational integrity in American literary history. In spite of the sudden success of his early novels (the story goes), the author's popularity waned even as his artistry and originality grew. This is the Melville who, after the mixed reception of *Moby-Dick* in 1851, decided to turn his back on the artistically and politically bankrupt literary market-place and accordingly suffered the consequences of choosing to tell the "truth uncompromisingly" (*Billy Budd*, 67). Left behind by a public who could not appreciate his genius, he shifted away from commercially viable prose to poetry "eminently adapted for unpopularity" (*Correspondence*, 483).[1] Melville struggled to support his family through his writing and was eventually forced into finding alternative employment as a deputy customs inspector in post-Civil-War Manhattan. Typically, those twenty years—from 1866 to 1885—have been associated with an enforced

---

[1] Herman Melville to James Billson, October 10, 1884. This phrase is Melville's own retrospective assessment of his epic poem *Clarel* (1876).

artistic decline, as evidenced by the sum total of his creative output only amounting to the odd collection of peculiarly uneven poetry. The chronicle ends with Melville's retirement from an oppressively conventional day job enabling a return, with *Billy Budd*, to his long-stifled true calling as the author who would be recognized belatedly as one of the greatest America ever produced.

To be fair, there are those moments when Melville contributes to his own myth-making as a tragic icon of a pure poetic vocation in a constant struggle to rise above economic circumstance. Writing at a pivotal moment in his career, just before the publication of *Moby-Dick* in 1851, Melville explained to Hawthorne that

> Truth is the silliest thing under the sun. Try to get a living by the Truth— and go to the Soup Societies [. . .] In a week or so, I go to New York, to bury myself in a third-story room, and work and slave on my "Whale" while it is driving through the press. That is the only way I can finish it now,—I am pulled hither and thither by circumstances. The calm, the coolness, the silent grass-growing mood in which a man ought always to compose,—that, I fear, can seldom be mine. Dollars damn me . . . What I feel most moved to write, that is banned,—it will not pay. Yet, altogether, write the *other* way I cannot. So the product is a final hash, and all my books are botches.
>
> (Letter to Nathaniel Hawthorne, June 1, 1851, 191)

Melville finished this particular letter with the unforgettable line: "Though I wrote the Gospels in this century, I should die in the gutter." Samuel Otter writes that such passages have taken on an almost "incantatory" quality for Melville critics, summoning a "series of biographical images: the Thwarted Melville, the Torn Melville, the Botched Melville"— caught between the impulses of the exceptional individual author and the demands of an (often feminized) mass audience: "creator is set up against consumer, elite against popular, pure against contaminated, freedom against necessity, depth against surface" (7).[2] Melville handed down to his early critics a sublime vocabulary for articulating the various gutter/gospel antinomies that were, at the modernist moment of his revival in the 1920s, coming so sharply into focus. In this section, I see what happens to the Melville narrative when we cease to let his memorable complaints obscure other significant facets of his complex working life.[3] Indeed,

---

[2] Otter's landmark publication, *Melville's Anatomies* (1999) explores the ways in which Melville was less interested in upholding Manichean oppositions than revealing their ideological constitutions.

[3] Cody Marrs, discussing the limitations of a designation such as "Late Melville," has pointed out the challenges Melville's work presents to traditional literary critical approaches. The temporal spread (fifty years) and sheer formal variety (novels, novellas, magazine fiction, poems, ballads, etc.) of Melville's career is out of sync with the "field's

throughout his varied career, Melville persistently interrogated those logics of vocation and exceptionalism for which the poet so often serves as a potent agent.

In *Empire for Liberty: Melville and the Poetics of Individualism* (1989), Wai Chi Dimock flipped the script on Melville as the tragic genius in his garret to instead see him as a "something of a representative author" whose desire for authorial "sea-room" was actually inextricably bound to the prevailing nationalist, expansionist, and imperial agenda of Jacksonian America (6). Seeking to distance himself from his contemporaries and construct his authorial independence, Melville becomes ever more deeply implicated within the exceptionalist political discourses espoused by his contemporaries, "speaking for them and with them, most of all, when he imagines himself to be above them, apart from them, opposed to them" (6). This line of argument does much to complicate the familiar narrative of Melville's career. However, it overlooks the extent to which Melville was intensely self-conscious about, and suspicious of, the construction of authorship that Dimock suggests he unconsciously inhabits. By contrast, I suggest that Melville was not only intensely aware of this reactionary "poetics of individualism" but also that the critique of the same was a recurring thematic and formal feature of his work. My rereading, then, seeks to uncover a potentially radical "poetics of distraction" (that anticipates Benjamin's "reception in distraction") in Melville's writings and mode of composition. His distracted poetics, formulated and restaged at various defining moments in his literary career, expose and offer a counterpoint to the exceptionalist discourses that underwrite the reactionary politics of his contemporary milieu, including that of the poetic vocation. Melville in fact envisioned and practiced a mode of literary production that agitated against any future defined by what William V. Spanos describes in terms of the "indissoluble relationality between American exceptionalism, the calling, monumental history, and nationalism" (*Calling*, 11).

I begin this analysis by considering how Melville's ambivalence toward the "poet" and "poetry" emerged as a response to, and as a rewriting of, Emerson's vision of the national bard. Focusing on major and lesser known texts written before, during, and after his stretch of supposed confinement in an unexceptional day job, I investigate the ways in

patterns of division and specialization"—calling into question many of the standard distinctions related to genre and periodization (2). To isolate a discussion of Melville's work in terms of a before-and-after chronology or as corresponding to particular formal phases is to risk overlooking the many permeations, continuities, and feedback loops that defined an obstinately complex literary output and working life. See Cody Marrs' introduction to "Late Melvilles" in *Leviathan: A Journal of Melville Studies*, 18.3 (2016): 1–10.

which Melville engages the Emersonian poet as a locus for an extended anatomization—across both verse and prose—of the occlusive politics of authorial calling. A re-examination of various touch points in his career that are most suggestive of vocation—the writing of his initially misunderstood masterpiece *Moby-Dick*, his supposed decline and retreat towards *Clarel*, and his resurgent return to top artistic form in retirement with *Billy Budd*—illustrates how Melville never let himself or his characters inhabit a transcendent persona or abstracted sovereign position for long. Laced with intensely self-conscious dramatizations of an authority that is never allowed to face forward and fulfill its triumphant destiny, his writings instead cultivate a formal waywardness that always eventually declines the securities of "being" for the possibilities of "becoming."

The urge to subsume Melville's career within the parameters of vocational thinking has more often than not informed the various attempts to recover Melville the poet. In the historical note appended to the Northwestern Newberry edition of *Published Poems* (2009), for instance, Hershel Parker provides the following affirmative headings for his chapters concerning Melville's gradual vocational progression: "A Poet in Prose," "Melville's Progress as Poet," "His Verse still Unpublished, Melville defines himself as Poet."[4] Each confident reiteration of the moniker, I would suggest, rather forces the issue, emphasizing a triumphant emergence of an innate—and distinctively Emersonian—calling made all the more remarkable by the stifling proximity of that quintessence of "Capitol" and "Exchange," the Customs House.[5] Moreover, what this characterization overlooks is the ways in which Melville either tended to agitate against the epithets "poet" and "poetry" or avoid them altogether—a reluctance that is readily apparent even in his choice of titles. Apart from the unpublished and now lost 1860 *Poems*, there is *Battle Pieces and Aspects of the War*, *Clarel: A Poem and Pilgrimage in the Holy Land*, *John Marr and other Sailors with Some Sea-Pieces*, *Timoleon and Other Ventures in Minor Verse*, and *Weeds and Wildings and a Rose or Two*. There are only two further examples of Melville describing his efforts explicitly as "poems": "Fragments of a Lost Gnostic Poem of the 12th Century" in *Timoleon* (*Published Poems*, 201), and an uncollected piece called "In the Hall of Marbles (Lines recalled from a destroyed poem)."[6]

---

[4] See also the relevant chapter headings in Parker's *Melville: The Making of the Poet* (2008).

[5] While Parker is careful to point out Melville's skepticism towards Emerson, he nevertheless enfolds Melville the poet within the distinctively Emersonian "it is in me, and shall out" logic of individual promise and triumph.

[6] See Michael Jonik's discussion of this poem in relation to entropy and decay in *Herman Melville and the Politics of the Inhuman* (2018), 225.

In fact, Melville's poems (and this relates to the vocabulary of final "hashes" and "botches" he developed in 1851) most often refuse any confident generic designation. Melville describes his poems as lost, fragmented, or destroyed, configuring them as a variety of entangled aspects, speculative ventures, pieces, pebbles, fruit, weeds, wildings, and roses—detritus and ephemera that always seem to fall short of affirming a secure authorial identity.

Melville's own copy of Emerson's *Essays: Second Series* (1844) includes a telling moment of scepticism, in which he annotates the following passage from "The Poet":

> the poet, who re-attaches things to nature and the Whole,—re-attaching even artificial things, and violations of nature, to nature, by a deeper insight,—disposes very easily of the most disagreeable facts. Readers of poetry see the factory-village, and the railway, and fancy that the poetry of the landscape is broken up by these; for these works of art are not yet consecrated in their reading; but the poet sees them fall within the great Order not less than the bee-hive, or the spider's geometrical web.[7]

To the left of his underlining, Melville writes dryly: "so it would seem. In this sense Mr E. is a great poet" (523). Over the page he continues: "[Emerson's] gross and astonishing errors and illusions spring from a self-conceit so intensely intellectual and calm that one at first hesitates to call it by its right name" (524). While Melville was sympathetic to Emerson's call for a formally innovative "meter making argument" (24), the supposedly necessary disposal of "the most disagreeable facts" (the factory village, the railway—all symbols of commerce and labor) within narratives of wholeness and manifest destiny constituted a troubling and ultimately unacceptable erasure. Judged in terms of a widely celebrated, yet politically occlusive "symbolic" style, Melville implies, Emerson was indeed a great poet, capable of quietly overlooking anything he wished (including the institution that was so disagreeable it did not even make it onto Emerson's list: slavery). By Melville's own politically charged "allegorical" standards however, Emerson's "deeper insight" constituted a form of amnesia that not only disposed with the most troubling aspects of his society but also seemed oblivious to the integral implications of his own privileged social standing.[8] Emerson's "illusions" concerning the American

---

[7] Walker Cowen, *Melville's Marginalia in Two Volumes*, Vol. 1 (1987), 524–5.

[8] Cindy Weinstein claims that in its numerous representations of labor, Melville's writing adopts a consistently "allegorical" style. Accounting for the muted contemporary critical reception received by much of his oeuvre, she argues that the arbiters of cultural taste in nineteenth-century America tended to praise, as "seamless" and "artless," a style of "symbolic" writing that depicted pristine pastoral landscapes and timeless human nature.

poet self-conceitedly floated in a space of naive "intellectual calm." In such a context, it is of course not particularly difficult to envision a poet who is able to "lie close hid with nature" and "abdicate a duplex and manifold life" (283). Unable to rely on a stable source of income (and unwilling to write in such a way as to secure such an income), the increasingly culturally visible designation of Emerson's capacious poet was not only unavailable to the later Melville, but also unconscionable—a persona that bogusly claimed political remove while actually reinforcing all the familiar divisions between elite and popular, intellectual and manual, freedom and necessity. Although Melville might at times have valorized the "the silent grass-growing mood in which a man ought always to compose," he also apprehended this fiction as the silencing (and possibly even bovine) pasture in which Emerson's poet gained cultural traction.

Melville's "archives of distraction" might not be as readily available as Whitman's, but there is an important sense in which Melville has already anticipated and incorporated the implications of such ephemera as the structuring principal of his writing. His botches and hashes—weeds and wildings—gesture to a necessarily contingent literary production process that is disenchanted with the exceptional horizon of personal calling and interested instead in envisioning a conception of labor that drifts away from so limiting a promise. In *Billy Budd*, the narrator claims that:

> The symmetry of form attainable in pure fiction cannot so readily be achieved in a narration essentially having less to do with fable than with fact. Truth uncompromisingly told will always have its ragged edges; hence the conclusion of such a narration is apt to be less finished than an architectural finial. (128)

Protected from the intrusions of fact, a "pure fiction" might indeed achieve the finish of a neoclassical finial. Yet the irony of this is that Emerson's poet, exempted from both Capitol and exchange, was actually more likely to reproduce the inherited forms of ages past (those, for example, that stylistically defined the Capitol building and most U.S. centers of Commerce). The ragged edges of Melville's "Truth uncompromisingly

As the elaborate infrastructures of factory production transfigured the American landscape, commentators praised "symbolic" texts for conversely concealing the labor of their own constitutions. By stark contrast, Melville's allegorical style had a habit of exposing the ragged edges of its own production; and, reacting to what they intuited to be a disruptive form of ideology critique, cultural critics consequently castigated his "labored texts" for a lack of skill, harmony, and depth. See Cindy Weinstein, *The Literature of Labor and the Labors of Literature: Allegory in Nineteenth-Century American Fiction* (1995), 1–13.

told" do not point to any predetermined solace, existential fulfillment, or final consummation: they are always liable to be "less finished," presaging the multiple frayings of a far less stable and suggestive futurity.

* * *

The tepid reception of *Moby-Dick* is often aligned with Melville's turn away from the literary marketplace and eventual shift to poetry. His magnum opus, it is *the* work that posthumously bestowed him with the moniker Great American Novelist and exalted him to that exceptional vocational category of Poet in Prose. Its close identification with Melville's transcendent genius is ironic considering that he opens the novel by carefully deconstructing the very idea of exceptional authorship. Right at the beginning of *Moby-Dick*, the author-narrator (the Melville of the title page) introduces two biographically resonant characters who, in providing the "Etymology" and "Extracts" on whales that open the novel, seem to have also had a role in the book's production. In fact, they seem to gesture to the counterfactual futures of the hypothetical Melvilles who, instead of shipping aboard the Acushnet in 1841, remained a teacher in New York with an interest in "all the known nations of the world", or eked out a living as a downtrodden clerk with a bookish interest in whaling trivia. The "Sub-Sub Librarian" and "Late Consumptive Usher to a Grammar School" are experiments, I want to suggest, in virtual biography—the specters of counterfactual vocational pathways that resonated with a man who tried his hand at both teaching and admin between 1836 and 1838.[9] In summoning these "threadbare" figures, Melville casts his authorial presence as a "crosswise interblending" (to adopt a phrase from the novel's "The Mat-Maker" chapter) of virtual biographical threads. He presents a carefully staged weave of alternative lifelines that not only serve to amplify the necessary occlusions that secure the construction of linear biography but also begins the process of anatomizing the political exclusion underpinning any exceptional calling.

Moby-Dick's dedication to Nathaniel Hawthorne—in "admiration for his genius"—is not without a degree of jocular self-consciousness. Indeed Melville's opening play on the biographical "what might have been" was a witty adaptation of one of Hawthorne's recently published sketches. In "P.'s Correspondence"—included in *Mosses from an Old Manse* (published in 1846 and reviewed by Melville a year later)—Hawthorne's narrator

---

[9] There is also something of Melville the local newspaper polemicist in these representations. See Delbanco, 26. And Parker, "Clerk, Farmer, Teacher, Polemicist: 1836–May 1838" in *Herman Melville: A Biography*, Vol. 1: *1819–1851* (1996), 104–24.

introduces us to the addled eponymous character P., who has apparently "lost the thread of life, by the interposition of long intervals of partially disordered reason" (*Tales*, 1006). Appropriately enough, P.'s rambling letter to the story's narrator relates the counterfactual lives of a series of iconic poets. In this parallel world, P. (an initial that suggests the titular character is also a poet figure) reminisces about a promising "lad just from college, Longfellow by name," who "scattered some delicate verses to the winds, and went to Germany, and perished, I think, of intense application, at the University of Gottingen" (1020–1). In a series of playful reversals similar to that which he has enacted on the (in reality, long-lived) Longfellow, P. offers revised histories for famous British poets that undermine their Romantic mystique as defiantly individual, tragic geniuses. Shelley, having survived a boating accident in Italy, has subsequently turned to the Church; a morbidly obese and aging Byron is currently preparing a heavily censored version of his complete works for market; and an eighty-seven-year-old Robert Burns, still full of the joys of spring, is currently being (prematurely according to P.) "embalmed in biography" by his literary followers. Through enacting these inversions, P.'s ramblings humorously reveal the extent to which exceptional biographies implicitly shape our understanding and valuation of poetic production, "embalming" prevailing conceptions of "genius" in the process. Melville's opening to *Moby-Dick* takes a cue from Hawthorne's sketch to present a quietly counterfactual parody of his own authorial biography, offering in turn a trenchant critique of the very idea of the literary genius at work.

Thinking about "what might have been," or the alternative virtual histories of persons or events has certainly had its detractors. E. P. Thompson memorably dismissed "counterfactual fictions" as "Geschichtswissenschlopff," or, "unhistorical shit": narratives that tend to "hobble along programmed routes" and bear no relation to the irrevocably contingent processes that define the course of history (145). Yet, in Melville's hands, such counterfactual reverberations accomplish something very different, tending to short-circuit rather than reify any such "programmed routes." His experiment in virtual biography in *Moby-Dick* draws attention to the fragile or arbitrarily arranged present, exposing the various deselections that unpin any foregrounded biographical narrative. Thomas Carlyle, in his 1830 essay "On History" (an essay that Melville read), wrote that

> Our own biography... study and recapitulate it as we may, remains in so
> many points unintelligible to us [...] actual events are nowise so simply
> related to each other as parent and offspring are; every single event is the
> offspring not of one, but of all other events prior or contemporaneous, and
> will in its turn combine with all others to give birth to new: it is an ever-
> living, ever-working Chaos of Being, wherein shape after shape bodies itself
> forth from innumerable elements... Narrative is, by its nature, of only one

dimension; only travels forward toward one, or toward successive points: Narrative is linear, Action is solid. Alas for our "chains," or chainlets, of "causes and effects," which we so assiduously track through certain hand-breadths of years and square miles, when the whole is a broad, deep Immensity, and each atom is "chained" and complected with all! (59–60)

Bound within the limits of one-dimensional sequencing, the biographical narrative always constitutes an arbitrarily delimited "chainlet" of cause and effect. According to Carlyle, an infinity of virtual eventualities is always in some way already encoded and implied within any such limited biographical narrative, with the reverberations of the what might have been offsetting the "bodying forth" of what apparently did come to pass. Melville, at the beginning of *Moby-Dick*, not only plays on this particular historical perspective, but also starts weighing the political dimensions of this foregrounding process in relation to his own status as an author. The author-narrator that opens the novel initially seems to pompously hold forth about his own exceptional status in relation to two other "Sub Sub" workers:

Etymology (Supplied by a Late Consumptive Usher to a Grammar School.) [The pale Usher—threadbare in coat, heart, body, and brain; I see him now. He was ever dusting his old lexicons and grammars, with a queer handker-chief, mockingly embellished with all the gay flags of all the known nations of the world. He loved to dust his old grammars; it somehow mildly reminded him of his mortality.]
   Extracts (Supplied by a Sub-Sub-Librarian.)
   [It will be seen that this mere painstaking burrower and grub-worm of a poor devil of a -Sub appears to have gone through the long Vaticans and street-stalls of the earth, picking up whatever random allusions to whales he could anyways find in any book whatsoever, sacred or profane. Therefore you must not, in every case at least, take the higgledy-piggledy whale statements, however authentic, in these extracts, for veritable gospel cetol-ogy. Far from it. As touching the ancient authors generally, as well as the poets here appearing, these extracts are solely valuable or entertaining, as affording a glancing bird's eye view of what has been promiscuously said, thought, fancied, and sung of Leviathan, by many nations and generations, including our own.
   So fare thee well, poor devil of a Sub-Sub, whose commentator I am. Thou belongest to that hopeless, sallow tribe which no wine of this world will ever warm; and for whom even Pale Sherry would be too rosy-strong; but with whom one sometimes loves to sit, and feel poor-devilish, too; and grow convivial upon tears; and say to them bluntly, with full eyes and empty glasses, and in not altogether unpleasant sadness—Give it up, Sub-Subs! For by how much the more pains ye take to please the world, by so much the more shall ye for ever go thankless! Would that I could clear out Hampton Court and the Tuileries for ye! But gulp down your tears and hie aloft to the

royal-mast with your hearts; for your friends who have gone before are clearing out the seven-storied heavens, and making refugees of long-pampered Gabriel, Michael, and Raphael, against your coming. Here ye strike but splintered hearts together—there, ye shall strike unsplinterable glasses!]   (9)

Instead of presenting us with a traditional dedication, composed by an omnipotent and disembodied author, Melville distracts the reader with a tragicomic dramatization of the decidedly unglamorous underbelly of intellectual labor. "Supplied by" manages to provide us with a host of passive and active possibilities that entangle the professional proximities between author and his sub-subs. If the usher was indeed tasked with actively supplying the "Etymology", his efforts were certainly uneven. He first thought it appropriate (befitting his role as a school teacher and not an etymologist) to provide a pedagogical note by Richard Hakluyt on the importance of making sure that students spell "whale" with an "H", "which almost alone maketh the signification of the word" (8). He then supplies two more recognizably etymological quotations drawn from Webster's and Richardson's Dictionaries, but seems to stray from his brief again with his interesting though uncommented-upon list of the word "whale" translated into twelve different languages. Despite his threadbare state and approaching end, this usher still has his eccentric preferences. The final version of the etymology is not the work of a total nonentity, but rather the uneven product of someone who operates outside the remit of any easily definable occupational category; a contingent laborer who is quietly inscribing his paratextual work with his own ambiguous agency. Assistant teacher, part-time curator, part-time contracted (or hobby) etymologist—"threadbare in coat, heart, body, and brain" (7)—this phantom-like member of the precariat eludes any clear-cut identification, but is still counted as forming part of the book.

The other shadowy figure of this opening fares marginally better with his task. Apparently employed to hunt down and supply allusions and references to whales, the Sub-Sub librarian's findings are valuable only insofar as they constitute a kind of cursory overview, affording the author a "glancing bird's eye view" of what has variously been said, sung, and written of whales. The author quickly downplays the labor of this "grub," and subsumes it within familiar condescending laboring hierarchies. However painstaking the Sub-Sub may have been in his efforts, this collection of "higgledy-piggledy whale statements" constitutes only the most superficial or manual of literary beginnings; the "authentic" mindful work starts now with the work of the author.

Charmingly though, author-Melville begins a process of reconciliation and rehabilitation when he describes himself at the beginning of the following paragraph as the Sub-Sub's "commentator": "So fare thee well, poor devil of a Sub-Sub, whose commentator I am." He seems to be struggling with a sense of betrayal: commentators are usually of subsidiary significance to the thing or person they are commenting on, and so Melville reverses the hierarchy he has been seemingly at pains to establish. The author, Herman Melville, several rungs above the grub in the pecking order, now casts himself as the Sub-Sub's subsidiary. Thinking about the "remarkably practical and unromantic notion of a writer's work," and particularly this use of "commentator," Wyn Kelley suggests that Melville based his conception of authorship on an idea put forward by thirteenth-century theologian St. Bonaventure: "[a commentator] is the man who 'writes both others' work and his own, but with others' work in principal place, adding his own for purposes of explanation'" ("Writ," 401). Kelley notes that even though "we may struggle with the idea of Ishmael *only* as a commentator," Melville is continually experimenting with a more capacious and collaborative conception of authorial labor.

At this moment of relinquishment, Melville reverses Emerson's injunction in "The Poet"; rather than "abdicate a manifold and duplex life," Melville instead abandons his exceptional calling and joins his threadbare comrades. What emerges right at the beginning of *Moby-Dick* is the playful staging of a sovereign vocational crisis that acknowledges an often hidden interdependence of labor, a moment in which a transcendent persona laments his own detachment from the other forms of contingent work that have also been essential in this book's construction. Melville's alienated work as an author—or more precisely an Emersonian poet—is above the everyday laboring of a grub-worm, but this particular "Poet in Prose" is also unwilling to disavow the excluded extra-literary part of himself that has so diligently gone about his work of burrowing compilation. Despite any faults, the Sub-Sub is in fact a type "with whom one sometimes loves to sit, and feel poor-devilish, too; and grow convivial upon tears." Melville imagines drunkenly commiserating with an earthbound embodiment of contingency. The Sub-Sub eventually emerges in the passage as the unacknowledged and uncelebrated hero of the piece, even though consigned to live in the pristine and abstract author's shadow. Melville longs to chew the blubber and reconnect with that part of himself that he has been forced to disown. The author-narrator assures the "poor devil" that, if he could, he would clear out heavenly palaces to accommodate him, displacing the "long-pampered" (read "idle" or "decadent") Archangels so that the Sub-Sub can toast, with other shadowy types of his kind, his proper dues.

The passage turns into a comradely prophecy of royal and heavenly overthrow, a turning out of would-be-poets from their parapet. Echoing recent tremors of the 1848 European uprisings, the final parenthetical sentences describe a Miltonic rebellion against the established sovereign by a silently oppressed majority. Perhaps the most significant thread to pick up on in this respect is the way in which these characters' parenthetical dramatizations also serve to illuminate their partially emasculated and racialized attributes, or, their off-whiteness. The usher's first descriptive characteristic is his effeminate paleness (no doubt the result of being a consumptive), but "pale" is also deployed in connection with the Sub-Sub: "Thou belongest to that hopeless, sallow tribe which no wine of this world will ever warm; and for whom even Pale Sherry would be too rosy-strong." The implication here is that the complexions of these contingent laborers have been brutalized into their off-whiteness by the kind of work they have been compelled to undertake. There is also in these paragraphs a subtle and consonant reassignment of gender. Foreshadowing the gendered divisions of labor that come to be depicted in the "Paradise of Bachelors and the Tartarus of Maids" (1855), Melville's contingent virtual selves, with their pallid complexions, queer handkerchiefs, and inability to take their drink, also become emasculated just at the point at which their complexions are drained of color.

The conspicuous working-class embodiment of these menials is juxta-posed with the unmarked author and his angelic colleagues in their seven-storied heavens. Pure authorial labor is implicitly coded in terms of a heavenly whiteness, the ultimate standard from which other forms of work defer, fading gradually to black as they reach the nadir of a manual grub-worm condemned to underground toil: "poor devil of a Sub Sub." Of course, the hyperbolic nature of the author-narrator's descriptions of inferiority here (there is no such position as a "Sub Sub librarian") puts the supposed binary between exceptional, sovereign vocation and embodied labor into high relief, challenging that foundational dialectic relationship by caricaturing it. Furthermore, insofar as the author-narrator assumes a tone of intimate understanding with the reader, we become implicated in the construction of his suspect sovereignty, forcing us to question our own participation in reifying the dialectical logic of vocation. Via this peculiar staging, then, Melville unpicks the exclusionary violence of white male biography as it uncouples itself from the tarnished and occluded facets of the self that are apparently incompatible with tran-scendent being. Resisting biography as an ideological "embalmment," as a shoring up of the ideal Emersonian calling, Melville envisions a multiply complected and deeply politicized weave of biographical chainlets, sum-moning the virtual shadows of what might have been so as to extend and announce the range and self-awareness of the voice or voices that begin: "Call me Ishmael."

* * *

If Melville picks a fight with Emersonian vocational logic in *Moby-Dick*'s self-effacing opening, it is an argument he continues to stage throughout the novel's narrative, especially when it comes to framing the monomaniacal Ahab as an icon of individual calling. Such a reading broadly aligns with a critical tradition that stretches back to the arguments put forward by F. O. Matthiessen in his *American Renaissance: Art and Expression in the Age of Emerson and Whitman* (1941). In his classic take on the novel, Ahab becomes the symbolic "embodiment" (447) of Emersonian sovereignty taken to its violent extreme. According to Matthiessen, Melville thus forecasts the rise of various political tyrants who came to power in the first half of the twentieth century.[10] Modifying this analogy, I want to consider the ways in which Melville's dramatization of Ahab's monomania not only criticizes the occlusive politics of Emerson's Poet, but also foreshadows debates about subjectivity and form that emerged with the cultural advent of literary modernism. This is not to posit Melville as a "proto-modernist", as a mainline of Melville scholarship has repeatedly suggested, but rather to figure his contribution as anticipating some much later critiques of modernism's partitioning cultural work.[11] Specifically, I see Melville as positing an early resistance to what Virginia Jackson has referred to as the "lyricization" of poetry, in which "lyric" form became a synonym in the modernist era for a once more socially embedded and capacious "poetry." According to Jackson, during the print, pedagogical, and institutional transformations that defined the first half of the twentieth century, the scope of poetry narrowed, and became inextricably associated with a particular mode of individuated, disembodied self-expression (see 1–16).

In order to draw out this claim, I initially want to explore the argument that seems to underpin Jackson's helpful account of modernism's cultural legacy; namely György Lukács's "The Ideology of Modernism" (1957). In this essay, Lukács outlined what he saw as a modernist capitulation to a default conception of interior and individuated consciousness. By this he meant the instantiation of the human as an a priori interior being that

---

[10] See Samuel Otter's thoughtful paraphrase of Matthiessen's argument in "The American Renaissance and Us", *J19: The Journal of Nineteenth-Century Americanists*, 3.2 (2015): 228–35.

[11] See Bryan Yothers' discussion of this critical tradition in *Melville's Mirrors: Literary Criticism and America's Most Elusive Author* (2011), 55–6.

responds to a variety of necessarily external sensations. This is a version of the human, according to Lukács, that is incapable of glimpsing a synoptic, connective historical totality that implies its own potential transformation.[12] Lukács leveled a critique at those artworks (particularly the work of Anglo-American modernists such as Joyce and Eliot) that in his view instantiated a particular version of human consciousness as the essentialist standard. This modernist representation of the self recursively emphasized "the perpetually oscillating patterns of sense and memory data, their powerfully charged—but aimless and directionless—fields of force, give rise to an epic structure which is *static*, reflecting a belief in the basically static character of events" (188). Writers such as Joyce fetishize a particular subject-relation; a work such as *Ulysses* constitutes an elevation of individual sense-datary experience over and above any meaningful externally embodied referent or relationship. Modernism's implicit claim was that this mode of representation was the way individual humans had always experienced the world; they were merely the first generation of artists to have most faithfully rendered and revealed this unmediated truth. For Lukács, the characteristic modernist dispersals, ambiguities, and dramatizations of a continuous interior [bourgeois] consciousness were static ends in themselves, rather than means towards an apprehension of possible historical transformation. Modernist literature universalized a historically specific and static version of exceptional, atomized man, thereby checking the possibility of imagining not only alternative subject-relations but also alternative modes of collective being in the world. When it came to the representation of human interiority, such writers implicitly dispensed with historical alternatives. What Lukács values in previous great realist representations of selfhood—"Achilles and Werther, Oedipus and Tom Jones, Antigone and Anna Karenina"—is that "their human significance, their specific individuality cannot be separated from the context in which they were created" (189).

The crucial demands made here of artwork are twofold: first it ought to cultivate a consciousness of how its version of the human has been historically determined; and second, that the work contains the possibility or, better, inevitability of its own historical supersession. Modernism in this respect ignores both of these requirements, and so propagates a historically static abstraction: "Man, for these writers, is by nature solitary, asocial, unable to enter into relationships with other human beings [. . .]

---

[12] See Lloyd Pratt's eloquent paraphrase and subsequent adaptation of Lukács's conception of "totality" in "Historical Totality and the African American Archive" in Dana Luciano and Ivy Wilson (eds), *Unsettled States: Nineteenth-Century American Literary Studies* (2014), 134–6.

man, thus imagined, may establish contact with other individuals, but only in a superficial, accidental manner; only, ontologically speaking, by retrospective reflection. For 'the others', too, are basically solitary, beyond significant human relationship" (189). The crucial word there is "contact"—the implicit disparagement of a social, material situatedness that might serve as a point of historical recalibration. This is not, of course, to deny the experience of solitariness—Lukács points to the lyrical dramatizations of inwardness in Tolstoy's Ivan Ilyich and Flaubert's Frédéric Moreau—but crucially, these works present solitariness as but "a fragment, a phase, a climax or anti-climax, in the life of the community as a whole" (189): "a specific social fate, not a universal *condition humaine*" (190).[13]

I want to suggest that Melville, while elaborating on his skepticism of the Emersonian poet, convolutes the proto-modernist politics of any default individuated "interior" or "lyric" self, along with the exceptional model of (poetic) labor it implies. Significantly, in *Moby-Dick*, it is Ahab that expresses himself in terms of this soliloquizing lyricism, a poeticized speech that throughout the novel is identifiable as a politically charged form of blank verse (Pease, 411).[14] As author-sovereign and captain of an alienated industrial workforce, Ahab lyrically involutes towards the eventual consummation of his monomaniac fear and desire: revenge on the white whale. Such self-obsession prefigures that ultimately reified state of historical oblivion depicted at the end of the novel: the liquid vortex in which "all collapsed, and the great shroud of the sea that rolled on as it rolled five thousand years ago" (499). Ahab allegorizes an unmarked, partitioned authorial labor that cannot apprehend or countenance alternative sympathies or continuities. His Sub Subs are so many sacrificial lambs at the altar of his self-obsessed vocational fulfilment.

If *Moby-Dick* provides a foil for Ahab in its narrator Ishmael, then Melville offers one of the most powerful examples of their juxtaposition in Chapter 87 of the novel. "The Grand Armada" initially depicts Ishmael

---

[13] Lukács frames his critique of modernism in contradistinction to realism. His endorsement of realism and stark distinction between the two modes have been challenged by subsequent critics. For instance, Fredric Jameson's account of the shift from realism to modernism stresses a specific historical continuity, describing a gradual weakening of realism's revelatory capacity to "eradicate inherited psychic structures and values." Realism's force "always comes from this painful cancellation of tenaciously held illusions." But later on "when the realistic novel begins to discover (or if you prefer, to construct) altogether new kinds of subjective experience (from Dostoyevsky to Henry James), the negative social function begins to weaken, and demystification finds itself transformed into defamiliarization and the renewal of perception, a more modernist impulse, while the emotional tone of such texts tends towards resignation, renunciation or compromise." See *Antinomies*, 4.

[14] See also Harold Bloom's description of Ahab's speech as "lyric poem" in *Herman Melville's Moby-Dick* (2007), 126.

(recoiling from trauma) succumbing to the security of lyric interiority; however, his is a temptation quickly superseded by an intuitive openness to the possibility of personal transformation through an encounter with another suffering species. Melville's depiction implicitly contrasts Ahab's destructively static, hermetically sealed subjectivity, and Ishmael's distracted receptivity to alternative subject-relations as two possible responses to the violence of industrial capitalism. And it just so happens that the "The Grand Armada" features one of the most shockingly brutal scenes of exploitation in the book, depicting in graphic detail the destruction of a large pod of whales. The crew employs a particularly lethal instrument of torture: floats or "druggs" that attach to the end of multiple barbed harpoons to prevent the whales diving for safety. Such labor seems to signal a point at which the brutality of the industrial production process becomes so gratuitous that it deserts any definable objective (in this case, the harvest and manufacture of spermaceti). As the action subsides, Ishmael admits that this particular engagement yields "only one" whale, though countless others are implied to have consequently died very slowly, painfully, and unnecessarily (347).

Ishmael's initial reaction to this violence is to begin equivocating at the precipice of what Lukács might conceive of as a modernist invitation to capitulate to lyric oblivion—a disposition to retreat towards an apparently universal interior sanctuary as modeled by Ahab. Surrounded by, and complicit in, this scene of industrial exploitation (and adopting lyric form), Ishmael begins reflecting on the consolation of a final, innate psychological refuge:

> amid the tornadoed Atlantic of my being do I myself still forever centrally disport in mute calm; and while ponderous planets of unwaning woe revolve around me, deep down, and deep inland there I still bathe me in eternal mildness of joy.   (346)

Ahab has already asserted that he'd "strike the sun if it insulted [him]" (159), operating within the assumptions of his own pre-Copernican paradigm, and here is Ishmael, similarly retreating towards a gravitational center which seeks to govern the orbit of external alien planets. Unlike Ahab though, Ishmael ultimately manages to resist this solipsism, probing instead the troubling politics of any such tendency to retreat towards the solace of a seemingly intrinsic "deep down" "inland." Rather than give in to the attractions of this ontological stability, Ishmael exposes the ways in which such a proto-modernist "core" is manufactured as a response to the labors of industrialized exploitation rather than preordained as any viable solution or truth.

Yet this is more than simply a condemnation of the logic of capitalism. Ishmael also begins apprehending the alternative sympathies and kinships that seem to emerge as a by-product of his alienated labors. Throughout the scene, he glimpses a variety of relocating borders—alternative and intersecting formations of geography, ethnicity, and gender. Ishmael experiences what might be framed in terms of "reception in distraction," a partially suspended state that momentarily refuses to yield to any inevitable outcome or easy essentialism. His narration provides neither a decisive critique of exploitation nor any affirmation of any pre-industrial organic refuge. Instead, he explores the imaginative implications of his own complicitous labors in order to move towards an apprehension of the various irreducible singularities that begin revealing themselves throughout the action. In Cesare Casarino's suggestive formulation, Melville's narrative approaches a "laboratory for that crisis that goes by the name of modernity" in which new "conceptual-affective and conceptual-perspective constellations" begin testing the limits of comprehension and representation (1).

"The Grand Armada" builds gradually, with the opening constituting a description of the *Pequod*'s intermediate geographical location. Passing through the constricting Straits of Sunda (a hundred miles northwest of present day Jakarta), Ishmael describes traversing the continuous line of contested territories stretching from the Peninsula of Malacca to the "long islands of Sumatra, Java, Bally, and Timor; which, with many others, form a vast mole, or rampart, lengthwise connecting Asia with Australia, and dividing the long unbroken Indian Ocean from the thickly studded oriental archipelagos" (339). At this topographic juncture, Ishmael begins speaking in consonantly archipelagic registers, switching between tones and even political perspectives. The first, the reactionary badinage of a generic crewmember, emphasizes all of the idealized self-sufficiency, xenophobia, and suspicion associated with a thoroughgoing imperialist perspective. A complicated geopolitical territory such as this is populated with "tawny," "oriental," "piratical Malays," "lurking behind the headlands," who in spite of the various "bloody chastisements" handed out by English and American vessels, continue to threaten Western ships (339). This version of Ishmael goes on to describe, with a certain degree of pride, how American whaling vessels such as the *Pequod* (so as to avoid contact with the locals), never load up with any foreign goods, or "alien stuff." Even after three years of continuous voyaging, the crew still insists on drinking its supplies of "clear old prime Nantucket water" rather than "the brackish fluid, but yesterday rafted off in casks, from the Peruvian or Indian streams" (341).

A different Ishmael then departs from this questionable repartee. While describing the pods of whales that tend to congregate in such locations, he provides a contrasting vision of international unity and cooperation.

Whales gather here "in extensive herds, sometimes embracing so great a multitude, that it would almost seem as if numerous nations of them had sworn solemn league and covenant for mutual assistance and protection" (552). By this point, Ishmael has already established and emphasized the possibility of the whale's superior intellectual and sensate range in comparison to man's. This is from "The Sperm Whale's Head—Contrasted View":

> How is it, then, with the whale? True, both his eyes, in themselves, must simultaneously act; but is his brain so much more comprehensive, combining, and subtle than man's, that he can at the same moment of time attentively examine two distinct prospects, one on one side of him, and the other in an exactly opposite direction? If he can, then is it as marvelous a thing in him, as if a man were able simultaneously to go through the demonstrations of two distinct problems in Euclid.   (298)

"Is his brain so much more comprehensive, combining, and subtle than man's . . . ?" The capacities of the whale extend well beyond the abilities of the comparatively narrow (and narrowing) human subject, particularly when it comes to assimilating and processing discrete perspectives simultaneously. No wonder Ishmael projects his enlightened vision of international "mutual assistance and protection" onto a pod of whales rather than the jingoistic subjects of liberal capitalism. Up until "The Grand Armada" chapter, Ishmael's narrative has repeatedly foregrounded a series of human and non-human reversals: whales can solve two Euclidian problems concurrently; they are more diplomatically subtle; their "brain[s] so much more comprehensive [and] combining." And then, by contrast, there is man, and as Ishmael reminds us, "there is no folly of the beasts of the earth which is not infinitely outdone by the madness of men" (342). There is however, in terms of the plot, a dramatic consequence to the whale's increased sensory refinement. If Ishmael has succeeded in "subtiliz [ing]" (299) the whale's affective range so as to rival and possibly exceed that of man's, then he has also simultaneously increased its potential to feel and react to pain. In expanding the whale's complexity, Melville heightens the sensory and intellectual similarities between non-humans and humans just before describing, in detail, the most intense passage of suffering in the book.

The hierarchies of man and beast partially dislodged—and now ecologically complected—the passage starts to depict a recognizable pattern of "natural competition": by chance, a Malay pirate ship starts giving chase to the *Pequod* just as the *Pequod* begins giving chase to the whales. This narrative circularity is only matched by Ahab's solipsistic, and reductive interpretation of the incident:

As with glass under arm, Ahab to-and-fro paced the deck; in his forward turn beholding the monsters he chased, and in the after one the bloodthirsty pirates chasing *him*; some such fancy as the above seemed his. And when he glanced upon the green walls of the watery defile in which the ship was then sailing, and bethought him that through that gate lay the route to his vengeance, and beheld, how that through that same gate he was now both chasing and being chased to his deadly end; and not only that, but a herd of remorseless wild pirates and inhuman atheistical devils were infernally cheering him on with their curses;—when all these conceits had passed through his brain, Ahab's brow was left gaunt and ribbed, like the black sand beach after some stormy tide has been gnawing it, without being able to drag the firm thing from its place".   (341–2)

With characteristic paranoia, Ahab interprets each component of this chase as informing the deterministic contours of his own personal quest. The defile topography becomes the narrow channel that leads towards his doomed vengeance; the collection of "remorseless wild pirates" and "inhuman atheistical devils" become conflated as the chorus of his own tragic destiny. Ahab can only imagine the external world in relation to his own central drama, a sovereign quest delineated in opposition to an increasingly amalgamated and monstrous population of Malays and animals (imbuing the ensuing violence with intersecting colonial undertones). The very pattern of such a chase, at least for Ahab, is evidence enough of the metaphysical competition in which he continually assumes to participate.

During the initial chase of the "The Grand Armada," "when all these conceits" "of chasing and being chased to his deadly end" "had passed through his brain," Ishmael also describes Ahab's brow as becoming "gaunt and ribbed, like the black sand beach after some stormy tide has been gnawing it, without being able to drag the firm thing from its place" (342). Looking as though it had been scoured by the gravitational forces of a tide—Ahab's brow is compared to an obstinate object left behind on a beach that will inevitably succumb (as Ahab eventually does) to the next subsuming current. These descriptions present an Ahab who formally embodies his own obsessions, a stubbornly static thing that refuses to acknowledge the outside forces acting upon it. Ahab stands in this moment as the irredeemably entrenched counter-embodiment to the tactile combinations that start to proliferate during the ensuing scene.

As the focus shifts away from the intellectually and materially retrenched Ahab, the pirate ship is simultaneously forgotten, outstripped by the much faster *Pequod*. In fact, it does not make a further reappearance in the narrative, as though having been willed into existence as a phantom of Ahab's centripetal drama. The crew subsequently lower their boats and begin targeting a sighted pod of whales that have now started swimming away in protective formation. Even while describing Ahab's involuting state of mind, Ishmael continues to stress the heightened sensate capacity of the animals, as "by some presumed wonderful instinct" (342), they become "notified of the three keels that were after them,—though as yet a mile in their rear" (342). Seeming to take evasive action, they start moving on in "double velocity," forming closer ranks and battalions" (342).

And yet it is at this point that the logic of the chase and competition is dismantled. Various members of the pod suddenly become immobile— "gallied"—apparently suffering a sensory overload that prevents them from fulfilling their role as the pursued. Ishmael describes this variously as a "strange perplexity of inert irresolution" (342) as well as a "still becharmed panic" (345) that results in their sudden inertia. Foreshadowing the later refusal of Bartleby to participate in any of the pregiven hierarchies or contracts of Wall Street, the whales seem to disengage and passively offer themselves up to the approaching slaughter. Their curious state, which leaves many whales "helplessly [floating] like water-logged dismantled ships on the sea", provokes other members of the pod into a chaotic "distraction of panic" (342). The entire pod eventually becomes stationary, entirely at the mercy of the three oncoming crews; the whales "neither advanced nor retreated, but collectively remained in one place" (342).

As he revised the manuscript for the 1851 English edition of *Moby-Dick*, Melville experimented with a self-reflexive formal enactment of this psychological retreat by "gallying" the narrative itself, dropping down to a footnote that provides a digression on this "old Saxon word": "*To gally, or gallow, is to frighten excessively,—to confound with fright" (343). While both text and animal, as though in preparation for the approaching massacre, respond by resorting to alternative psychological refuge, Queequeg throws the first harpoon. In this initial act of violence, the sensory complexity that Ishmael has so far been at pains to emphasize is immediately eradicated: "blind and deaf," the targeted whale suddenly "plunged forward" (343). At this moment of contact, Ishmael's account shifts its emphasis from the pursuit to an examination of rapidly forming lyric centers and circumferences. It becomes clear that the stricken whale is speeding towards the inner protective sanctuary of the pod: "as the swift monster drags you deeper and deeper into the frantic shoal, you bid adieu to circumspect life and only exist in a delirious throb" (343).

As the boat progresses towards the center of the herd, "further and further from the circumference of the commotion" (344), the darted whale breaks free, and the crew suddenly emerge into what Ishmael describes as a "serene valley lake," the "enchanted calm which they say lurks at the heart of every commotion" (344). This is one of the very few moments in the book in which Ishmael invokes the labor of women, albeit in the most traditional, functionary of settings, and in non-human form. Surrounded by circling members of the pod, the space constitutes a nursery that has until now been shielded from the ongoing carnage—the boat has been dragged to an inner domestic sanctuary: "keeping at the center of the lake, we were occasionally visited by small tame cows and calves: the women and children of this routed host" (345). Having unwittingly gained access to this zone of intimacy, there is an immediate suspension of antagonism. The juveniles of this pod display a "wondrous fearlessness" or else a "still becharmed panic," and the crew respond by setting aside their lethal ambitions, a momentary vision of that earlier hypothetical "covenant for mutual assistance and protection" (this time between species):

> like household dogs came snuffling around us, right up to our gunwhales, and touching them; till it almost seemed that some spell had suddenly domesticated them. Queequeg patted their foreheads; Starbuck scratched their backs with his lance. (345)

Even instruments of killing are converted in this becharmed domestic domain. As though increasingly under a spell, the crew are then given a glimpse of further, deeper interior, and with it, yet another affirmation of the potential overlapping behavioral characteristics of whales and humans:

> Far beneath this wondrous world upon the surface, another and still stranger world met our eyes as we gazed over the side. For, suspended in those watery vaults, floated the forms of the nursing mothers of the whales, and those that by their enormous girth seemed shortly to become mothers. The lake, as I have hinted, was to a considerable depth exceedingly transparent; and as human infants while suckling will calmly and fixedly gaze away from the breast, as if leading two different lives at the time; and while yet drawing mortal nourishment, be still spiritually feasting upon some unearthly reminiscence;—even so did the young of these whales seem looking up towards us, but not at us, as if we were but a bit of Gulf-weed in their new-born sight. Floating on their sides, the mothers also seemed quietly eyeing us. One of these little infants, that from certain queer tokens seemed hardly a day old, might have measured some fourteen feet in length, and some six feet in girth. He was a little frisky; though as yet his body seemed scarce yet recovered from that irksome position it had so lately occupied in the maternal reticule; where, tail to head, and all ready for the final spring, the unborn whale lies bent like a Tartar's bow. The delicate side-fins, and the palms of his flukes, still freshly retained the plaited crumpled appearance of a baby's ears newly arrived from foreign parts. (345)

Quietly alluding back to the sperm whale's capacity to "simultaneously go through the demonstrations of two distinct problems in Euclid", the infant whales (as with nursing human infants) seem to "lead two different lives at the time", gazing away from their mother's breast as if in some contemplative repose. With the final sentence of the paragraph, Melville heightens his unfolding drama of the senses by focusing on the delicacy of a newborn's ears. One apparent problem here though is that in spite of the scene's revelatory proximities and intimacies, this momentary retreat also seems to presume a default equivalence between the feminine and the maternal—an affirmation of intransigent gender roles, predicated on a distinction between public and private spheres. The infant ears have "arrived from foreign parts" (and elsewhere in the paragraph from "the maternal reticule" or woman's drawstring purse). Is Ishmael getting "bogged down" here framing this scene in terms of what Deleuze and Guattari would describe as a regressive retreat towards a default "Oedipal family" (276)?

The narrative begins to complicate the issue. As is so often the case when Ishmael invokes the delicacy of the senses (baby's ears in this instance), he is preparing an accentuation of a further moment of trauma. And sure enough, interrupting Ishmael's account of the underwater nursery is the sudden cry of Queequeg, who has mistaken an umbilical cord for a harpoon line. Queequeg demands (with apparent reproach and indignation in his voice) to know "Who line him! Who struck?"—reacting to a "haecceitic" moment in which the borders between life and death, sign and semiotic momentarily (in Deleuze and Guattari's sense) "string together" (276):

> As when the stricken whale, that from the tub has reeled out hundreds of fathoms of rope; as, after deep sounding, he floats up again, and shows the slackened curling line buoyantly rising and spiralling towards the air; so now, Starbuck saw long coils of the umbilical cord of Madame Leviathan, by which the young cub seemed still tethered to its dam. Not seldom in the rapid vicissitudes of the chase, this natural line, with the maternal end loose, becomes entangled with the hempen one, so that the cub is thereby trapped. Some of the subtlest secrets of the seas seemed divulged to us in this enchanted pond. We saw young Leviathan amours in the deep. (346)

Julia Kristeva describes "abjection" as constituting "a twisted braid of affects and thoughts" without correspondence to any identifiable "object" (1). Abjection is, of course, gendered: the "feminine body, the maternal body", "in its most un-signifiable, un-symbolizable aspect", which shores up, in the individual, "the fantasy of the loss in which he is engulfed or becomes inebriated, for want of the ability to name an object of desire" (20). As the transformative intensities of this passage escalate, the centered enchanted calm of the nursery flashes towards an abject conflagration of voyeurism, corporeal mutation, and the corruption of the maternal line. In retreat from the "rising", "spiraling" umbilical cord, the text once again defers to a footnote concerning the reproductive functions of whales. But instead of providing momentary respite, the detached documentary tone gives way to a description of female genital mutilation:

> [whales] in some few known instances giving birth to an Esau and Jacob: - a contingency provided for in suckling by two teats, curiously situated, one on each side of the anus; but the breasts themselves extend upwards from that. When by chance these precious parts in a nursing whale are cut by the hunter's lance, the mother's pouring milk and blood rivallingly discolor the sea for rods. The milk is very sweet and rich; it has been tasted by man; it might do well with strawberries. When overflowing with mutual esteem, the whales salute more hominum.   (346)

At this juncture the text reaches a kind of affective apotheosis: a mixture of strawberries, blood, mother's milk, and severed reproductive organs. In this moment, Melville approaches a representation of an abject total perspective, a momentary glimpse of the infinitely complected weave that constitutes Carlyle's chaos of being and history. And it is exactly at this point that Ishmael's account retreats inwards, breaking off in gallied reverie. The footnote does not lead back to historical time, but pulls towards an enchanted—Kristeva might describe this as an "inebriated"—enclave or the sheltered repose of the would-be lyric poet, abdicating the manifold and duplex life:

> And thus, though surrounded by circle upon circle of consternations and affrights, did these inscrutable creatures at the centre freely and fearlessly indulge in all peaceful concernments; yea, serenely revelled in dalliance and delight. But even so, amid the tornadoed Atlantic of my being do I myself still forever centrally disport in mute calm; and while ponderous planets of unwaning woe revolve around me, deep down, and deep inland there I still bathe me in eternal mildness of joy.   (346)

Amid abject horror, Ishmaels affirms a pristine inner sanctuary, which doubles in this instance as a surrogate womb or nursery; a gendered space which also aligns with an affirmation of essential national belonging (deep inland), as well as an essential core being. As though under a spell, Ishmael's speech formally approaches the lyric mode of Ahab, catching the blank verse rhythm of successive metrical beats: "while *pond*erous *pla*nets of un*wan*ing *woe* re*volve* a*round* me." Ishmael as sovereign lyric poet momentarily teeters at the edge of Ahab's monomaniac abyss—modernism's encroaching historical vortex of static interior being.

But rather than capitulating to the rhythmic undertow of this essentialist core, the narrative develops a consciousness of its own gravitational force. Ishmael's lyricism, it seems, waxes inadequate in this setting, and is soon exposed as a flight from suffering rather than any affirmation of ontological (gendered or national) certainty. Ishmael manages to snap out of his lyric reverie, and taking a lesson from the more synoptic and combining capacities of whales, breaks off with the dismissive and wide-awake volta: "Meanwhile, as we thus lay entranced" (346). He then proceeds to carefully document the process by which the now panicking whales begin to move "together in one dense body"—"violently making for one center" (346)—an analogous retreat to the one he has just experienced. He observes one whale dragging a cutting spade behind him "so that tormented to madness, he was now churning through the water, violently flailing with his flexible tail, and tossing the keen spade about him, wounding and murdering his own comrades" (346). These comrades then redouble their efforts to motion towards their own doomed center.

Ishmael now observes the reciprocal involuting reaction in whales, whereby a formerly coextensive and varied sensorium flies, under siege, towards an artificially constructed interior. His description evokes the process by which the violence of exploitation gives rise to the ideological seductions of stable interiority. All of those multiply-complected capacities and continuities are foreclosed upon as the whales resolve "into what seemed a systematic movement; for having clumped together at last in one dense body, they renewed their onward flight with augmented fleetness" (346). Melville explores the material and psychological effects of exploitation that are then often misapprehended as "natural" behaviors. Briefly though, in Ishmael's hands, this arena of murderous exploitation transforms into an opportunity to grasp a perpetually external and relational becoming of the human (rather than any essential core expression of man or woman). Ishmael's narrative, while drawn towards the lyrical solace, holds on to the promise of historical transformation—his is a reception in distraction that glimpses the outer bounds of our epistemic borders. In a sense, "The Grand Armada" undermines the promise of two discrete sanctuaries: it undermines any reasonable faith in the progressive or enlightened claims of capitalist modernity, but also suggests the impossibility of retreating to any universal refuge of belonging. What remains is an urgency to discern and hold on to the promise of the "not yet" that might be momentarily apprehended and rescued from the disorientating shocks of capitalism's ongoing brutality.

So, while the text emphasizes the allure of an inward retreat as a response to threatening external realities, it also envisions a series of provisional counterpoint deterritorializations—alternative material reconfigurations, and moments of non-dualistic becoming that are both made possible and then extinguished by the kinds of labor that underpin industry. In deconstructing the pacifying undertow of isolated interior being, Melville gestures toward new historical and ecological perspectives. This is not to suggest that Melville pulls back from his mystified lyrical retreat to the pure revelatory critique associated with Lukács's endorsement of realism (this is in no sense a critical unveiling of any clearly delineated historical "totality"); rather it demonstrates a commitment to exploring the potential for historical supersession—of grasping the premise and promise of renewing the future coordinates of self, community, and world.[15] Ishmael's narrative repeatedly suspends the seductions of any lyric, interior enchantment, and instead allows the traumatized industrialized self to feel and touch the alternative tractions that lead away from any prefabricated way of thinking or reacting. Ishmael could be said to divert the implications of his own work towards an apprehension of the potentially redemptive worlds that start trembling at the margins of modernity's perpetual crisis-state.

The resulting shifts in awareness produced in this context also aids in further refining a sense of Benjamin's "reception in distraction," a transformation brought about by the tactile, habitual experiences of an accelerated capitalist mode of production. As explored in the introduction, for Benjamin, the potential of "Zerstreuung" or "distraction," in decomposing the prison of the self, differed substantially from his intellectual contemporaries. George Simmel, in the well-known essay "The Metropolis and Mental Life" (1903) described an urban population, swamped by stimuli, retreating towards a defensive malaise, in turn manufacturing a default blasé state of anonymity and inwardness (324–39). For Siegfried Krakauer, "Zerstreuung" or any analogously "dispersive state" similarly signaled the reduction of the human to the state of a passive sensory recorder or static individual consumer.[16] By contrast, Benjamin saw the repeated tactile shocks of modernity as potentially unfastening the received coordinates of the self and producing new formations—formations that might prove unmanageable within the normative disciplinary regime of

---

[15] Jameson's critique of Lukács is that his defense of realism predicates itself on the notion of a graspable external reality (the very reality that Modernism seeks to question). See Fredric Jameson, "The Case for George Lukács". *Salmagundi* 13 (Summer 1970): 3–35.

[16] See "Kult der Zerstreuung: Über die Berliner Lichtspielhäuser" in Siegfried Kracauer, *Das Ornament der Masse: Essays Mit einem Nachwort von Karsten Witte* (1963), 311–17. Adorno also rejects distraction as a potentially redemptive state, preferring instead the possibilities inherent in the "shudder" or utmost tension produced by the artwork. See Theodore Adorno, *Aesthetic Theory* (2013), 333.

an emerging consumer culture. This is not the jolt that awakens or "unveils" but rather a state that might prove receptive to potentially divergent historical configurations. As part of a deeply disorientating scene of labor, which repeatedly subjects a workforce to the tactile, sensory shocks of industrial exploitation, Ishmael envisions the combinations of new worlds in a state of receptive distraction. Whereas Ahab succumbs—literally sucked under in an all-consuming whirlpool—Ishmael manages to resist the undertow of any such annihilation, developing a sensitivity to the tractions of the alternative pathways that begin unfolding in the course of performing his contingent labors.

*   *   *

Up to this point, I have suggested that in *Moby-Dick* Melville stages a distinction between being and becoming: between the self-confirming "lyric" reaction of Ahab and the alternatively networked receptivity that defines Ishmael's response to industrial trauma. Melville also articulates a version of this drama at the very beginning of the novel, whereby an exceptional, self-conceited author-narrator—a figuration of the Emersonian poet—ends up acknowledging his fundamental dependency on the contingent forms of labor that his authority seems to necessarily preclude. Persistently interrogating "natural" divisions and hierarchies of work, Melville complicates Emerson's transcendent vision of the American poet who cannot "be afforded to the Capitol or the Exchange"—who necessarily abdicates his relation to a "manifold or duplex life." To "centrally disport in mute calm," Melville warns, is to always risk capitulating to reactionary promises of ontological security and formal stasis. Only by resisting the draw of a centered refuge, such as the myth of stable vocation, might some form of redemption be salvaged. Anticipating the parameters of later arguments put forward by Lukács and Benjamin, Melville exposes his characters to the full force of modernity's sensory "shock," and then details the ways in which they either double down on prior self-conceits or allow themselves in such moments to be unfastened and remade. It is only in the midst of such chaos, rather than set apart from it, that Ishmael is able to articulate the radical continuities and affiliations that define a chapter such as "The Grand Armada."

A revealing comparison can be drawn with Whitman at this juncture. As I have already suggested, the forms of inclusivity that define Whitman's *Leaves of Grass* were shaped through his active participation in the non-literary market. This participation prevented whatever transcendent predilections he harbored from straying too far towards the banalities of backward-looking organic fictions. Whitman ends up repeatedly refolding "himself" into the fray, distracted by the new opportunities and intimacies that were materializing around him. While writing *Moby-Dick*, Melville was still relatively shielded from the necessity of having to find a job. Though financial pressures were beginning to mount at this time, he was still able to retreat to his Arrowhead farmhouse (secured with the assistance of his wife's family).[17] In the following letter to Nathaniel Hawthorne, dated June 29, 1851, Melville outlines the familiar distinctions between repose and urgency; between the "silent grass-growing mood" in which one ought to compose, and New York:

> Since you have been here, I have been building some shanties of houses (connected with the old one) and likewise some shanties of chapters and essays. I have been plowing and sowing and raising and painting and printing and praying,—and now begin to come out upon a less bustling time, and to enjoy the calm prospect of things from a fair piazza at the north of the old farm house here.
>
> Not entirely yet, though, am I without something to be urgent with. The "Whale" is only half through the press; for, wearied with the long delay at the printers, and disgusted with the heat and dust of the babylonish brick-kiln of New York, I come back to the country to feel the grass—and end the book reclining on it, if I may.   (*Correspondence*, 195)

Plowing, sowing, raising, painting, printing, praying, and writing. At first glance, this combination reads like a version of Marx's utopian, post-capitalist vision of flexible labor. What prevents this description from aligning with Marx's ideal, however, is the proximity of Manhattan, which stands in here as the contingent, exploitative counterpoint that always underpins such a vision. Melville never loses sight of this interdependency; never allows the transcendent ideal (however attractive) to uncouple from its often-obscured basis in production. As with Whitman— though always more self-consciously—visions of reclining (or loafing) on grass are never quite enough. Even when his financial situation deteriorated to the extent that he had to take his day job as deputy customs inspector, Melville resisted the consolation of an easy escapism or retreat to a creative garret held high above his stifling workaday world.

This assertion urges a reconsideration of Melville's verse epic *Clarel: A Poem and Pilgrimage in the Holy Land* (1876), a text that at first glance, in both its form and subject matter, seems to be precisely about trying to achieve some kind of poetic or spiritual transcendence. In closing this chapter, then, I would like to offer an alternate take on this seemingly

---

[17] See Hershel Parker's account of Melville's steadily worsening financial situation at this time in "Damned by Dollars: 'Moby-Dick' and the Price of Genius" in *Moby-Dick*, ed. Hershel Parker and Harrison Hayford (2002), 713–24.

anomalous work; one that suggests it is doing something like the opposite of fulfilling the divine personal quest referenced in its title. Instead, a close examination of Melville's experiment with epic form reveals the extent to which this poetic production is informed by (rather than stifled by or set apart from) his extra-literary labors and immediate material context.

One of the longest poems in the English language, *Clarel* was the only substantial work that Melville wrote as a member of the contingent workforce: right in the heart of "the Babylonish brick-kiln of New York." Unable to rely on an income from his previous writings, this was also the moment when he most fully embodied the chasmic division of labor articulated at the beginning of *Moby-Dick*: the distance between Author-Poet and Sub-Sub. In deciding to write an epic poem, Melville chose to probe and embody this dualism to the furthest extent possible, recognizing in this moment a unique opportunity to inhabit the grandest vocational mantel—epic poet—while encumbered with the demands of a six-days-a-week, four-dollars-a day job. Though *Clarel* appears as the ultimate retreat, from the text's transcendent setting to its anachronistic high literary form, the extremity of the supposed distance from the context of its production only serves to emphasize the inescapable connections, correlations, and interdependencies of the latter. Melville, I argue, manufactures this remove as an experimental illustration of how the contingencies of the workaday world, and his poetry, are inextricable.

Melville based *Clarel* on journal entries written during a visit to the Holy Land and its environs in 1857 (*Journals*, 82–94). The narrative follows a group of pilgrims as they travel from Jerusalem, to Mar Saba, to Bethlehem, and then back to Jerusalem. Walter Bezanson has likened reading the strict four-beat lines to a progression through a confined space, observing that "variations from the basic prosodic pattern are so infrequent as to keep the movement along an insistently narrow corridor" (569). Bezanson's analogy also speaks, to Melville's own experience as worker in New York, with the metrical makeup of the epic emphasizing and responding to a sense of constriction. Throughout the narrative, words, ideas, geography, and bodies buckle under the pressures of this persistent "meter." Melville does not merely retreat towards the transcendent refuge of epic poet of the Holy Land; rather, as with *Moby-Dick*, his poem registers and formally reproduces the restrictions and pressures of production, probing the possibilities that might emerge from such an oppressive "brick-kiln."

As newly appointed deputy customs inspector in 1867, Melville began commuting from his home at 104 East 26th Street to his new office, further south, on the Hudson waterfront at 207 West Street, not far from

Pier 34.[18] Six days a week he patrolled what was then the most densely populated area in the world, with an estimated 290,000 people per square mile (Burrows and Wallace, 883). Walking west to the Broadway intersection, he turned left, and, following the crowd down the city's main artery, continued until he came to either Leonard or Franklin Street. Taking a right turn down either of these, Melville found himself in the vicinity of Harrison Street with easy access to the waterfront docks. On the day he started, the front page of *The New York Times* read "CELLAR POPULATIONS—DENS OF DEATH". The Council of Hygiene and Public Health had just published its report on the "Sanitary Condition of the City." This dual vision of the "Sunshine and Shadow" city was billed as a comprehensive account of the effects of New York's population increase. It included "graphic illustrations of localities well known to the police and the medical inspector" but "*terra-incognita* to the general public." This was an exposé of "the 'mysteries and miseries' of the city's overcrowded population" vividly painted in statistics.[19] Inspection district 3A of the Council of Hygiene's *Report* corresponded to the 5th District of Manhattan—Melville's beat—which was bounded on the north by Canal Street, on the east by Broadway, south by Reade Street, and west by the Hudson River.

For Michel de Certeau, a "place" is designated by the status quo, authenticated by maps, architectural drawings, and laws. Two things cannot be in the same place because two authenticated elements—stable, proper, autonomous identities—cannot overlap. "Space," for Certeau, forms an opposition to this conception of place: unlike a place, several spaces can coexist simultaneously. Each human being forms throughout the day "the strange fables of [their] own private stories," stories created by the individual's movement in space (112). As he commuted to work and made his rounds, he traced such stories: thousands of decisions that tracked a particular course through the city, creating his own unique narrative of

---

[18] In 1867, he moved offices to Harrison Street just around the corner from West Street, opposite pier 34. See Garner, *Civil*, 292.
[19] *Report of the Council of Hygiene and Public Health of the Citizens' Association of New York upon the Sanitary Condition of the City* (New York: D. Appleton and Co., 1865). Wyn Kelley discusses the popular writings that helped establish a dual vision of the city: works like Matthew Hale Smith's *Sunshine and Shadow in New York* (Hartford, CT: J. B. Burr and Company, 1868) and George Lippard's *New York: Its Upper Ten and Lower Million* (Cincinatti, OH: H. M. Rulinson, Queen City Publishing House, 1853). For Kelley, "authors and artists everywhere exploited the sunshine-and-shadow, mystery-and-misery theme." See *Melville's City: Literary and Urban Form in Nineteenth Century New York* (1996), 49. In the above extract, the *New York Times* actually alludes to a specific work in this genre: E. Z. C. Judson's *The Mysteries and Miseries of New York: A Story of Real Life* (New York: Berford and Co., 1848).

consciousness in time. The greater the restrictions of designated place, such as the crowded, enclosed thoroughfares of downtown New York, the more a commuter's stories shape themselves according to the confines of the city. When place closes in, when a commuter repeatedly negotiates crowded rush-hour passageways—stories in space begin to form a consensus. Benedict Anderson (via Benjamin) would describe this in term of the production of "homogenous empty time" associated with the experience of simultaneity that defines individual experiences of cohesion within the nation state (25). Melville needed to be in a certain place at sunrise along with much of the industrial workforce, and to get there he had to take the roads used by everyone else. An increasing homogeneity of "when" and "where" developed; Melville's personal rhythms were forcibly impinged upon by the places he walked and the times he had to keep. His stories in space were subject to the pressures of temporal conformity—to the pressures of the workaday world.

Indeed, there is a perceptible analogy, detectable in Melville's writing, between the consensus that defines "place" and the regulations that govern poetic form. John Hollander makes a place/space distinction when he writes of "meter" and "rhythm" in poetry:

> The word of flow, 'rhythm', characterises the series of actual effects upon our consciousness of a line or passage of verse: it is the road along which we read. The meter, then would apply to whatever it was that might constitute the framing, the isolating; its presence we infer from our scanning.
>
> (*Vision*, 135–6)

Meter serves as place in a poem—an imposed standard that conforms to the validated patterns of prosody. Rhythms, by contrast, are the stories of words as they encounter the metrical frame: "the road along which we read." The identities of both meter and rhythm are dependent on their mutual interaction: meter is only sustained if the rhythm of words sets a metrical precedent and rhythm is only sustained if the poet prevents the flow of words from colliding with obstacles (beats) that it has itself produced. The linguistic consensus that Melville shapes in *Clarel* is the four-beat line, with the rhythmic stories of words, animated in time by the process of reading, moving through a place established by their own precedent.

Various critics have claimed that *Clarel*'s four-beat frame intentionally constricts the text's expressive potential.[20] Walter Bezanson, for example,

---

[20] Joseph G. Knapp has argued that Melville "deliberately chose a verse form that was constricting [. . .] Instead of choosing blank verse, which would have permitted him the freedom and mobility needed for a long poem, Melville chose a rhyming octosyllabic line."

argued that "an essential part of the poem is that the verse form is constricted and bounded, that the basic movements are tight, hard, constrained" (568). Why did Melville opt for four instead of five beats for his epic poem? He was of course engaging in a form that had been used by Scott, Byron, and Tennyson earlier in the century. However, as with most of Melville's artistic decisions, his adoption of tetrameter points to more than a simple formal inheritance. Intensifying the lyric involution that defined Ahab's and at certain moments Ishmael's response to sensory shock, Melville has his drama unfold within the stifling orbit of a distinctively urban meter in order to test the limits of epic form.

Derek Attridge, explaining why poets have traditionally used the longer line for their more ambitious works, says that

> pentameter is the only simple metrical form of manageable length which escaped the elementary four-beat rhythm, with its insistence, its hierarchical structures, and its close relationship to the world of ballad and song [. . .] to understand the special character of the five-beat line [. . .] it is essential to be aware of the properties of the four-beat rhythm which it escapes.
>
> (*Rhythms*, 124)

He is specific about what kind of "escape" this is, emphasizing that "longer" does not mean freer. He quotes Ruskin: "upon adding the fifth foot to our gradually lengthening line, we find ourselves fallen suddenly under hitherto unfelt limitation [. . .] no poet has ever attempted to write pentameter in any foot but the iamb" (125). A transition from four to five beats is not liberation, rather a continuity of restriction—not jumping out of a straitjacket, but rather jumping into another with different buckles and belts. Attridge's "escape," rather, is from the pull of the elemental metrical frame in English: the 4×4 pattern.[21] He distinguishes between verse that engages with "the constant temptation of the four-beat movement" and verse "that doesn't." The "4×4" verse structure is "already deeply familiar to us," comprising four metrical beats per line over four lines and usually involving a rhyme scheme that enforces a sense of finality in the last word. Because four-beat verse lends itself so readily to this 4×4

See Knapp, *Tortured Synthesis: The Meaning of Melville's Clarel* (1971), 23–4. Knapp suggests that poems of epic length are traditionally associated with the freer five-beats per line of blank verse and so the majority of Melville's 18,000 four-beat lines are therefore consciously truncated. Vincent Kenny similarly argued that "the verse pattern and the language choice work intentionally against the epic effect because Melville's purpose was to show the modern tragedy of constriction in verse", *Herman Melville's Clarel: A Spiritual Autobiography* (1973), 98.

[21] See *Rhythms* for an overview of the critics who have claimed that the four-beat line does not require formal training to pick up and is "natural" to all English speakers (124).

pattern, it becomes a struggle to prevent the contents of a four-beat line poem from being contaminated by a persistent virtual meter.[22] For Attridge, the 4×4 meter is "quite apart from its embodiment in language, and as readers of verse we find ourselves falling into it whenever the words allow us to do so" (*Poetic*, 153). When William Bysshe Stein complained about *Clarel's* "countless infelicities of execution: grotesque inversions, tortured ellipses, banal rimes, expedient archaisms, distorted word forms, and limping rhythms" (98), he was in fact pointing to the effects created by a tension between the rhythms of speech and the structural demands made by the 4×4 formation. Melville's poetic place is the 4×4 metrical frame; his space is created by the rhythm of words as they struggle against metrical expectation. Melville relished this opportunity to be *in* a meter that warped content; he wanted to see what stories do when closed in— discover new margins of expressive possibility within encroaching circumferences. In this way, he created a formal allegory of his city: the strictly imposed regulations of his verse align with the corporeal pressures of his brick-kiln metropolis.

Hershel Parker, describing *Clarel's* period of composition, observes that "For four or five years [...] Melville walked two sets of passageways at once, the squalid, jammed streets of Manhattan Island and the narrow streets of Jerusalem and its environs" (695). The presence of New York is felt as a meter that shadows the ostensible features of Jerusalem, forging a palimpsestic urban representation. By organizing bodies into homogeneous consensus, Manhattan created a kind of metrical consistency. While preoccupied daily by the gridded, crowded streets (compelled by financial necessity), Melville experienced his city as a metrical pattern—a pattern that then translates into a suitable formal model for epic urban verse.

Clarel's opening Canto begins in a Jerusalem hostel: a student sits thinking in his cell-like room:

> In chamber low and scored by time,
> Masonry old, late washed with lime—
> Much like a tomb new-cut in stone;
> Elbow on knee, and brow sustained
> All motionless on sidelong hand,
> A student sits, and broods alone.   (1.1.1–6)

The first line comprises four rising beats and sets the metrical precedent for the majority of poem's lines, a synthesis of metrical and urban

---

[22] A virtual meter can be "experienced without being realized in language" (*Rhythms*, 62). The 4×4 metrical structure is so strong that you can tap, or even walk, along to it.

structures. The "chamber low," an enclosed place, is also a play on the poet's choice of form, which is accordingly "scored by time": either the chamber is scratched and striated, or given a time signature of four beats per line. It is out of this urban and prosodic confinement that the verse begins materially sculpting its representation of the subject—or the subjected—with Manhattan's urban geography haunting various features of the Holy Land. The anastrophe "In chamber low" elides "In *a* low chamber" so that the line can accommodate the first two rising beats of the four-beat pattern. The effect of this opening is one of compaction; the sentence begins "In chamber low" and finishes six lines later with "A student sits, and broods alone." The distance between the initial preposition "In" and its immediate governance, the "Masonry old," is relatively easy to follow, but then the semicolon at the end of line three forces the connotation of the preposition forward, so that it appears also to govern "the student": "In chamber low and scored by time [. . .] A student sits and broods alone." The function of "In" is stretched to the end of the passage, and the reader, in search of grammatical resolution, compresses the intervening lines.

The chiastic movement of the passage produces an unmistakable brick-kiln compaction. Everything is ambiguously jammed in until the squeezed and disjointed subject becomes indistinguishable from his environment. *Clarel* begins with something complete, a "low chamber"; the second and third lines then dismember this totality into parts or qualities: it has lime-washed masonry, it resembles a tomb. The semicolon marking the mid-point of the six lines then quietly switches the referent, so that lines four and five now begin anatomizing the student: elbow on knee, brow sustained on sidelong hand. Line three, however, has introduced a metaphor—the chamber is "much like a tomb"—so a confusion arises as to whether "Elbow on knee and brow sustained" is an extension of this metaphor or something else. Does it refer to a sustaining beam that is holding up the brow of the tomb-like chamber? Or does it refer to a person? The passage lacks grammatical orientation: it is only when the fully formed student appears in the last line that we can definitely say: there is a student sitting in a room. The text's subtle chiastic shift of "whole, parts; parts, whole'"—organized by the meter—compresses and elides subject and object. The student, embedded in his linguistic and physical surroundings, emerges as a fossil in the walls.

The "walls" of the poem are metrically made up of sixteen strongly felt beats over the first four lines, and a rhyme scheme that sets up the expectation of a resolution (aab[b]): time/lime/stone/[?]. Melville invokes the pull of a 4×4 pattern, but then prevents its completion with "sustained": the flow of the sentence is sustained, as its rhythm, unwilling to be shaped by the 4×4 structure, jags across the place of an expected, rhyming counterpart to "stone." The resulting assonance of the half rhyme "stone/sustained" fires the poem's ongoing conflict between petrifaction (stone), and that which perpetuates rhythmic flow (sustain). "Sustained" clashes with metrical place; its spoken rhythm is momentarily congested by the gravitational pull of the 4×4 structure. A petrifying, assimilating force attacks its rhythmic autonomy. And yet it also embodies its own conflict: caught between two connotations of architectural structure and musical flow. In other words, "sustained" is forcibly packed with two oppositional functions that provide a reflexive commentary on the poem's formal tensions.

In Canto 5, Melville again explicitly calls attention to the effects of "place". The student looks out across the rooftops and sees an array of clogged urban structures. It is as though he were looking at the indistinguishable fossils of buildings and humans in a cross-section of sedimentary rock:

> Blind arches showed in walls of wane,
> Sealed windows, portals masoned fast,
> And terraces where nothing passed
> By parapets all dumb. No tarn
> Among the Kaatskills   (1.1.163–7)

The passage imbues urban forms with human qualities: the arches are blind; the parapets are dumb—this is another conflation of body and place. No organic rhythms flow here; opportunities to look out of a window, or walk through an arch—to tell the stories of self—are "masoned fast", entombed within the congested city arteries. Notice that no tarn runs through the *Kaatskill* mountains. The narrative briefly switches continents as though now looking out from some vantage point toward a surrounding New England landscape. Manhattan, latent in the poem's metrical arrangement, is briefly allowed to bleed into the ostensible Jerusalem setting.

In Canto 27 of Part 3, "Man and Bird," the narrator frames a particularly acute representation of human petrifaction. Set in a monastic cell, a "crazed" monk Habbibi, has carved his despair into the walls:

> "How like you it—Habbibi's home?
> You see these writings on the wall?
> His craze was this: he heard a call
> Ever from heaven: O scribe, write, write!
> Write this—that write—to these indite—
> To them! Forever it was—write!
> Well, write he did, as here you see.

What is it all?"
      "Dim, dim to me,"
Said Derwent; "ay, obscurely traced;
And much is rubbed off or defaced.
But here now, this is pretty clear:
'*I, Self, I am the enemy*
Of all. From me deliver me,
O Lord.'—Poor man!—But here, dim here:
"*There is a hell over which mere hell*
Serves—for— a—heaven.'—Oh, terrible!
Profound pit that must be!—   (3.27.112–28)

Four voices—the narrator's, Habbibi's and Derwent's—and Ahab's—jam together to maintain the four-beat pattern: as in "'*Serves—for—a—heaven.'*—Oh, terrible!" This cell forces echoing call and response patterns that—cave-like—bounce back and forth between the various margins and contours of the verse. Derwent's repetition of "write", which paraphrases Habbibi's vocational injunction from heaven, disperses a reverberating "I" that echoes the monk's carvings on the wall: "*I, Self, I am the enemy | Of all. From me deliver me, | O Lord*". In this place, Habbibi only manages to articulate tortured lyrical tautologies that rebound back and forth between "me" and "me".

Melville's epic opens with a material merger of human and stone, word and meter, the metrical frame experimenting with the tactile shocks and adaptations of the body as it negotiates a new urban terrain. *Clarel* enacts the deformations of the body as it is subjected to the pressures of this new urban conformity. As a member of the workforce, writing while distracted by other labors, Melville inscribes into the very fabric of his epic poem a process through which a subject buckles and embeds within a particular political and economic context. *Clarel* once again demonstrates his reluctance to enforce any easy imaginative escape or repose. Instead, the poem gives form to an alternative conception of creative production that does not conform to any pre-existing or discrete division of labor. It offers a local model of distracted, and always contingent poetics, illustrating how writing an epic poem as part of the workforce in the New Jerusalem necessarily alters the possibilities of poetic self-expression. This is what poetry looks like when the abdication from a duplex life proves impossible.

4

Billy Budd and Melville's Retirement

Accounts of "The late Melville" continue to make for maudlin reading. For the last twenty years of his working life, serving first as a deputy customs inspector then as a district inspector, Melville performed tedious governmental jobs that were not only beneath him (see *The Night Inspector* by Frederick Busch for confirmation of that) but also potentially compromising to the progressive political credo of his writings.[1] While he might once have offered a "meditation on the meaning of the state of exception as it pertains to America" (Spanos, *Exceptionalist*, 4), he was now apparently making sure, on a daily basis, that the Ship of State was paid its dues. Such work might charitably be construed in terms of a progressive civic duty, but it was also unavoidably complicit in funding America's expanding colonial and imperial ambitions of the era. Consequently, Melville the customs inspector has often been depicted as a disappointed and conflicted genius. Disillusioned with his unfulfilling work and family life, not to mention the world at large, he wanders the banks of the Hudson, writes indifferent poetry, and longs for the day when he can be released from the daily grind. Robert Milder goes so far as to portray the workaday Melville as finally succumbing to the invitations of Ahab's proto-modernist lyric refuge: "collapsing inwards toward a center of private musing, which in his physically and emotionally weakened state he nurtured carefully against inordinate hopes and the chance of real or imagined slights" (*Exiled Royalties*, 222). It was only after he retired in 1885 (so the story goes), that Fallen Melville found the long-awaited period of leisure to turn away from verse and re-channel his true calling as the "Poet in Prose" in the form of *Billy Budd*.

This chapter considers what happens to our understanding of Melville's later texts (as well as his biography) when the contours of this portrait are redrawn. In doing so, it proposes an alternative account of Melville's later career, one that resists the implicit Romantic privileging of literary labor over other forms of work and complicates the familiar late Melvillean

---

[1] See *The Night Inspector*, a novel in which the central protagonist befriends a particularly beset and dejected Herman Melville.

narratives of disillusionment, withdrawal, nostalgia, and transcendence. A wistful nostalgia does permeate the "retirement club" feel of *John Marr and Other Sailors* (1888), and *Billy Budd* does gesture towards the heavens, but there is also something else at play in these texts—something more engaged and genial, akin to what John Bryant has described as the "warm sparking of Melville's artful repose" (267). In spite of any perceived professional disappointments, Melville the writer and retired Customs Inspector continued to experiment across a variety of formal approaches, personas, and counterpoint geographies,[2] working through his retirement to develop late writings that were not simply retreating from the indifferent world "out there," but actively engaged in responding to the contingencies of his political and economic environment. Indeed, there is also a perceptible continuation of Melville's earlier preoccupations with undermining the possibility of lyric repose. *Timoleon* (1891), *Weeds and Wildings Chiefly: With a Rose or Two* (unpublished), *Billy Budd*, and *John Marr* were written more or less conterminously, and when read in conjunction, and in the context of Melville's retirement sensibility, they help readjust our sense of old-man-Melville occupying "a convent-like retreat... carefully protected against incursions from the disorderly world without" (*Exiled Royalties*, 223). Melville approached literary composition and revision, in his later years, as an extension of (rather than a release from) other forms of work, an approach that makes his writings remarkably imbricated and coextensive with one another. What emerges from these later works is a sustained exploration of alternative allegiances and complicities that radically undermine narratives of vocational fulfillment.

Scholarship on Melville's late career—and especially *Billy Budd* scholarship—is indebted to Harrison Hayford's and Merton M. Sealts's landmark genetic text (1962). Dissatisfied with Raymond Weaver's early edition of the novella, they returned to the unfinished and jumbled manuscripts that had been kept in a family breadbox for decades following Melville's death and illustrated for the first time how interconnected his final projects eventually became, how they resonate both outwards and inwards towards one another in something akin to a textual feedback loop.[3] They revealed that Melville had initially intended a much shorter version of *Billy Budd* to be included in *John Marr and Other Sailors*. Unable to let the piece go in 1888, he picked up various strands of the

---

[2] For Wyn Kelley, Melville "seems to have been looking for a new way to tell stories that was neither wholly prose nor wholly lyric" (*Introduction*, 160).

[3] See the second volume of Parker's *Biography* for a detailed description of the interrelated way Melville worked on his last projects (880–3). Parker notes, for example, that "the blank verso of a cancelled sheet of poetry from *Weeds and Wildings* was reused in the *Billy Budd* manuscript" (880).

story, extended them, and began blunting their moral legibility, opening up ever widening margins of possible interpretation. In what the editors call Stage B of revision, Melville transformed Billy, the wily old mutineer of the ballad, into a youthful "illiterate nightingale"; at Stage C, he endowed Claggart with his malevolent grudge; and in subsequent revisions, he bought Captain Vere forward to deliver the final, fraught sentence. As the project took shape, Melville freighted each character with increasingly conflicting responsibilities for Billy's downfall—rewriting, crossing out, and even overlaying palimpsestic redrafts (with pins) as he went. What this breadbox archive revealed, then, was a productively distracted mode of composition informed by his experiences of simultaneous labors.

The genetic text revealed the construction of *Billy Budd* as a process of meticulous revision and suspension, an observation that was then both intuited and capitalized on for the purposes of several subsequent landmark interpretations.[4] John Wenke, for example, argued that "even in the latest fair-copy inscriptions—at Stages F and G—Melville was not simply tinkering with words and phrases but making decisive alterations that seem *designed* to thwart determinate readings."[5] And Barbara Johnson, in her well-known essay "Melville's Fist: The Execution of *Billy Budd*," noted how "the story ends by fearlessly fraying its own symmetry, thrice transgressing its own 'proper' end." What *Billy Budd* demonstrates, according to Johnson, "is that authority consists precisely in the impossibility of containing the effects of its own application" (569). Melville's retirement provides an unexplored context for such apprehensions of deferral, fraying—and distraction—through his recuperative experimentation between alternative forms of labor and between alternative and coextensive texts.

In writing his final works, Melville was not simply relishing the opportunity to turn his back once and for all on a twenty-year customs career; and, in a similar way, *Billy Budd* does not represent a clear-cut decision to revert from poetry to his supposedly preferred medium of prose. Rather, he held these differing perspectives and approaches in collaborative suspension, often articulating an idea in one forum so as to realize its generative potential in another. These final texts and contexts function

---

[4] Robert Ryan, another early critic to carefully look at the late manuscripts, revealed that the poems eventually collected in *John Marr* and *Weeds and Wildings* were initially bound together in a volume probably entitled *Meadows and Seas* (16).

[5] Wenke examines the "bifurcated readings" that have so often defined the criticism of *Billy Budd*, pointing to the variety of "either/or," "liberal" or "conservative" interpretations the text has inspired (115). Yet Wenke is by no means the first critic to emphasize the text's indeterminacy or provisionality; one of the earliest and most perceptive readers of *Billy Budd* was Paul Brodtkorb, Jr who called into question the very notion of a definitive version of the text. See his "The Definitive *Billy Budd*: 'But Aren't It All Sham?'" *PMLA* 82 (December 1967): 600–12.

as discursively resistant, multifaceted anatomies of one another rather than as inevitable or discrete literary or biographical events. Melville's late works strive towards junctures of indeterminacy in which new permutations might coalesce, blunting the very idea of mastery over a text.

Adjectives such as "late," "last," and "final" have a habit of instilling this part of his career with a linear determinism and sense of self-realization, retrospectively curtailing the multifarious interdependencies that Melville began mobilizing at this moment. His retirement did not release him into a terminal creative garret where he focused on achieving a monumental ending. Rather, his departure from the workforce provided another series of simultaneous perpectives with which to experiment with further proliferating connections. In this light, "late Melville" extends beyond its function as biographical epithet, signalling instead the cultivation of a vital untimeliness—an insistence on never quite arriving at the stipulated place, time, attitude, or disposition. The only promise to be found in these texts is the radical imperative to apprehend the promise of one more provisional combination, to draw attention to literary labor as something that drifts irretrievably sideways and away from any discernible terminus of personal consummation.

Melville was partly relieved to stop work and partly frustrated with his failing body, but he was also aware of the social and political pressures that were pushing men like him out of the workforce by the mid-1880s. His job, sometimes exasperating, had been a significant and complicated part of his life for nearly two decades: it was neither something he merely tolerated nor something that he wanted desperately to escape. Much credence for the view of Melville as professionally frustrated—as fundamentally at odds with his day job—is drawn from a single letter written in 1873 by Melville's brother-in-law John Hoadley to the newly elected Republican Secretary of the Treasury. Elections usually spelled trouble for civil servants, and Hoadley argued that Melville, working under impossible circumstances, ought to be allowed to avoid the inevitable round of political sackings. Cast in this letter as saintly defender of free commerce and governmental interests, Melville was apparently surrounded by "low venality" and repeatedly offered bribes, "quietly returning money which has been thrust into his pockets behind his back, avoiding offence alike to the corrupting merchants and their clerks and runners, who think that all men can be bought" (Leyda, 731). In trying to save Melville's job, Hoadley necessarily overstated the case, providing just one more highly politicized account of an always politicized writer. Given the nature of his work, it does seem naive to think that Melville remained morally impervious to this most notoriously Byzantine of occupations; we also know that he was not so pure as to be above handing out signed copies of his works to ease his social passage into this profession in 1865 (Parker, *Biography*, ii.604–5). Melville knew as well as the next employee how to negotiate the patronage system, and he may well have even sympathized with his more unscrupulous co-workers. Many of his colleagues saw such backhanders as a just means of remuneration and retaliation for, as one prominent reformist put it, the "despotic and piratical use of official authority" by the Republican administration in generating funds (Eaton, 26). Customs inspectors like Melville were forced to pay protection money or risk losing their jobs: two percent of their annual wages went to the New York Republican State Committee and, for two years leading up to the general election in 1885, a similar amount went to the national Republican Party (Garner, "Surviving," 12). A report from 1881 sympathized with the plight of corrupt inspectors, arguing that their current state of affairs was the direct result of being "unprotected against arbitrary exactions from their salaries" (Eaton, 26). John Hoadley's diagnosis of the "low venality" that surrounded Melville necessarily pandered to the Republican administration's view that the problem lay with the faulty morals of employees, and not with their own questionable policies.

Andrew Delbanco narrates the story of Melville's retirement as an escape from morally bankrupt colleagues and a demeaning position, enabled by his wife's timely inheritance:

> Melville's tone in *Billy Budd* toward the cheats and sneaks among its minor characters suggests that his mood toward his colleagues at the Customs House was more weary than incensed. There was something grim about holding a job in which graft was a matter of course, since to acquiesce was demeaning while to hold oneself aloof was self-punitive. He retired on the strength of his wife's inheritance from her aunt Martha Marett, who died in 1878, and her half brother Lemuel Shaw, Jr. who died in 1884.   (292)

Seven years before Melville retired, the family received the substantial sum of $20,000 from Marett: Lizzie inherited $10,000, with the children dividing the remainder between them (Parker, *Biography*, ii.836). If Melville's job was as burdensome as Delbanco claims, why did he not seize upon this increased financial stability and retire in 1878, or at least take this opportunity to search for something else? Melville's retirement seems difficult to attribute directly to the inheritance of 1884 because payment—amounting to some $80,000—was only made in the fall of 1888, three years after he stopped working (895). For the last few years of his career, Melville it seems did not go to work merely out of financial necessity.

Why retire in 1885, then? In January 1886, Lizzie explained to Kate Lansing that "for a year or so past he has found the duties too onerous for a man of his years, and at times of exhaustion, both mental and physical, he has been on the point of giving it up, but recovering a little, has held on, very naturally anxious to do so, for many reasons" (Parker, *Biography*, ii. 878). Few accounts of his attitude to his job exist, but we may venture a few reasonable speculations concerning the reasons for wanting to continue. Melville patrolled a Manhattan waterfront that at this time constituted one of the great thresholds of transnational traffic, an increasingly complex epicenter of emerging global flows. As representative of the New York Custom-House, he found himself occupying a politically conflicted—given his consistent penchant for deconstructing national exceptionalisms—but no doubt engaging role as apparent gatekeeper of the national interest.[6] He was also surrounded by men who spoke the language of the sea, and as Stanton Garner speculates, in "some ways, it was an agreeable occupation: close to the ships and the seamen he loved" (291). His work thus offered him a point of access to the absorbing arena that had always occupied such a central role in his life and writing. Disadvantages aside, his occupation allowed him to be paid to do what he had always done: observe and interact with a city that had continually fascinated him. No wonder he was in some ways keen to hang on. During slow periods, it was not necessary that all inspectors be on duty, meaning that Melville often had half-days to himself. According to Garner, his colleagues "could mind the office while Melville tended to his personal business of inspecting bookstores, combing through libraries and art galleries, strolling through streets to observe the human comedy and tragedy enacted there and to peer into the store windows, or perhaps even returning home for lunch" (281).

This slightly more generous account of Melville at work casts a very different light on the following letter written by Lizzie on July 29, 1885 (the year of his retirement):

> Herman's position in the Custom's House is in the Surveyor's Department—a *district inspector*—his work is all on the uptown piers nearly to Harlem, and he has held office since Dec. 1866. Of course there have been removals, and he may be removed any day, for which I should be very sorry as apart from anything else the *occupation* is a great thing for him, and he could not take any other post that required head work, & sitting at a desk
> (Parker, *Biography*, ii.871)

Lizzie's insistence that Melville's "*occupation*" was a "great thing for him" ought to be taken seriously, rather than dismissed—as Parker dismisses it—as the misjudgment of an estranged and insensitive wife. Parker, in one of the more troubling passages from his biography, insists that "Lizzie knew so little of her husband that she could assert that his work at the Customs House was still 'a great thing for him' when in reality it was

---

[6] See, for example, Spanos, *Calling*, 13–15.

wearing him down, more brutally every year" (871). But Lizzie's letter
implies that conjugal communication channels were open; Melville kept
her up to date with news of his work—of these imminent "removals" or
redundancies. It also suggests that even as late as July, the option of
Melville's retirement did not immediately present itself. Note also that
Lizzie does not seem at all concerned about the financial impact this
removal might have on the family.

Lizzie was concerned for her husband because in March 1885 the
Democrat and former Governor of New York Grover Cleveland had
become the twenty-second President of the United States. With the new
administration came the usual round of political dismissals (Hawthorne's
sackings in 1849 and 1857, from respective official posts as surveyor-
inspector and consul, are the cases in point). The figurehead of what would
become known as the pro-business Bourbon Democrats, Cleveland ush-
ered in a new era of reforms that sought to eradicate barriers to competition and free trade. This movement also coincided with the appearance
of another social phenomenon that levied distinct pressures on Melville's
position. William Graebner suggests that "in the two decades before 1900,
age discrimination grew virulently, as the owners and managers who made
personnel decisions for American corporations redefined the work force to
achieve increased efficiency" (15). Even as a public-sector worker, Melville
would have felt the ubiquitous impact of this increasingly competitive
marketplace. Reforms within the civil service had already been implemented during the late 1870s and early 1880s in order to keep up with
the demands of an accelerating economy. The most significant of these, the
Pendleton Civil Service Reform Act of 1883, was a major step in transforming what until then had previously been a spoils system into something more meritocratic (Grossman, 259). Melville's job had been secured
through the patronage of Henry A. Smythe, his former traveling companion, who wrote a successful letter of support to the Republican Secretary of
the Treasury in 1866 (Parker, 603). By the 1880s, a district inspector like
Melville was considered part of the old guard, representative of a corrupt,
exclusionary, and backward system. As the new Democratic administration came to power in early 1885, a younger and more vociferous
workforce was beginning to dominate America's job market, clamouring
for better working conditions, better pay, and for the older generation to
step aside.[7] This offers an alternative explanation as to why so many of

---

[7] Larry J. Reynolds has pointed to the labor unrest that erupted in Chicago and New
York City (along with several other cities) in May 1886 as a possible influence on the first
drafts of *Billy Budd*. See "*Billy Budd* and American Labor Unrest: The Case for Striking
Back" in Donald Yannella (ed.), *New Essays on "Billy Budd"* (2002), 21–48.

Melville's late poems locate themselves either in the classical past or in the midst of the Renaissance—namely the defining moments of the patronage system. Melville plays on the rearguard social and economic stance he occupies in a poem such as "At the Hostelry" when he experiments explicitly with the address of flattering poet to patron: "TO M. DE GRANDVIN... Pardon me, Monsieur, in the following sally I have endeavoured to methodise into literary form, and make consecutive, upon one of your favourite themes, something at least of that desultory wit, gaiety, knowledge, and invention so singularly yours" (*Works*, 355).

The late nineteenth century also saw retirement increasingly touted as a "panacea for the ills that beset... particular fields" (Graebner, 13). For business leaders, retirement meant a younger and more efficient workforce capable of learning new skills, as well as higher rates of staff turnover; for the church it meant a more galvanized and dynamic priesthood; and for the millions of new immigrants who continued flooding into New York City, it meant work.[8] In 1878, statistician Carroll Wright made the first serious attempt to count the reserve pool of labor. His 1887 report issued as the U.S. Commissioner of Labor introduced the "idea of a permanent and potentially dangerous residual unemployment" (Graebner, 16).[9] As Graebner puts it, this allowed "employers, scientific managers, economists, and physicians to emphasise the benefits of employing superior workmen and the liabilities of keeping inefficient ones, instead of seeking to use all workers in a tight labor market" (16).

One of the most divisive public debates at the time of Melville's retirement centered on officers in the military. A *New York Times* article of 1881, "Compulsory Retirement," argued that "even granting the serviceable qualities of all the veterans, the fundamental fact to note is that their retirement is the only way just now to secure that steady and equable flow of promotion without which any military service will first fret with disappointment and then stagnate with despair" (np). This argument acquired its potency from the increasingly competitive and mobile workforce. In almost all sections of the working population, retirement was purportedly key to preventing economic stagnation. If senior positions became more readily available, so the argument went, more individuals would be galvanized into working harder, increasing efficiency within the institution and in society as a whole. Whether or not he was explicitly asked to hand in his notice, it seems likely, given the sustained upward pressure of the labor market, that Melville was beginning to sense his own untimeliness.

---

[8] Between 1880 and 1900, the population of New York City increased from 1.2 million to almost 3.5 million people. See J. Allen, 910.

[9] See also Leiby, 66.

Working on the Hudson waterfront, Melville also witnessed the radical changes that were occurring in the shipping industry: sailing ships were being retired from active service and being replaced by more efficient machines. Maritime historian Richard Runciman Terry claims that "by the end of the seventies steam had driven the sailing ship from the seas. A number of ailing vessels lingered on through the eighties, but they retained little of the corporate pride and splendor that was once theirs" (1). Donkey engines and steam winches had transformed the work of sailors; no longer was it necessary to man the windlass and halyards and sing their various shanties and work songs. The "sailor" was replaced by the more specialized engineer. During the last years of Melville's career, then, a confluence of pressures was brought to bear: fatigue, ill health, and weariness—but also cultural, technological, and administrative changes combined with an increasingly pervasive ageism. At last, in December 1885, and with a host of conflicting sentiments, his twenty-year career came to a close. It is in this context that Melville presents us with a cast of nostalgic and reluctant retirees and writes of ailing vessels forced into redundancy, lingering in their old age as a new world supersedes them. *John Marr and Other Sailors* (1888) constitutes something of a retirement club—a series of ballads, tales and shanties—that continually struggle to memorialize the passing of a maritime culture, and come to terms with the loss of a profession and identity so intimately connected with that culture.[10] In "Bridegroom Dick," for example, a jovial old man delivers a rather satisfied and racy monologue to his wife about his career at sea: "This stripped old hulk here for years may survive" (*John Marr*, 47). Next we get "Tom Deadlight" who sings a capstan shanty of a broken-down "hulk" steering towards the "Deadman"; and then an ecstatic reminiscence of an old sailor called "Jack Roy," a shanty-man, who could "ascend in love-ditty, kissing fingers to your ladies!" (80).

Melville wrote one of the earliest canceled drafts of the ballad "Billy in the Darbies" (composed in the immediate aftermath of his retirement and alongside these other retirees), on the back of a manuscript sketch called "Daniel Orme," a story, like *Billy Budd*, initially intended for inclusion in the *John Marr* collection:

> In his retirement the superannuated giant begins to mellow down into a sort
> of animal decay. In hard, rude natures, especially such as have passed their
> lives among the elements, farmers and sailors, this animal decay mostly

[10] In 1867, Melville's brother Thomas became governor of "Sailors' Snug Harbor" on Staten Island, a retirement home for former sailors (see *Correspondence*, 410). See Parker's chapter entitled ' "Old Fogy and Imaginary Companions" for the possible connection with the conception of *John Marr* (*Biography*, ii.815–44).

effects the memory by casting a haze over it; not seldom, it softens the heart as well, besides more or less, perhaps, drowsing the conscience, innocent or otherwise.   (Parker, *Biography*, ii.882)

On one side of this draft, we have this meditation on the "animal decay" of a senior citizen, and on the other, we find the earliest versions of a ballad about the impending execution of an old sailor—a Melvillean hanging to match the beheading that Nathaniel Hawthorne used as an analogy for his own loss of a patronage position. Hawthorne's customs career was consigned to a fate not unrelated to Melville's; he fell victim to the politicized accusations of corruption that followed the victory of the Whig President Zachary Taylor in 1849. Smarting at having been so abruptly "turned out of office," Hawthorne wrote to Longfellow that he felt "pretty well since [his] head has been chopt off" (*Letters*, 283).[11] A beheading subsequently appeared in the alternative title the narrator offers for *The Scarlet Letter* (published a year later): "THE POSTHUMOUS PAPERS OF A DECAPITATED SURVEYOR" (43).[12] Melville's last works, analogously bound up with a personal laboring history, are the product of a sixty-six-year-old man coming to terms with his own ousting from the workforce. He was not simply a writer newly liberated from tedious work and finally free to fulfill his true vocational ambitions.

Melville, then, was dwelling on what it means to stop work when he started writing "Billy in the Darbies." The older Billy, not the youthful credulous Billy of the prose, sings of the sentence just passed down to him and his imminent fate:

> Good of the chaplain to enter Lone Bay
> And down on his marrow-bones here and pray
> For the likes just o' me, Billy Budd.—But, look:
> Through the port comes the moonshine astray!

[11] Sacvan Bercovitch connects this, and the novel's other recurrent "allusions to scaffold and guillotine," to the recently ousted Democratic Party's identification with the victims of the 1848–9 European revolutions. See *The Rites of Assent: Transformations in the Symbolic Construction of America* (1993), 218. See also Jonathan Arac's discussion of the successive rotatory axings of the Custom-House in "The Politics of *The Scarlet Letter*" in Sacvan Bercovitch and Myra Jehlen (eds), *Ideology and Classic American Literature* (1986), 253.

[12] Hawthorne was soon publically resurrected when he wrote the partisan *Life of Franklin Pierce* (Boston, MA: Ticknor, Reed and Fields, 1852). When Pierce was elected President in 1853, Hawthorne's reward was the position of United States consul in Liverpool—an office he held for four years until another change of administration in 1857 swiftly decapitated him again. See Brenda Wineapple, *Hawthorne: A Life* (2004), 342–5. It was towards the end of Hawthorne's appointment that he and Melville last met. Aside from "Futurity and Provenance, and of everything that lies beyond human ken," the two men may also have discussed Hawthorne's imminent "execution." See *Journals*, 628.

It tips the guard's cutlass and silvers this nook;
But 'twill die in the dawning of Billy's last day.
A jewel-block they'll make of me tomorrow,
Pendant pearl from the yardarm-end
Like the eardrop I gave to Bristol Molly—
O, 'tis me, not the sentence they'll suspend.
Ay, ay, all is up; and I must up too,
Early in the morning, aloft from alow.   (132)

Limping along in uneven triple meter, this singer has a convincing solemnity about him. The romantic muse, "moonshine," filters through the port and illuminates this garret, inspiring one final poetic utterance. But Billy's lyrical ballad hangs in the balance: he suspends "suspend" between a reprieve and a hanging; "Die in the dawning" carries the paradox of ceasing at the beginning; and "aloft from alow" inverts Billy's fated progression from cell to yardarm. These reversals partially dislodge the sequence of events; they serve as waylaying reprieves, confusing Billy's advance towards his final fate and denying any sense of release or transcendence by weaving together a tangled network of preoccupied associations: a nautical "jewel-block" becomes a "pearl" that dangles from the yardarm, before transforming into an earring that hangs from the ear of an old flame, Bristol Molly. He thereby defers his own death by suspending a string of connections that lead away from the terminal reality of the noose and back to dry land. The ballad concludes with Billy's moving request: "Just ease these darbies at the wrist, | And roll me over fair! | I am sleepy, and the oozy weeds about me twist." In his final somnolent state, Billy apparently confuses his manacles for the weeds that will eventually twist about his body when he is rolled overboard. The ballad thus begins with him trussed in the manacles of the judiciary and ends with him twisted in the fronds of natural decay—and Billy, condemned, dangles somewhere in between, gently agitating against the finality that will define his inevitable end.

Something else is going on here as well though. Notice that when this "moonshine" (not moonlight) comes through the port, it "tips" the guard's cutlass and "silvers this nook." Is that really the solemn poetic light of the moon? Or is it contraband liquor (this usage of "moonshine" was common by 1885)?[13] Is the apparently anonymous guard, or even the chaplain, supplying this treacherous old sailor on the quiet here? It certainly makes you rethink the last line of the revised ballad: "I am sleepy,

---

[13] The OED dates "Moonshine," "smuggled or illicitly distilled liquor," from 1782, and provides an American usage from 1875.

and the oozy weeds about me twist." One explanation is that he may be under the influence (there is even some "port" mixed in, too).

The very things that aestheticize and sanctify this solemn creative garret of the sovereign singer—the priest, the moonshine silvering the nook, tipping the guard's cutlass (just by his trouser pocket)—are all very pretty and pious, but they are also a decoy: a distraction. The interjection "But look!" forces a metrical pause over a line break, and while our solemn attentions are drawn, the ballad starts quietly dealing on the sly. The speaker relies both on his listeners sympathetically following the meandering contours of his metrics and on their getting distracted by a transcendent poetic light that emanates through the port. But this is the song of a treacherous old sailor, and he has been trying to smuggle something past us here as someone who knows the tricks of the trade. Melville wrote this just as he was forced into inhabiting what he'd begun ambivalently referring to as his realm of "unobstructed leisure."[14] And yet, he writes a ballad that refers us back to his former place of work: the "low venality" of the docks of Manhattan, populated by those "corrupting merchants and their clerks and runners, who think that all men can be bought."

In establishing this collusion between his solitary singer Billy and a shadowy extra-authorial presence, Melville hints at the type of literary experimentation he undertakes in these final years. This is not the work of a downtrodden retiree—it is the light-footed self-consciousness of a writer engaged in a process of creative interplay, who scans his predicament for new thresholds of expression and potential intersections across apparently separate texts, personae, and settings. It also enumerates one more way in which Melville situates his writing askance the priorities of an exceptional national framework; in this instance, by experimenting with a black-market poetic persona that seeks to put one over on the officialdom.

* * *

By far the least read work of Melville's later years, though composed in tandem with *Billy Budd*, is *Weeds and Wildings Chiefly: with a Rose or Two*. If he returns once more to ships and sailors in *Billy Budd*, Melville in *Weeds* takes on a distinctly different voice and style that plays on ideas of having been put out to pasture or having gone to seed. As Wyn Kelley suggests, "these poems include flowers, children, small animals, and the influences of pastoral scenes and narratives" and while "they exhibit wit affection and charm", "on the surface, at least, they do seem less fraught with conflict than Melville's published collections" (*Introduction*, 171);

---

[14] See Melville's letter to Professor Archibald MacMechan, December 5, 1889, *Correspondence*, 519.

indeed, "it is hard to recognize or locate the Melville many readers know in these seemingly charming ditties and musings on flowers" (172). One way to approach this collection is (to adapt Melville's own metaphor here) to read it as a kind of adjunct literary seedbed—a forum in which he cultivated certain ideas in order to test their possibility in alternative settings. This creative process is continuous with an idea put forward by Harrison Hayford in "Unnecessary Duplicates: A Key to the Writing of *Moby-Dick*" (1978). Hayford's apprehension of certain textual anomalies or doublings in *Moby-Dick* led him to claim that the novel is the result of Melville having spliced separate narratives together (thus accounting for the often erratic formal qualities of the work). The interrelated network of texts that Melville cultivates at this moment also bear the traces of a coterminous, mutually constitutive process of production, suggesting that at this late stage, Melville continued to network his literary labor across seemingly discrete narratives and literary forms.

"The Rose Farmer," one of the longest poems in *Weeds and Wildings*, and one that again decamps its narrative to a seemingly exotic to the Middle East, relays a meandering narrative of a retiree who inherits a rose farm from a recently passed friend. The speaker, another playful surrogate for the author, is unsure how to manage and market his crop:

> But, ah, the stewardship it poses!
> Every hour the bloom, the bliss
> Upbraid me that I am remiss.
> For still I dally,—I delay,—
> Long do hesitate, and say,
> "Of fifty thousand Damask Roses,—
> (For my rose-farm no great matter),—
> Shall I make me heaps of posies,
> Or some crystal drops of Attar?
> To smell or sell or for a boon
> Quick you cull a rose and easy;
> But Attar is not got so soon,
> Demanding more than gesture breezy.
> Yet this same Attar, I suppose,
> Long time will last, outlive indeed
> The rightful sceptre of the rose
> And coronations of the weed.   (45)

Having been belatedly forced into the role of farmer, the narrator's dilemma provides a telling allegory of creative labor that places the stereotypical fodder of poetry (the rose) into a distinctly commercial context. The work or "stewardship" involved in running this farm seems daunting, and with every hour that passes, he imagines that his flowers reprimand him for being "remiss." He dallies and delays—unsure of whether to turn a quick profit by selling his flowers as they are, or attempt something more ambitious like extracting "crystal drops of Attar", a product that will outlive the ephemeral but "rightful sceptre of the rose." What is the suitable way forward? To make up his mind, he asks a Persian (a "gentleman-rose-farmer" living nearby) for advice. Before answering, the Persian subjects the speaker to a dose of ageism, doubting his ability to create anything at all: " 'And you?—an older man than I? | Late come you with your sage propounding: | Allah! Your time has long gone by' " (46). The speaker promptly defends himself with an assertion of his enduring youth and vigor: "these gray hairs but disguise, | Since down in heart youth never dies— | O, sharpened by the long delay, | I'm eager for my roses quite" (46). He then asks the Persian what he thinks of the possibility of producing "Attar," which provokes the following discouraging response:

> "Attar? go ask the Parsee yonder.
> Lean as a rake with his distilling,
> Cancel his debts, scarce worth a shilling!
> How he exists I frequent wonder.
> No neighbor loves him: sweet endeavor
> Will get a nosegay from him never;
> No, nor even your ducats will;
> A very save-all for his still!
> Of *me*, however, all speak well:
> You see, my little coins I tell;
> I give away, but more I sell.
> In mossy pots, or bound in posies,
> Always a market for my roses.
> But attar, why, it comes so dear
> 'Tis far from popular, that's clear.   (46)

The isolated Parsee is motivated by concerns other than financial—no "ducats" will sway him from his ambition to distil the rose's essence. The Persian wonders how the ascetic Parsee actually manages to stay alive; he produces Attar at the cost of making a decent living. It requires such effort ("comes so dear"), yet is not even sought-after. The Persian, by contrast, flourishes: he is well thought of; always finds a market for his fresh flowers; and figures his blooms as coins, arranging them in pleasant-looking "mossy pots," or bunches, for popular consumption. The speaker presents two parables of literary labor here: the Persian produces something that is saleable and pleasing, and consequently reaps both financial and social rewards; and the Parsee, in doggedly attempting to extract the ideal essence of his crop, forfeits wealth and popularity for a life of rejection and struggle. Though the Parsee's sacrifice might seem virtuous—he follows his vocation and creates something that is ultimately more durable and valuable than the rose itself—the wealthy Persian calls his ascetic aesthetic practice into question:

> "I flourish, I; yon heavens they bless me,
> My darlings cluster to caress me."
> At that fond sentence overheard,
> Methought his rose-seraglio stirred.
> But further he: "Yon Parsee lours
> Headsman and Blue Beard of the flowers.
> In virgin flush of efflorescence
> When buds their bosoms just disclose,
> To get a mummified quintessence
> He scimetars the living rose!"   (47)

At the fond "sentence" of the self-aggrandizing Persian, his "rose-seraglio" stirs: either his flowers comically swoon at his praise and attention, or they shudder because his "sentence" means their inevitable decapitation and destruction. He accuses the Parsee of beheading his flowers to get at a synthetic "mummified quintessence" that is a pale reflection of the real thing, but is this any better than beheading them to turn a quick profit? Of course, the temptation is to read the Parsee of this allegory as a thinly veiled retrospective on Melville's own career as a writer, but the equivocating speaker of this meandering poem ensures that it is impossible to know where any allegiance lies. Though potentially ironizing the populist approach of the Persian, he also resists affirming the dogmatic pursuit of any quintessence. In aligning the latter with "attar," the poem further illustrates how any such exemption is always ultimately imbricated with those market forces it presumes to rise above. While it seems like the transcendent product of a labor significantly detached from the world of moneymaking, the attar will eventually become a commodity whose consumption is reserved for the elite few. Melville, then, playfully presents a dilemma that cannot readily be solved, pointing to the need for an alternative conception of production that exceeds this familiar opposition.

It is at this moment, while distractedly weighing these alternatives, that the Persian provides what sounds like a reformulation of Billy Budd's hanging, aligning the Parsee's choices with the moral dilemma of Captain Vere: the "headsman" Parsee scimitars the living rose "when *buds* their bosoms just disclose." Billy's killing of Claggart is divinely "just" but Vere realizes that the "quintessence" of the law must be upheld; indeed, Vere knows what he must do as soon as Billy lashes out: "Struck dead by an angel of God! Yet the angel must hang!" (100). The rose farmer articulates Billy's fate in verse, from the vantage point of a seemingly discrete text, literary form, and geographical location. Melville works through alternative takes of this climactic ending and then leaves traces of their collaborative formulation in both works. Indeed, if we see a residual articulation of Billy's outburst in "The Rose Farmer," we also see a corresponding metaphor blossom at the moment of Billy's death: "Billy ascended; and, ascending, took the full rose of the dawn."

Melville's feedback-loop experimentations allow such metaphors to extend and develop across ostensibly discrete projects. At this apparently late stage, he displayed an intellectual receptivity that muddles the possibility of resolving these labors within any sentimental "swansong" narratives that have hitherto been associated with "late Melville". The faux-Romantic garret of "Billy in the Darbies"; the aesthetic/financial impasse faced by the rose farmer: each frustrated representation of the artist tests Emerson's affirmation of the unilateral, pre-ordained calling: "Doubt not, O poet, but persist. Say 'it is in me, and shall out' . . . God wills that thou abdicate a manifold and duplex life." Melville's conception of the writer-cum-poet ran counter to this vision; for him, artistic labor constituted the continual embrace of manifold life, rejecting the sanctities of any guaranteed being for the contingencies that animated his art of distracted complicity. Deleuze has suggested that while "we belong to the *dispositifs* and act within them," by which he means the material and social apparatuses that produce the human subject, the crucial aspect of self-production is the ethical imperative to apprehend, and as far as possible, resist allowing subjectival precedents to define us. What matters ultimately "is not what we are but rather what we are in the process of becoming—that is the Other, our becoming-other" (164). Even in his retirement, Melville continued to be alive to this distinction; and in so doing and becoming, his work stands as a challenge to the myth of the inward-looking Melville that modernism subsequently revived in its own political image.

PART III

HART CRANE, JUNIOR COPYWRITER

5

Classical Modernism and Impersonal Poetic Labor

In the publicity poster for James Franco's biopic *The Broken Tower* (2011), a tortured-looking Hart Crane (played by Franco himself) sits at his desk on the fourteenth floor of the J. Walter Thompson advertising agency in midtown Manhattan, staring at several vials of perfume.[1] The boss had asked him to extol their virtues for a forthcoming cosmetics campaign. Franco based the scene that follows on a recollection of Crane's friend Matthew Josephson: "the perfumes nauseated him so much that one day, when he had come to work with a bad hangover, he snatched up the whole collection and threw them out of his office window" (262). Tellingly used for the film's trailer, this scene presents a symbolic distillation of that archetypal conflict between the individual poetic genius and a feminized mass culture. Paul Mariani, one of Crane's principal biographers (and script consultant on *The Broken Tower*), goes so far as to diagnose Crane's debilitating alcoholism as a direct result of thwarted vocation. He writes that "*nothing* killed the imagination as fast as copywriting. To have to write each damned day of Fox furnaces and Pittsburgh hot-water heaters and Seiberling Tires just to make ends meet. No wonder he drank, drank whatever the hell he could get hold of" (102). Mariani speaks of "a mind divided, as Crane found himself divided each day by his job [...] his day 'partitioned' into chronometrical units." By contrast, "there was that other world of night" in which Crane—"the modern Faustus, the poet, the visionary, the alchemist"—created art "in spite of these quotidian mercantile forces that seemed bent on destroying his peace" (98). For the purposes of Hollywood, it is of course more captivating to focus on Crane's sometimes violent allergic reactions to the obvious contaminations of "quotidian mercantile" labor: what, after all, could be more synthetically revolting to the delicate sensibilities of a poet

---

[1] See *The Broken Tower*, dir. James Franco (RabbitBandini Productions, 2011).

Fig. 5.1. The Broken Tower, James Franco as Hart Crane on US advance poster art, 2012 © Focus World/ courtesy Everett Collection.

than the noxious odor of cheap commercial perfume? The fact that such tragic representations are imminently marketable shows how they pose no threat to the consumer culture that is the alleged object of critique. The myth of the thwarted exceptional vocation is one that sells. Such anecdotes reinforce a parable of ultimately frustrated calling, in which Crane is employed (somewhat ironically) to advertise the cosmic injustice of a delicate vocational soul battling against the contaminating incursions of the workaday world.

In relation to Crane, what this familiar account glosses over, I think, is a creative output that was in fact intricately bound up with the material implications of having to make a living. Indeed, to grasp the subversive continuities that informed Crane's literary labor, Mariani's idea of a "mind divided" between "mercantile" and "visionary" requires re-evaluation. Crane's mode of poetic production, I want to suggest, tended to obstinately vacillate at the threshold of apparently discreet divisions of labor. While he did often articulate his allegiance to various "impersonal" distinctions that were contemporaneously being drawn between the verbal icon and the poet—and between discreet forms of poetic and quotidian labor—he also persistently agitated (and continues to agitate) at the margins of these influential distinctions.

Writing about Crane's development as a poet, Langdon Hammer contrasts T. S. Eliot's successful holding down of a job with Crane's failure to "embrace this division of everyday life" (18).[2] Hammer sees Eliot as thriving "by separating his economic and his literary productivity" into "two independent spheres of activity" (17). Banking enabled Eliot "in his capacity as a man of letters, *not to make money*, and so to conserve the special value literature did have" (15). In this way, Eliot cultivated stability in his daily life, which in turn, allowed him to wrest his artistic ambitions away from the marketplace: "Eliot's Bond Street suits confirmed his membership in English society at the same time, then, that they signified his refusal to compromise the highness of his literary calling" (15). Eliot recognized that the best way of dealing with the dilemma of producing art in a consumer context was to embrace that context fully, thereby maintaining a productive distinction between the two opposing (but mutually constitutive) domains. Hammer goes on to suggest that, by contrast, Crane did not see that the aspiring artist's life was "held together by being held apart" (21), claiming that his "life recurrently illustrated the truth (for him) that one cannot make both money and poetry at the same time" (18). Although this account is helpful in pointing to the logistical

---

[2] Hammer is one of several critics eager to engage work as a formative influence on Crane's poetry. His successive jobs are often seen as draining his creative energies; Brom Weber for example wrote that "like many young writers pressured by the need to earn a living, he was unable to foresee that in fashioning advertising slogans and paragraphs, he would of necessity be weakening his integrity as a writer, as well as sapping his creative energies". See *Hart Crane: A Biographical and Critical Study* (1948), 112.

difficulties Crane faced, it passes over the fact that this conflict constituted in itself an alternative aesthetic stance, albeit a turbulent one. In contrast to Eliot the banker, or Stevens the insurance executive, Crane refused to accept the partition between what he envisioned as the still fluid boundaries of literary and non-literary domains. Crane consequently stands at the forefront of a modernist counter-tradition that repudiated an emerging bourgeois conception of poetic calling. Instead he strove in his poetry to envision a mode of production that continually looked towards the more capacious and utopian work that poetry might yet become.

In order to contextualize Crane's contribution, I want to initially revisit the careers of Wallace Stevens and T. S. Eliot, and think again about the powerful political legacy of their particular career choices. These choices were integral to the development of their "impersonal" poetics, as well as the emergence of a specific cultural rehearsal of vocational thinking—"classical modernism"—the legacies of which still shape dominant conceptions of the division between literary and extra-literary work. Classical modernism's disciplinary partitioning of labor in the early twentieth century constituted a specific manifestation, in the cultural sphere, of "reserve anxiety": the reaction of privileged white men to the perceived contaminating threat presented by the contingent labor force. Classical modernism's enduring cultural legacy was to restage an iteration of this broader political crisis and enshrine individual poetic sovereignty as a timeless ideal. In taking up their now-iconic day jobs, Stevens and Eliot found a way of paying for their non-marketable literary experimentations while benefiting from growing perceptions that this arrangement constituted an existential threat to their innate poetic calling (even though the work was stable, well-paid, and socially enabling). But crucially, the perception of unexceptional, extra-literary work as "impediment" to the poet also worked retroactively, folding the careers of poets past into the consolidating classical modernist fold. In a sense, my incorporation of various "archives of distraction" have so far sought to unfasten a series of default assumptions that gained traction at precisely this early twentieth century moment.

Undergirding the consolidation of this cultural movement was a transatlantic network of reactionary thinking that merged an ascendant U.S. nativism with the influences of an anti-democratic traditionalism that had been emerging in France since the turn of the century. Indeed, it was the specific cultural energies surrounding the rise of Action Française that T. E. Hulme drew on for his influential 1911 essay "Romanticism and Classicism," which T. S. Eliot then adapted for his 1916 lecture series: "The Reaction Against Romanticism" (1916). Hulme had positioned Romanticism as that which spoils an otherwise respectable dinner party:

You don't believe in a God, so you begin to believe that man is a god. You don't believe in Heaven, so you begin to believe in a heaven on earth. In other words, you get romanticism. The concepts that are right and proper in their own sphere are spread over, and so mess up, falsify and blur the clear outlines of human experience. It is like pouring a pot of treacle over the dinner table. Romanticism then, and this is the best definition I can give of it, is spilt religion.   (62)

Confusing issues of rank, troubling aesthetic parameters, blurring "the clear outlines of human experience", Romanticism represented a menace that destabilized "natural" social spheres. Glossing such lines, Eliot in turn called for the re-establishment of "form and restraint in art, discipline and authority in religion, centralization in government" (*Essays*, 3). Exactly what was being restrained in this instance remained clouded by euphemism, though it is likely not a coincidence that Hulme's sticky black treacle is a particularly difficult stain to remove from a pristine white tablecloth (think back to Henry James's assessment of Whitman's poetry as the discharge of a blotting-book's undigested contents into the lap of the public). For all its refinement, this figuration of reserve anxiety is not particularly subtle in conveying the underlying racist, misogynistic, and classist suppositions that constituted increasingly foundational distinctions between restraint and indulgence: containment and excess.

It was an ideologically motivated act of segregation, transposed onto the question of how to make a living as a poet, that informed the professional decisions that Eliot and Stevens took at precisely this juncture: Eliot accepted his position at Lloyd's Bank in 1917, while Wallace Stevens had started at the Harford Accident and Indemnity Company a year earlier. In choosing these paths, they decisively turned away from those literary precursors who had, in Hulme's sense, allowed their art to spill into their lives and vice versa. Whether implicitly reacting against figures such as de Nerval walking a lobster along the Left Bank, Verlaine the rag picker, or Whitman loafing at his ease in New York City, Eliot and Stevens seized an opportunity in their professional arrangements to cleanse and reinvent the parameters of a poetic persona that had become steadily aligned with a politically suspect superfluity.[3]

In the literary marketplace, the opportunities presented by the rise of Progressive-era professionalization and the mass media simultaneously began altering perceptions of poetry, casting it as an increasingly decadent and

---

[3] See James E. Miller's discussion of Eliot's classicism in *T. S. Eliot: The Making of an American Poet 1888–1922* (2005), 262–5. Miller demonstrates just how vehement Eliot's anti-romanticism was at this stage, and how easily this sentiment pivots towards a thoroughgoing social conservatism: "Romanticism's 'germs' were to be 'found in Rousseau'."

effeminate cultural curiosity. The new "dominant professional style" constituted a renewed "masculinization" of literary culture, leading many cultural commentators to "worr[y] that contemporary poetry had become not only emotionally soft and intellectually slack, but also sexually suspect" (Newcomb, 27). Christopher Wilson describes this cultural shift in the following terms:

> the occupational ideological consequences of the new [literary] scene were considerable indeed [...] literary endeavor could be cut loose from its Romantic, aristocratic, or part-time moorings and reestablished in a cult of professional expertise and democratic activism. Literature, therefore, could be conceived as a product of labor rather than romantic inspiration. (3)

The career choices of Eliot and Stevens manifest an anxiety towards this transformation, partially conceding to some of its terms in order to maintain the exceptional integrity of their poetic labors. Anxious to avoid being too-closely associated with a suspect romanticism, but also wary of the very notions of democratic participation and the rise of the "hack writer", these banker- and lawyer- poets secured a legitimizing "masculinity" through their taking up of extra-literary jobs. As white, Harvard-educated, middle-class men, they saw the possibility of gaining well-paid and professionally stabilizing work as one of the more palliative solutions to modernism's much-debated money problem (that is, how to fund art that seeks to extricate itself from the dominant trends and ideological pressures of the consolidating mass market). A strictly divided occupational model offered itself to them in the following appealing terms: section off and carefully manage the borders of the professional realm so as to offset any socially problematic implications of their "true" vocational ambitions. Classically structured, their lives foregrounded a transcendent art of individual calling while neutralizing the social and political contingencies that Stevens would so casually dismiss in that most capacious of terms: the "merely personal" (*Letters*, 413). This means that, far from representing a defiant or heroic confrontation with the public sphere, these jobs were, in an integral sense, the making of these poets— not only in terms of funding but also in terms of sculpting the very contours of their subsequent literary hagiographies.

In one of the short essays collected in *Mythologies*, Roland Barthes turns his attention to an analogous dialectical staging of the modernist writer's transcendent vocation. Why, Barthes asks, might the readership of *Le Figaro* be so interested by the idea of André Gide on holiday? What is it about the author function that invites, or even requires, a mundane counterpoint for the maintenance of his discursive parameters? With characteristic acuity, Barthes reads the article as manufacturing a "proletarianization" (19): a staged encounter for this celebrity winner of the 1947 Nobel Prize for literature with the masses. For Barthes, the point is that the juxtaposition "André Gide on holiday" serves to negatively construct and maintain the contours of something like the anonymous proletarian's opposite: the exceptional, creative agency. Far from socializing Gide as someone who does as everyone else does, the juxtaposition reinforces the division "between a prosaic condition [...] and the glamorous status which bourgeois society liberally grants its spiritual representatives" (20). The discrete aura of a writer's "vocation", Barthes continues, "is never better displayed than when it is contradicted—but not denied, far from it—by a prosaic incarnation: this is an old trick of all hagiographies" (21). Expose literary luminaries to the apparent ordinariness of daily life—contrast those mundane aspects of their existence to their public perception as exceptional creative individuals—and entrench their reified status as fallen angels condemned to wander among us.

For Barthes though, there is another, more politically pressing aspect of this vocational dialectic. The writer who is brought into contact with the prosaic also simultaneously delineates and then maintains a silently oppositional, and disenfranchised quotidian "reality." "The spectacular alliance," Barthes suggests, "of so much nobility and so much futility means that one still believes in the contradiction: since it is miraculous, each of its terms is miraculous too" (22). Gide on holiday, Eliot the bank clerk, Stevens the insurance salesman: such anecdotes "would obviously lose all interest in a world where the writer's work was so desacralized that it appeared as natural as his vestimentary or gustatory functions" (22). This is not merely the affirmation of one faculty of agency over and above others; it is rather the instantiation of mutually sustaining, dialectically opposed spheres of being. In other words, the poet-function intensifies a drama of proximity, whereby political exception and difference come into close contact with one another and thereby reaffirm the nature of their ontological distinction.

Stevens' and Eliot's day jobs, while no doubt tedious on a Monday morning, continue to offer the ideal "prosaic conditions" against which to reify their transcendent poetic personas. Having secured remunerative jobs during an era of unprecedented social disorientation, these figures perversely benefited, and continue to benefit, from a belief that theirs was some kind of fated misfortune, inviting us imagine the wonders that would issue forth if the labors of true poetic souls commanded a higher price in our world. It is with this revisionist perspective in mind that I now want to turn to a couple of moments in Stevens' and Eliot's careers when they were invited to reflect on their lives as poets and professionals. Each of their reluctant responses robustly moves to secure the political parameters of their own "impersonality," signalling the emergence of the critical doctrine that still structures our thinking about the exceptional and discrete work that poets supposedly do.

* * *

In "The Noble Rider and the Sound of Words" (1951), Stevens wrote that "it is a violence from within that protects us from a violence without." Poetry was about "self-preservation," "the imagination pressing back against the pressure of reality," an articulation of a pre-formed opposa- itional stance towards an ephemeral reality that continually threatens to convolute the effort to contrive a moment of perceptual or subjectival clarity (36). Variations of this theme define many of Stevens' genial displays, whether they involve the subject comically jousting with the "polyphony" beyond Crispin's conceptual "baton," or the personal pro- nouns attempting to keep up with the chicanery of thirteen parallax blackbirds: his poetry often dramatizes a self and world in intense and reciprocal constitutive play. There is, however, at least one (epistolary) exchange in which the default oppositional dialectics of Stevens' literary persona were explicitly questioned. In 1942, the "pressure of reality" presented itself in the form of a request by the playwright and poet Harvey Breit for Stevens to contribute to an article for *Harper's Bazaar* about poets and their jobs. William Carlos Williams had suggested to Breit that Stevens might be interested in contributing—he was not. Stevens' response, alongside the characteristic cleverness and charm of his page persona, is also rife with an illuminating impatience:

> Williams wrote to me and did his best. Since he likes the idea, it is embarrassing for me to say that I don't and particularly to say why I don't. It has nothing to do with either you or him, or even Harper's Bazaar; I just don't like personal publicity...In order that you shall not miss the oppor- tunity that Harper's has given you, let me make a suggestion: Edgar Lee Masters is, or was, a lawyer...Masters is far better known than I am. Of course, I don't know whether Bill Williams would want to pair off with him, but he might...After all, what is there odd about being a lawyer and being or doing something else at the same time? I am sorry not to be willing to go along with you; there are a good many reasons that I am not taking the trouble to speak of. (*Letters*, 412–13)

Obliged, because of the Williams connection, to respond cordially to Breit's invitation, Stevens immediately and "impersonally" deflected attention on to others like him; he certainly wasn't the only one to balance legal and poetic careers. This happened to be a rather common and perfectly natural arrangement. He was, however, unable to dismiss the topic out of hand; what, after all, was there odd about doing or being two things at once? This was surely too perfunctory (or perhaps too foundational) a topic to rehearse out loud. Why was he even being asked a question like this; what did it say about the popular conceptions of the poet, and a poet like himself, if Breit thought this a worthwhile matter for intellectual debate? Stevens quickly followed his initial paragraph with a postscript: "P.S Archibald MacLeish is a lawyer," and "if Bacon was Shakespeare, then, since Bacon was Lord Chief Justice, what better instance could you want? W S" (*Letters*, 413). A facetious note to end on, but Stevens' broader point here is that artists (who are implicitly not like everyone else) are also capable of having unremarkable and anonymous lives—just like everyone else (with "everyone" there most likely meaning people like him).[4]

Emboldened by this response, and having clearly tickled a nerve, Breit asked Stevens to expand his theme, an invitation that Stevens duly accepted, setting out the familiar modernist doctrine of impersonality:

> You must know without my telling you how one struggles to suppress the merely personal. Having disciplined myself to that over a long period of time, how can I be expected to be indifferent? Again, I want to keep out all that. And still again, one is not a lawyer one minute and a poet the next. You said in your first letter something about a point at which I turned from being a lawyer to writing poetry. There never was any such point. I have always been intensely interested in poetry, even when I was a boy. While I don't know you, I haven't the slightest doubt that that is also true of yourself.
>
>   No one could be more earnest about anything than I am about poetry, but this is not due to any event or exercise of will; it is a natural development of an interest that always existed.   (*Letters*, 414)

What, exactly, does Stevens occlude in the struggle to suppress "the merely personal" or the even broader: "all that"? Cast in terms of a self-sacrifice—a subsumption of the trivial within higher holistic aims of the poet—Stevens cranks the dialectical mechanics of the modernist day job into action. In other words, he dismisses as a subject worthy of discussion the very privileges that enable him to stabilize as well as isolate the territory of poetic production. Realigned in this way, it now constitutes an act of semi-exasperated condescension to reflect on irrelevant biographical detail;

---

[4] Wallace Stevens' career in insurance and law has been the subject of several critical studies: see especially James Longenbach's "Surety and Fidelity Claims" in *Wallace Stevens, The Plain Sense of Things* (1991), 105–20. The critic who has done most to rejuvenate a sense of Stevens' career is Alan Filreis, first with *Wallace Stevens and the Actual World* (1991), and then *Modernism from Right to Left: Wallace Stevens, the Thirties, & Literary Radicalism* (1994). The aspect of each of these studies I want to historicize is the implicit vocational partition that serves as the starting point for each of their enquiries.

his poetic inclinations have, it turns out, always been prior—"a natural development of an interest that always existed." This is the poet defining himself in relation to a simultaneously denigrated "all that," a reified past and present now relieved of any potential to direct or determine the integrity of the unmarked, untethered sovereign creator.

Having carefully managed and realigned the terms of the discussion, Stevens then takes the opportunity of identifying the "real" subject of Breit's proposed essay as attempting to demystify popular (and specifically Romantic) conceptions of the poet:

> I think that your real subject is the destroying of the caricature in people's minds that exist there as the image of the poet. You say in your letter that there are thousands of people who . . .
>
> "can't reconcile a man of sound logic * * * with the exploration of the imagination",
>
> and who think . . .
>
> "that a poet is altogether an idler, a man without clothes, a drunk, a 'fantasist'—or on the other hand he is an untouchable, a seer".
>
> The peculiar thing about all this is that the people of sound logic whom I know, and I know lots of them, don't really think of a poet as an idler, a man without clothes, a drunk, etc. The conception of the figure of the poet has changed and is changing every day. It was only a few years ago when Joaquin Miller or Walt Whitman were considered to be approximations of a typical image. But were they? Weren't they recognized by people of any sense at all as, personally, poseurs? They belong to in the same category of eccentrics to which queer looking actors belong. When you think of an actor, do you think of him as the typical figure or do you think of him in terms of the ordinary men and women round you? Assuming that you think of him in terms of the ordinary men and women around you, why shouldn't you think of a poet in the same way: in terms of the ordinary men and women around you?
>
> As a matter of fact, the conception of poetry itself has changed and is changing every day. Poetry is a thing that engages, or should engage, not the human curiosities to whom you have referred, but men of serious intelligence. I think that every poet of any interest considers himself as a person concerned with something essential and vital. That such a person is to be visualized as "an idler, a man without clothes, a drunk" or in any way as an eccentric or a person somehow manqué is nonsense. The contemporary poet is simply a contemporary man who writes poetry. He looks like anyone else, acts like anyone else, wears the same kind of clothes, and certainly is not an incompetent.   (*Letters*, 413–14)

Classical modernist rhetoric at its most apparently reasonable; and yet we glimpse in these sentences a series of sleights of hand that orientate the contemporary poet and poetry in terms of some very specific social and political cleansing. Having established that an interest and talent for poetry is innate, Stevens is able to redirect popular conceptions of a formerly marginal or precarious poet (and the imagination) towards a center-ground of apparently "ordinary men and women" (with Stevens again standing as representative of the "ordinary"). Thus, Stevens sets up an "ordinary," which refers to the reified securities and privileges of his own social milieu, while subjecting the embodied representatives of difference to the strictures of his exclusionary logic. In enumerating the familiar decadent list of idlers, men without clothes, drunks, fantasists, queer looking actors, human curiosities, poseurs, incompetents, Millers and Whitmans, and persons manqué, Stevens writes off any person who is not a member of his own normative bourgeois sphere. He then secures the purity of his own essential poetic vocation by casting these suspect others as pseudo-poets who have chosen to live a lives of caricaturist fantasy, who indulge in effeminate play to his masculine seriousness and rectitude, and who have allowed life to spill into art. In this moment, it is not only Romantic poseurs that are cast out, but also any creative soul who is not so fortunate as to achieve Stevens' professional stability.

But all of the above is moot anyway, because after all, the merely personal must be erased so as to let the work of poetry speak for itself. What Whitman and Miller had done was to muddle the ontological distinction between the poet and poetry, compromising the classically pristine and essential characteristics of the latter. When Stevens claims, then, that the "the conception of the poet [and poetry] itself has changed and is changing every day," he was not referring to a particular temporal shift (and certainly not historicizing), but rather claiming that poetry had arrived at its unmediated teleological end, and was at last able to exist uncontaminated by the distractions of the personal. Stevens secures poetry, and along with it a conception of poetic labor, as having reached its final vocational terminus. Poetry was for those who lived, or who were able to live, stable and unremarkable lives (and, in order to achieve this distillation, it helped if you were white, male, Harvard-educated, straight, and brilliant). Such a poetry, then, in the process of becoming sanctioned as *the* kind of poetry, relied on static and pre-established social distinctions. It was not for those who agitated, failed, spilled treacle, paraded, or otherwise made a spectacle of themselves.

Stevens ends his letter on a final consolatory note:

> I hate to let you down and I have written this letter so that, if you care to do so, you can quote from it, or quote all of it. But I am definitely against an interview and photographs and that sort of thing. You say that your article is "essentially an idea". This is at least a contribution to your idea. If we could get rid of all the caricatures of the past: the caricatures not only of the poet and the actor but also the caricatures of the business man and the barkeeper

and of a lot of other people, we should only be seeing what we see every day, which is not so easy after all.   (*Letters*, 414–15)

The conclusion continues to be cast in the most seemingly fair-handed, commonsensical of terms: let us rid ourselves of the caricatures of the past; let us try to see what we see every day (not so easy after all). For Stevens, this is about dispensing with any distracting representations in favor of the supposedly unmediated work he is doing. While denigrating a wayward precarious past and promoting the eminent suitability of a smooth-functioning present, Stevens forcibly mystifies himself as the representative poet. Having challenged the frivolous mythologies surrounding the pseudo-poet, the reasonable, ordinary, everyday, just-like-everyone-else and ultimately "unmarked" Stevens enshrined, qua Barthes, both his own vocation and his common-sense habitat.

* * *

The position that T. S. Eliot took up at Lloyds in 1917 functioned in similar terms. This was a job that kept on giving. When in 1918 he unsuccessfully attempted to volunteer for the U.S. Army and Navy, his employers were only too happy to have him back, raising his salary to £500 per annum and entrusting him with the bank's role in administering Germany's post-Treaty of Versailles war reparations.[5] When Eliot's health began deteriorating in 1921, they were again very accommodating:

> I have seen the specialist (said to be the best in London) who made his tests and said that I must go away *at once* for three months . . . So I have been given leave by the bank for that period, very generously—they continue to pay my salary. I am going in about a week, as soon as I have taught enough knowledge of my work to a substitute.   (*Letters*, 586)

The pattern continues throughout the early 1920s: after Eliot returned from Paris to London, in early 1922 (with the Ezra-Pound-edited *The Waste Land* in hand), Lloyds took him back again, and there he stayed until Faber and Gwyer offered him the editorial role in 1925.

Banking offered to Eliot a political and economic manifestation of "form and restraint." There is a particularly revealing exchange between that influential acolyte of Eliot's I. A. Richards, and a colleague at the bank. Richards had taken an opportunity of visiting the poet at work, and struck up a conversation with one "Mr W.," who had heard rumors of

---

[5] For an account of Eliot's banking career, see Joseph McLaughlin's *Writing the Urban Jungle: Reading Empire in London from Doyle to Eliot* (2000), 172–7, or J. R. Winton's *Lloyds Bank 1918–1969* (1982), 38–40.

there being a poet on the premises. Mr W. asked Richards whether Eliot was in fact a "good poet":

> I.A.R. Well, in my judgment—not everyone would agree, of course, far from it, he is a good poet.

> MR W. You know, I myself am really very glad indeed to hear you say that. Many of my colleagues wouldn't agree at all. They think a Banker has no business whatever to be a poet. They don't think the two things can combine. But I believe that anything a man does, whatever his hobby may be, it's all the better if he is really keen on it and does it well. I think it helps him with his work. If you see our young friend, you might tell him that we think he's doing quite well at the Bank. In fact, if he goes on as he has been doing, I don't see why—in time, of course, in time—he mightn't even become a Branch Manager.   ("On TSE", 5)

"Most gratifying", was Eliot's remark upon hearing the report, a reply that, while seemingly imbued with gallows humor, was actually perfectly sincere. Mr W.'s comments tell us a good deal about the profitable dynamics of Eliot's segmented professional life. The irony here is that if you invert the terms under discussion, and swap banker for poet, and hobby for job, the logic governing this conversation remains remarkably intact (of course at Faber, he did indeed become a Branch Manager of sorts). Structuring the exchange is a series of strict, mutually constitutive binary distinctions; between avocations and vocations, between banking and poetry (with poetry for the less open-minded of Mr W.'s colleagues also coded in terms of effeminacy and queerness), and also between "good" and "bad" poetry. Put another way, there are polite "disagreements" here and there; not everyone thinks Eliot is a good poet; not everyone thinks that bankers ought to write poetry; but overwhelmingly, the exchange operates in terms of a mutual assurance and social tautology. The just rewards of doing well at the bank—of prospering in the professional realm—were to structure the parameters of his avocation, which literary history then forcibly reaffirmed as his "real" vocation. The thought of Eliot one day becoming a branch manager should not just be read in terms of Richards' sense of irony. To excel in the masculine, normative sphere was to neutralize any suspicions that might otherwise trouble his growing literary reputation as poet.

   The principal threat to Eliot's productive vocational arrangement during this period actually came from Ezra Pound, who tried to intervene in what he saw as a travesty both against literature and vocation. Regimentally intensifying the partitioned terms of the debate, he wrote:

> No use blinking the fact that it is a crime against literature to let him waste eight hours vitality per diem in that bank [...] the boy hasn't got my

constitution, certain sorts of prolific outpouring can't (thank god) be expected of him. It is a question of saving three or four books like his volume of poems from remaining in the limbo of not getting written.

(Gallup, *Collaborators*, 14)

The crime against literature: the contamination of vital promethean time and space that might be spent writing poetry. Pound went on to complain that Eliot was "not an affirming revolutionary"—"he don't, as I at moments, get mistaken for a labor-leader or bolshy bomb-thrower" (14)—if only this behavior could somehow be reclaimed in the name of radical aesthetic experiment. It turned out, though, that Eliot did not need or want rescuing, and that actually, the bank provided the congenial conditions in which his literary ambitions flourished. So much so, that when Pound tried to publish dissenting sentiments while attempting to raise alternative financial means for Eliot (the well-known "Bel Esprit" project, which constituted an early attempt at crowdfunding), Eliot responded:

> I hope this Circular has not gone out, will you please delete *Lloyds Bank*, to the mention of which I *strongly object*. If it is stated so positively that Lloyds Bank interfered with literature, Lloyds Bank would have a perfect right to infer that literature interfered with Lloyds Bank. *Please see my position.*
>
> (*Letters*, 712)[6]

Pound had not realized that Eliot had come to a workable and structurally integral arrangement at Lloyds. It all appeared "fairly simple" to Pound, who could not grasp what all the fuss was about. In a "Paris Letter" of 1922, he wrote with an air of mild surprise: "I am somewhat submerged in the number of minor objections and misunderstandings presented to me since the inception of the scheme. Market applied to the arts has NOT worked." And with a final parting shot at Eliot: "Nobody with any knowledge of poetry or the fine arts has ever I think, claimed that it did work."[7] Eliot's appeal that Pound see his "position" is a request for him to understand the implications of a stabilizing vocational dynamic: again, Eliot the bank clerk and Eliot the poet were mutually exclusive but mutually ensuring identities. This position afforded him a platform against which he could orientate and legitimate his "true" poetic nature.

---

[6] Lawrence Rainey describes the failure of "Bel Esprit" as "marking the end of efforts to transform patronage into a public activity [. . .] its demise also ended the possibility of reintroducing elements of reliability, predictability, or trust into the institutional logic of the avant-garde." (108). See Lawrence Rainey, *Institutions of Modernism: Literary Elites and Public Culture* (1998).

[7] See *The Dial*, Vol. LXXIII (1922).

Pound had unnecessarily disturbed the fabric of Eliot's vocational design, compromising the classical modernist injunction to impersonally distinguish between, and divert interest away from, poet to poetry. The subsequent publicity was, Eliot thought, unnecessarily revealing; it directed public (and potentially his employer's) attention towards the implications (material and ideological) of his stable and therefore productive arrangement. The most embarrassing aspect of the Bel-Esprit affair culminated in the whole story being leaked to *The Liverpool Post*, who falsely claimed that Eliot had taken the considerable sum of money raised by Pound's project and also kept his job. Eliot immediately asked for a retraction from the newspaper (and got it), though by this time it was too late, and the story had circulated across the Atlantic, eventually appearing in the comment pages of *The New York Tribune*. Though Eliot was not explicitly named, there was little doubt about who Pound's now effeminate "Coddled Author" referred to:

> The Coddled Author: Is he likely to repay coddling? Mr. Ezra Pound, an amiable oracle, is of the opinion that he is. At all events he sketches in a Paris letter to *The Dial* a delectable scheme for keeping the wolf from the door of the literary artist, where its howls disturb the serenity of creative composition. It appears that once upon a time "there was a man in a small town who had Pisanello, Pier Francesco and Mino da Fiesole working for him at one time or another." These three, as is well known, worked to good purpose. Ergo, thinks Mr. Pound, there must have been something helpful about the man who hired them, so he would revive the functions of the wise patron.
>
> "The modus of Bel Esprit," he tells us, "is a simple annual subscription of $50 yearly; the society has no running expenses (or at least none chargeable to members) and the aim is to free, one at a time, as many writers and artists as possible; this by giving them the deficit difference between a reasonable cost of living and the amount they can make by the sale of their best work and nothing but their best work under current conditions. This means that they are not expected to interrupt serious work by doing the vendible trivial, and that they will not be penalized (on the pocket) for destroying their inferior stuff."
>
> Could anything be lovelier for the beaux espritt [sic]? First they catch their Pisanello or their Chatterton, which, of course, ought not to be difficult in an era bursting with them. And then they treat the case according to its requirements. We would give a wilderness of monkeys to see them doing it, helping to decide between the best and the inferior stuff, pigeonholing "the vendible trivial" (for the great man's heirs to sell at a profit the moment the breath is out of his body) and altogether putting the artistic conscience on a solvent basis. "This appears fairly simple to me," says Mr. Pound, of his big-hearted scheme. But we wonder how many authors there are left in the world who really want to be "freed" by any committee of beaux espritt? Authors, that is, who would be worth freeing.

"Hardship is a good incentive", says Mr. Pound, "until it kills". A good axiom, no doubt, and in the abstract there is everything to be said for the support of your true artist. The world owes him a living. But your true artist will persist in wanting to work for coddling makes for flabbiness? It lies in the soul of the poet, the artist, and never yet was quenched by fear of butcher's bills. Hardship is indeed an incentive that sometimes kills, but even while it slays it consecrates. Its discipline has, if anything, put the victim on his mettle. How much real spiritual sustenance there is in coddling you may learn by plugging through the desolating stuff which so often masquerades as "success." To coddle an author is to reduce him to the level of a Pekingese. It is on his just dues that he thrives, the reward is of the sweat of his brow, not on a subsidy. Ancient, platitudinous philosophy this, but is one not sometimes driven to platitudes by the paradoxes of the beaux esprit of this world? Piranello and Pier Francesco and Mino were not "kept." They did a job of work and got paid for it. If the pay hadn't been forthcoming they would have raised a nice, rumply Renaissance row. The kind of man who would let the bill collector get between him and the making of a masterpiece would doubtless have some use for a parcel of beaux espritt. But a born author, a born artist, would see them hanged first. (*New York Tribune*, December 3, 1922)

In casting Eliot as a Pekingese, the emperor's effeminate lap dog, this editorial obviously responds to, and plays on, Pound's charmingly decadent sense of poetry's inflated self-image. But perhaps most noteworthy to this particular correspondent is the herculean social condescension that characterizes all work other than the production of great art as "the vendible trivial" of a hack writer. Turning over the implications of the insult, this self-consciously vendible editorial mounts a rather eloquent challenge to Pound's decadent conception of pure artistic "freedom." Artists and their work grow "flabby" if they are not made to do a bit of work—pitching a masculinized Progressive-era American work ethic against Pound's decadent and sexually suspect Imperial Chinese court. In proposing the Bel Esprit project as a viable alternative for Eliot, Pound had not appreciated the degree to which an unassuming and unspoken proximity to the "vendible trivial" served to legitimate the cultural claims of modernism much more effectively than openly oppositional, sexually suspect polemic. Pound's stance left him exposed to ridicule and suspicion—the quiet, dignified negotiations of Eliot by contrast increasingly ensured a reverence among an expanding band of acolytes. To be known among friends as a mere bank-clerk was useful in all sorts of ways, but to have the mechanics of this productive material arrangement probed, exposed, and railed against threatened to undermine one of classical modernism's lasting interventions: the figure of the tragic poet who paradoxically intensifies his claim to possess an inner poetic calling by maintaining close contact with the supposedly threatening realm of quotidian work.

To be fair to Pound, he was not the only one to explicitly voice their concern for Eliot the banker. Virginia Woolf also attempted to "rescue" him with a similar initiative: a Bloomsbury Group "Eliot Fellowship Fund" worth £500 a year. And Eliot again refused this offer. Rachel Foss, the curator of the 2009 exhibition *In a Bloomsbury Square: T. S. Eliot the Publisher* claims that "this idea that Eliot should be freed from the drudgery of work misses the point that he was actually very interested in the minutiae of everyday life—he was a commentator on the quotidian, and really thrived on the routine of office life at Lloyd's."[8] More than this, his poetic reputation also thrived on the supposedly oppressive proximity of this quotidian world, and particularly the way his friends and acolytes perceived this contact. Aldous Huxley struck exactly the right note when he visited Eliot in Lombard Street, describing himself as descending into some kind of Dantean hell: "he was the most bank-clerky of all bank clerks." Quite possibly alluding directly to the precarious workers who feature at the beginning of *Moby-Dick* (he had just read the novel), Huxley continued: "[Eliot] was not on the ground floor nor even on the floor under that, but in a sub-sub-basement sitting at a desk which was in a row of desks with other bank clerks" (qt. Tate, 59).[9] With each articulation of ordinariness and inconspicuousness, he reinforces a clean split between reified realms, papering over the critique of poetic sovereignty that Melville had unfolded some seventy years earlier. Just as Eliot consolidated his expanding coterie reputation as one of the leading poets of the era, it should come as no surprise that he was simultaneously capable of being the most "bank-clerky of all bank clerks": a "sub sub." The more bank-clerky Eliot appeared, the more Christ-like and self-sacrificing he became; condemned to patrol the irredeemable sphere of quotidian labor as an impersonal, vocationally sacrosanct poet. The day job of the poet was now deified as the great crime against literature—the (rather well paid) descent into hell of Saint Eliot.

By the time Eliot finally left his position at Lloyds and took on the editorial role at Faber and Gwyer, the bank had fundamentally aided in securing the mythic terms of his reputation. It also simultaneously spoke directly to, and bolstered the various priorities of, his critical persona. Here, for example, are three well-known sentences from "Tradition and

---

[8] Quoted in Alison Flood, "T.S. Eliot rejected Bloomsbury group's 'cursed fund' to work in bank," *The Guardian*, September 2, 2009.

[9] Aldous Huxley first mentions *Moby-Dick* in a letter to Robert Nichols in 1923. See *Letters of Aldous Huxley*, ed. Grover Smith (1969), 215.

the Individual Talent" (1921), in which he suggests, famously, that "diverting interest" from the poet to the poetry is a "laudable aim":

> for it would conduce to a juster estimation of actual poetry, good and bad. There are many people who appreciate the expression of sincere emotion in verse, and there is a smaller number of people who can appreciate technical excellence. But very few know when there is expression of *significant* emotion, emotion which has its life in the poem and not in the history of the poet. The emotion of art is impersonal. And the poet cannot reach this impersonality without surrendering himself wholly to the work to be done. (25)

Terry Eagleton has identified a radical potential in Eliot's affirmation of the impersonality of poetry in its assault on "the whole ideology of middle-class liberalism, the official ruling ideology of industrial capitalist society. Liberalism, Romanticism, Protestantism, economic individualism: all of these are the perverted dogmas of those expelled from the happy garden of the organic society, with nothing to fall back on but their own paltry individual resources" (*Introduction*, 34). A typically generous reading, but missing from this account of Eliot's maneuvering is the necessary privilege that enables impersonality with its concomitant insistence that we turn a blind eye to the integral conditions of production and erase all forms of contingency and difference. This is much the same blind eye that Wimsatt and Beardsley ask us to turn in this influential and intimately related statement on the "New Criticism":

> Judging a poem is like judging a pudding or a machine. One demands that it work. It is only because an artifact works that we infer the intention of an artificer. "A poem should not mean but be." A poem can *be* only through its *meaning*—since its medium is words—yet it *is*, simply *is*, in the sense that we have no excuse for inquiring what part is intended or meant. Poetry is a feat of style by which a complex of meaning is handled all at once. Poetry succeeds because all or most of what is said or implied is relevant; what is irrelevant has been excluded, like lumps from pudding and "bugs" from machinery. (469)

Most startling about the "intentional fallacy" was the confidence with which it occluded the conditions of poetic production. In two similes (poems like machines and puddings), Wimsatt and Beardsley allude to the main constituencies that tend to fall victim to all such ontological affirmations of the immaculate product: those expendable representatives of difference who work in kitchens and factories. "One demands that it work," rather than know who made it. The result was a further mystification of the now unmarked context that defined the social and economic stability of the speaking subject. Furthermore, impersonality enshrined the existential and vocational coherence of the "poet" now being turned away from; in other words, they insisted that interest be diverted from a labor that was now self-evident and without need of paraphrase. This in turn paved the way for the subsequent wholesale rejection of a politically troubling "personal"; or precisely those materials that my archives of distraction seek to fold back into the reconsideration of a thoroughly reified poetic labor.

As my various readings have thus far sought to demonstrate, we are still living with, and thinking through, the impersonal doctrine that was one of classical modernism's most influential cultural productions. In some ways, however, it is misleading in this context to think of the "classical" and "romantic" in strictly oppositional terms. The achievement of the classical modernists was to secure and thereby extend what was essentially a Romantic conception of the poet as detached from the contingencies presented by a "manifold and duplex life". Defending and extending the sense of calling that underpinned Emersonian Romanticism, classical modernism had an integral role in shutting down—and rendering illegible—the continuities and interdependencies that proliferate in the work of Whitman and Melville. Jacques Rancière might describe the achievement of Eliot and Stevens (along with their subsequent followers) as instantiating a specific "distribution of the sensible"—marking the horizon of intelligibility in a particular environment and determining those elements within a political and social field we either privilege or denigrate, foreground or background (*Politics*, 9). The smooth functioning of this distribution is fundamental to the reproduction and maintenance of vocational "precorporation," whereby poets immediately become subject to the "pre-emptive formatting and shaping of desires, aspirations and hopes by capitalist culture" (Fisher, 9). This default precorporation forecloses on our ability to apprehend the subversions of those who construed contingent labor as an opportunity to imagine beyond and test the limits of exceptional vocational fulfillment. In turning now to Crane, I want to provide a different account of this supposedly late Romantic poet's career. Romanticism in this instance, however, was not actually about securing the vocational integrity of the poet; but rather allowing the implied coherence of this moniker to be warped into more capacious form by the very element Crane's contemporaries were so anxious to contain: the day job.

6

Making Ends Meet

Hart Crane's Job

Hart Crane did in fact comprehend the substantial potential benefits of maintaining a strict classical career partition: at various stages throughout his short adult life, "copywriter/poet" was an identity he very earnestly experimented with. Ultimately though, he rejected this strictly bifurcated arrangement—at once unable and unwilling to maintain this kind of bourgeois discipline, but also intuiting the creative confines and political compromises that such an existence entailed. Many of Crane's poems consequently crystallize an impasse whereby the necessary material conditions are never securely enough in place to realize the sought-after impersonal ideal; that is, as he once wrote in his short essay "General Aims and Theories": "to establish the [the poem] as free from [his] own personality" (*Complete*, 161). Crane's poetry instead displays an acute responsiveness to the shifting contexts of its own continually compromised production, straying in some politically provocative directions that often end up revising, and offering an alternative to, the cultural project of his classical modernist peers.

Explicitly framing Crane's characteristic volatility and perceived imbalance in terms of a malfunctioning impersonality, Alan Trachtenberg has suggested that "in a manner quite different" from his contemporaries, "Hart Crane demands to be taken personally, in the double sense of a speaker uttering poems from the immediacy of experience and a reader receiving a new personal experience by that very act" ("Legend," 2). Crane, he continues, is "not quite at ease" in the company of his peers, perhaps too "personal" and gauche in his thrusting of emotion before the reader. Several critics have convincingly ascribed this critical apprehensiveness to the sometimes latent, sometimes overt homophobia that has tended to characterize the reception of his work.[1] By writing poetry, Crane was, in his own eloquent estimation, interested in "the so-called illogical

---

[1] See discussions of various early homophobic receptions of Crane in Langdon Hammer's *Janus-Faced Modernism*, particularly in relation to early reviews by Allan Tate and Yvor Winters (51).

impingements of the connotations of words on the consciousness (and their combinations and interplay in metaphor on this basis)" (*Selected Letters*, 278). This famous defense against *Poetry* editor Harriet Monroe's charge of willful obscurity (appropriately enough, in reference to his homage "At Melville's Tomb") celebrates the power of poetry to trouble conscious interpretations of language. When aligned with his notorious "roaring boy" reputation, contemporaries such as Allan Tate and Yvor Winters understood Crane's poetics as an unwanted encroachment—an example of ungainly intimacy and excess that often resembled the "real" thing (in that it displayed many of the challenging characteristics of an avant-garde style), but that actually threatened to undermine the impersonal conception of the poem as self-contained object for critical appreciation.

If the New Critics were disturbed by the troublingly personal nature of Crane's writing, this is precisely what has made him such a significant figure in the subsequent emergence of queer theory. Before *No Future: Queer Theory and the Death Drive* (2004), Lee Edelman wrote *Transmemberment of Song: Hart Crane's Anatomies of Rhetoric and Desire* (1987), which detailed Crane's exploration of the ways in which language might begin articulating new subversive thresholds of intimacy.[2] And, anticipating and perhaps even forming the precursor to Edelman's "no future" thesis, Thomas E. Yingling subsequently investigated the problematic assumptions that informed early assessments of Crane's work, especially the tendency to cast his alternative epic of America, *The Bridge*, as a "failure." Such assessments, Yingling argued, belied a widespread critical attitude that tacitly aligned the exceptionalist unfolding of U.S. nationhood with a rigidly heterosexual, reproductive future (11).[3] In what follows, I want to extend what I see as the subversive non-capitalist potential of Yingling's insight, which broadly conceives of Crane's contribution as an implicit challenge to normative futurity—and, by extension—any future governed by the tenets of vocational modernity. Refusing to cast Crane as a poet who tragically fell short of his innate potential, I suggest that Crane's particular mode of poetic production works to disturb vocational thinking, reconceiving in the process the kind of work that poetry might become (as well as the kind of futurity it might imply).

It is not a coincidence that the suspicion towards Crane's poetry has often tended to manifest as an accusation concerning the failure of his work ethic and inability to transcend his unseemly bodily appetites. In the following *New York Times* review from 2007 of the Library of America's

---

[2] See also Michael Snediker's essay on Crane's use of the smile and its relation to 1920s cruising strategies: "Hart Crane's Smile", *Modernism/Modernity* 12.4 (2005): 629–58.

[3] For a recent discussion of Crane's relationship to the history of queer theory see Niall Monroe, *Hart Crane's Queer Modernist Aesthetic* (2015), 1–16.

Complete Poems and Selected Letters, notice, for example, the way in which
the critic aligns a suspect sexuality with a compromised artistry:

> Crane tried on various identities as a young man and failed at most of them.
> He was frank about his homosexuality only with close friends—his sexual
> appetites were voracious and involved far too many sailors. (The definitive
> work on the United States Navy's contributions to cruising has yet to written.)
> Crane dreamed of being a poet much more often than he sat at his desk and
> wrote poems; and he was forever complaining in letters that he had no time to
> write, though he found plenty of time to drink. He conceived his major poem,
> "The Bridge," as early as 1923 but made only desultory progress towards it.
> (Remaining drunk all through Prohibition proved surprisingly easy.) It was
> hard work, avoiding real work; but Crane became an expert at writing cadging
> letters to his parents and playing one against the other.[4]

The title of this piece—"Hart Crane's Bridge to Nowhere"—is a prime
example of what Lee Edelman would see as an anti-gay indictment of "no
future," very obviously opposed to the exemplary and productive destiny
that characterizes the legitimate "real work" of his classical hetero-modernist
peers. Yet, by framing his homophobic reaction in terms of a faulty work
ethic, the reviewer helpfully identifies another key facet of Crane's poetry—
namely its capacity to threaten the "real" (read "impersonal") work of poetry
that, even as late as 2007, obstinately seems to stand in as the ideal. Of
course, the bridge to "Somewhere" is the straight white line of the
unmarked vocational future, leading inexorably toward the consummation
of that valedictory designation "poet" (bestowed with so much assurance
upon Eliot and Stevens). If it hadn't been for the excessive cocktail of sailors,
moonshine, and personal excess (so the story goes), Crane might have got
somewhere, and become "someone." Instead, and serving as a cautionary
tale to us all, he allowed those too personal and extraneous elements to
distract him from the real, sacrosanct work of poetry.

It is, however, possible to put an alternative spin on such an account.
Indeed it was because rather than in spite of these various distractions that
Crane managed to reimagine the limiting vocational parameters of his
contemporaries and offer something radically different. Yes, the sailors,
drink, and tantrums all played their disruptive part, but the process of
undermining the vocational future also operated at a more sober level. In a

----

[4] William Logan's "Hart Crane's Bridge to Nowhere: 'Review of Hart Crane: Complete
Poems and Selected Letters,'" *New York Times*, January 28, 2007. Logan's title is either
explicitly alluding to Yvor Winters' early estimation of Crane, or he is simply restating
Winters' accusation of failure: in the review essay, "The Progress of Hart Crane" (1930),
Winters wrote that Crane's epic "headed precisely for nowhere, in spite of all the shouting"
[in *Hart Crane: A Collection of Critical Essays* (1982)]. See also Edward Brunner's discussion
in *Splendid Failure: Hart Crane and the Making of the Bridge* (1985).

curious reversal, it was actually the unwieldy proximity of Crane's contingent labor—particularly the work of copywriting—that became the subversive means through which he prevented his own poetic labor from conforming to the impersonal preconceptions of his contemporaries. In this context, Crane's poetry and central motifs (the vortex and suspension bridge) formalize the momentary interruption of separating modernist realms. Refusing any capitalist future that might be dependent on extracting the poet as a detached vocational exemplar, he established his unwieldy quotidian working environment as a primary site of counter-vocational imagining.

* * *

In 1919, *The Little Review* editors Margaret Anderson and Jane Heap suggested that an eighteen-year-old Hart Crane might try and sell advertising space for their magazine. The job was on a commission-only basis but Crane quickly accepted, reasoning that any association with the publishers of Wyndham Lewis, T.S. Eliot, James Joyce, and Ezra Pound constituted an excellent opportunity to further his own literary ambitions. He'd been hanging around the Manhattan office for a while now looking for opportunities to get involved, and both Heap and Anderson grew increasingly fond of him, recognizing his potential when they accepted an early poem "Shadow" in December 1917:

Dear Hart Crane, poet!!
        I'm using 'Shadow' in the December issue, now going to press. It's the best you've sent yet: I'll tell you details of just why when you come. It's quite lovely. Hurrah for you!! MCA (qt. Unterecker, 89).

This was a period of cultural apprenticeship for Crane, with Anderson taking it upon herself to tutor the aspiring "poet!!" in the current literary trends. She would show him "just why" she had liked "Shadow" and indicate what he had got right this time (prior rejections had been numerous). Crane sent his poems in, not only for the promise of publication, but also critical assessment, shaping his ideas and his poetry according to the magazine's influential aesthetic strictures. He soon caught something of its editors' polemical tone; in a letter defending Joyce against the charge of "decadence," he wrote: "Sterility is the only 'decadence' I recognise. An abortion in art takes the same place as it does in society,—it deserves no recognition whatever,—it is simply outside. A piece of work is art, or it isn't: there is no neutral judgement" ("Joyce and Ethics," 65).[5]

---

[5] Richard Poirier refers to this particular brand of repartee as representative of the modernist "snob's game." See *The Renewal of Literature: Emersonian Reflections* (1987), 98. See also Catherine Turner's discussion of the ways in Anderson and Heap courted

Anderson and Heap's editorial policy, which seized upon every opportunity to respond to attacks from mainstream critics, spurred on Crane's disputatious bravado. In the same issue as Crane's "Shadow," Anderson printed the full verdict of a New York judge who had recently ruled against them in an indecency case for publishing Wyndham Lewis's short story "Cantleman's Spring Mate." Anderson's article, entitled "Judicial Opinion (Our Suppressed October Issue)," indignantly stated that "it would be ridiculous for me to conceal my complete disagreement with Judge Hand and the Post office."[6] Both Heap and Anderson understood the value of this sort of publicity, and such attacks presented an opportunity to affirm their project as vital and misunderstood (to engage in debate with this old-guard judge would be beneath them). Complaints and accusations were printed in the magazine's "Reader Critic" section and then dispatched with pithy, dismissive remarks, usually by Jane Heap. In the May/June edition of 1920, one Helen Bishop Dennis of Boston (potentially an alias of Heap's) wrote in, and claimed that

> The only cure for the nausea [Joyce] causes is the thought that "only a few read him." I think *The Little Review* has become a disgustingly artificial and affected publication [...] You are like a crowd of precocious, "smarty cat", over-wise children, showing off. I know of no one who has anything for you now but pity, mingled with contempt and disappointment.[7]

The editors immediately seized upon these opportunities—their droll and economical rejoinder to this particular letter went: "Yes, I think you must be right. I once knew a woman so modest that she didn't wear underwear: she couldn't stand its being seen in the wash" (74). Crane quickly learnt how to take part in this kind of repartee; in "Joyce and Ethics," the eighteen-year-old Crane dispatches Oscar Wilde with a single sentence: "after his bundle of paradoxes has been sorted and conned,—very little evidence of intellect remains" (65). Swinburne receives similar treatment and is judged as not "possessing anything beyond his 'art ears'" (65). Crane recognized and effectively mimicked the polemical tone of *The Little Review*, fashioning a critical and aesthetic persona that wholeheartedly embraced the role of precocious "smarty cat."

---

criticism as a badge of honor: "they seemed particularly pleased by the negative responses of the philistines in the literary sections of the *New York Times* and the *New York Herald*." See *Marketing Modernism Between the Two World Wars* (2003), 176.

[6] Margaret Anderson, "Judicial Opinion (Our Suppressed October Issue)," *The Little Review* 4.8 (December 1917): 46–9 (48).

[7] Helen Bishop Dennis, "The Reader Critic: The Modest Woman," *The Little Review* 7.1 (May/June 1920): 73–4 (74).

If Crane's early involvement with *The Little Review* aided in the formation of an increasingly strident aesthetic outlook, it certainly didn't earn him any money. His canvassing for the magazine gleaned a grand total of thirteen ads—one publicizing a performance by his dancer friend Stanislaw Portapovitch, and a further twelve he somehow managed to convince his father to buy. Between May 1919 and December 1920, twelve full-page advertisements for his father's brand—"Crane's Mary Garden Chocolates"—appeared in all but one issue of the magazine. This means that subscribers of *The Little Review* came across the Crane family name four times in connection with the arts (two poems and two short comment pieces) and twenty-four times in connection with confectionery ("Crane" appeared twice in each ad). The ad shows a profile of the internationally renowned opera star Mary Garden, with the Crane company insignia above her head, staring downwards as if at a box of Crane's chocolates (Fig. 6.1). The presentation bow fastening the box is positioned suggestively close to Garden's cleavage, (not particularly subtly) aligning the process of opening the chocolates with the disrobing of Garden herself. Beneath this, there is a signed endorsement: "'Your chocolates really are the finest I have ever tasted anywhere in the world' [signed] Mary Garden." This was in fact not her first appearance in *The Little Review*. Never the victim of the editors' acerbic critiques, her singing had been rapturously celebrated by both Anderson and Heap throughout 1918: "there is an over-beauty which she creates out of herself like the beauty created out of a poem or a picture or a piece of sculpture by itself if it possesses the eternal quality of Art."[8] Heap even went so far as to acclaim "the timbre of her great existence" (65).

Lawrence Rainey has suggested that little magazines of the period offered neither unequivocal resistance nor capitulation to the pressures of consumerism. Instead, *The Little Review* and *Poetry* occupied a position that was "temporarily exempted from the exigencies of immediate consumption prevalent within the larger cultural economy," relying on a "different economic circuit of patronage, collecting, speculation, and investment." This exemption often generated "momentary equivocation"; quietly conflicted (and often potentially productive) confluences of complicity that help us to reconfigure an understanding of the extra-literary forces at play in artistic inception (3). Here, then, is one such moment of potential equivocation: in contrast to the timbre of Mary Garden's "great existence" was her proclivity for lending her name to all manner of consumer

---

[8] See Jane Heap, "A Letter," 64, and also Margaret Anderson, "The Chicago Grand Opera Invades New York," *The Little Review* 4.10 (February 1918): 61–3.

Fig. 6.1. "Crane's Mary Garden Chocolates" advertisement, *The Little Review* 6.1 (May 1919): 2. Courtesy The Modernist Journals Project.

products, from cosmetics to confectionery to musical instruments.[9] You might think, given their absolutist praise, that this would have at least tested the editors' opinion of her as a pure representative of eternal "Art," perhaps qualifying the extremities of their enthusiasm. Not so; Heap and Anderson were comfortable with these endorsements (Garden's successful poster-girl career seems not to have even registered). For them, her talent occupied a qualitatively separate sphere, with their conviction in art's self-evident difference allaying any "anxiety of contamination" that might otherwise have emerged.[10]

It is this categorical intransigence that consequently exposed the magazine to what now seem like rather glaring ideological cross-currents. In a delicious irony, the Crane chocolate ads were placed in such a prominent position that they frequently appeared in the "front advertisements" section of the magazine, between the title page and the first contribution. So Pound's iconic front-page slogan, "Making No Compromise with the Public Taste," was followed just two pages later by Mary Garden's "Your chocolates are really the finest I have ever tasted anywhere in the world."

It is perhaps a little too easy to poke fun at this unfortunate arrangement (though especially tempting when Ezra Pound is the butt of the joke). What I think needs probing here is why such moments can be apprehended by us, and yet missed by the combined editorial intelligence of Anderson and Heap? The answer has something to do with the potential of this moment's generative illegibility. In describing this arrangement as "ironic," I incongruously filter these latent modernist tensions through a distinctively postmodern lens, when many of the tensions surrounding the opposition between a modernist "high" and "low" have been fully articulated and retrospectively deconstructed. In fact my anachronistic apprehension of irony forecloses on a potential moment of alternative imagining; if they can't see the potential contradiction of the chocolate ad, then we can't see the subversive potential of them not seeing it. To carefully read these unmediated gaps in the modernist awareness is to realize that the consolidating "great divide," the distribution of what is sensible in relation to aesthetic credo and consumer marketplace, was still in a state of ambiguous adolescence. The familiar modernist stance of an assumed aesthetic remove was not yet fully worked out; the "impersonality" gaining cultural ground under the terms of classical modernism was

---

[9] In 1922, *The Little Review* included another Mary Garden ad; this time, her full-page portrait touted the "Steinert Piano." It was "complete perfection in every detail that a piano should be—it was a revelation to me [signed Mary Garden]." "Back Advertisements," *The Little Review* 9.1 (Autumn 1922): 63.

[10] That now familiar term put forward by Andreas Huyssen in *After the Great Divide: Modernism, Mass Culture, Postmodernism* (1986), vii.

still subject to potential modulation and redirection. At this moment, an inability to apprehend the potential infiltrations of the marketplace also constituted an obverse power to see and imagine alternative continuities between art and that market, and specifically the ways in which the sanctified work of the poet might be pulled in other, more elliptical directions.

Crane took this generative historical credulousness with him into the rest of his working life—in this instance, approaching *The Little Review*'s offer of ad work with a fervor usually associated with his attitudes towards poetry. On April 2, 1919, he explained to his mother (parroting the decidedly professional tone of the era) that he would develop his own "department systematically."[11] What the publication had "lacked from its inception" was "someone with business initiative ability to develop the advertising and subscription departments of the magazine" (126). Two weeks later, Crane announced that he had employed a "subordinate": "a man turned up at *The Little Review* office last Wednesday [...] and having had several years' experience, he is proving a wonder." The pair expected to haul in several year-long contracts worth "no less than $480 each": "We are after all the great establishments on Fifth Ave., and I am learning a few things in going about."[12] Crane believed, entirely fancifully, that if he could "fill up the allowable space" of thirty-two pages then he could get $4,000 per year on commissions.[13] The figure of $480 was most likely based on the amount he charged his father for the year-long, twelve ad contract—a considerable sum to pay for a regular readership of just 1,200 or so. When Clarence Crane found out about this, he was outraged. What he had viewed as a deal between a businessman father and his ad-man son had turned into a rather innovative piece of literary patronage.

This episode reveals a pattern that would replay itself throughout Crane's short life, namely his distracted struggle to apprehend a way in which art and moneymaking might in some way coalesce, might arrange themselves in such a way as to reveal another viable career path. The Mary Garden chocolate episode had provoked a host of responses in Crane; and these can be observed quietly stirring in a poem accepted in the September 1920 issue of the *The Little Review*. "Garden Abstract," which coincidentally appeared in the same issue as the last ad for his father's confectionery, demonstrates Crane's early unspoken commitment to testing the shifting proximities between apparently separated spheres. A reader of this issue

---

[11] Hart Crane to Grace Hart Crane, April 2, 1919, *Letters of Hart Crane and His Family*, ed. by Thomas S.W. Lewis (1974), 126. Hereafter *LHCF*.
[12] Hart Crane to Grace Hart Crane, April 20, 1919, *LHCF*, 132.
[13] Hart Crane to Grace Hart Crane, May 3, 1919, *LHCF*, 134.

was first presented with Crane's characteristically absolutist review of the Cleveland photographer H. W. Minns: these photographs conjured the point at which "craftsman merges into the artist,—where the creative element becomes distinct."[14] A few pages later, Margaret Anderson contributed another celebration of Mary Garden: "It took [critics] years to acclaim [her] [...] they never recognize essential quality."[15] Printed alongside these two assertions of "distinct" and "essential" aesthetics (in an edition that concludes with the twelfth and final advertisement for Mary Garden chocolates) is Hart Crane's "Garden Abstract":

> Garden Abstract
>
> The apple on its bough is her desire,—
> Shining suspension, mimic of the sun.
> The bough has caught her breath up, and her voice,
> Dumbly articulate in the slant and rise
> Of branch on branch above her, blurs her eyes.
> She is prisoner of the tree and its green fingers.
>
> And so she comes to dream herself the tree,
> The wind possessing her, weaving her young veins,
> Holding her to the sky and its quick blue,
> Drowning the fever of her hands in sunlight.
> She has no memory, nor fear, nor hope
> Beyond the grass and shadows at her feet.[16]

Mary Garden, the poem's sublimated namesake here, haunts the constitution of an Eve/Daphne amalgam. This ethereal figure, held in a pensile state, is not quite the tree and not quite herself—not fully representative of the temptation of Eve or the transformation of Daphne. This partial merger finds form in the momentarily confusing syntax; you initially assume that it is her dumb articulations that are doing the slanting, potentially transcendent rising. However, with the "Of" that begins the following line, the referent is clarified, and we realize that it is actually the branches above her that "slant and rise." The poem continually threatens to dissolve this figure as though some desirous Apollonian force were provoking her into arboreal metamorphosis: she begins to "dream herself the tree"; the wind possesses her; and the sun drowns the fevered temptation of her hands. Quietly modulating the tone of this "Garden Abstract" is the language of spectacle, theatre, and desire. The phallic "Bough" in the first line also puns on the verb to bow; and there is also the

---

[14] Hart Crane, "Discussion: A Note on Minns", *The Little Review* 7.3 (Fall 1920): 60.
[15] Margaret Anderson, "Marguerite D'Alvarez", *The Little Review* 7.3 (Fall 1920): 74.
[16] Hart Crane, "Garden Abstract," *The Little Review* 7.3 (Fall 1920): 78.

hint of a stifled operatic voice rising to crescendo ("caught her breath up, and her voice | Dumbly"). In desiring the apple, this disorientatingly composite "She" gets more than she bargained for, becoming increasingly bound to the object of her desire. The poem ends up strung out somewhere between Eve's temptation (with its attendant implications of a transcendent judgemental Father inscribing the fundamental limitations of embodiment), Apollo's frustrated lust, and a host of other consumerist implications in "the fever of her hands." In these allusory and illusory cross-currents, abstracting this particular "Garden" into a higher realm proves impossible. Instead, the poem's conclusion gestures away from any linear or aspirational narrative, as the "She" is left with "no memory" (past) or "hope" (future) beyond the murky earth below her. Crane's poem registers an impasse; and rather than entertain the possibility of any easy escape to a higher plane, it can only remain in and experiment with the poetic opportunities presented by its own entangled complicity.[17]

The poem represents an ongoing and productive tension in Crane's life; namely his inability to extricate his writing from the exigencies of his own political and economic circumstance. He is an important modernist poet exactly because he perpetually negotiated and even courted financial instability (providing an insight into the importance of the necessary privileges and personal consistencies that Eliot and Stevens managed so carefully). The implications of having to make a living as an advertising underling in Manhattan provoked Crane into a series of uneasy compromises. He persistently wrestled at the fraught intersection of avant-garde aesthetics and the pressure of having to make a living—never foreclosing on the possibility that the two were in some way resolvable. Always operating, in Raymond Williams' sense, within the fluctuating bounds of particular material limits and pressures ("Base", 4), he unfolded a poetics of brinkmanship that at once exposed the occluded privileged trappings of his contemporaries, and began gesturing to what else a poet might work towards.

---

[17] In contrast to the predominantly "lopsided picture we have of [Crane] as a religious visionary or mystic," Michael Trask has emphasized the intensely materialist strain that runs through *The Bridge*. This has been frequently passed over by critics because, he suggests, "Crane imagined material relations, particularly those involving manual labor, as oddly immaterial—that is, as fragile, ephemeral, and liable to implosion or breaking apart" (10). Trask goes on to posit a nexus between the increasing transience of the early twentieth-century labor market and Crane's own attractions to "cruising." His mythopoetic realm, so frequently taken at face value by critics, was in fact an "alibi" for the "alternative" dynamic realm he explores. See "Hart Crane's Epic of Anonymity" in Michael Trask, *Cruising Modernism: Class and Sexuality in American Literature and Social Thought* (2003), 108–41.

Crane managed to secure a succession of advertising jobs during the early 1920s, and each one proved impossible to hold on to. With every attempt, he first displayed enthusiasm, grateful that he had an income. In September 1921, he even enrolled in an advertising course—a series of evening classes that comprised his only formal higher education. The Advertising Club in Cleveland introduced topics such as "The Consumer," "The Tools of Advertising," and "The Common Carriers of Advertising" (Fisher, *Life*, 133). Crane enthused to Gorham Munson: "I am taking a course in advertising two nights of every week until next May which is very good and ought to help me to get started...I am now pretty sure of making advertising my real route to bread and butter, and have a strong notion that as a copy writer I will eventually make a 'whiz'" (*Selected Letters*, 65). Early the following year, Crane started work at Corday and Gross for $25 a week, a position he managed to keep for six months. He wrote to Sherwood Anderson—a little proudly—"Now I am working as a copywriter for the Corday and Gross Co., here which you may have heard of."[18] Crane responded positively to the new sense of independence that the work provided. He once explained to his mother that "the time spent in idleness when out of a job was always a worse strain than the hardest kind of labor."[19] Unemployment was not only about financial insecurity for Crane, it was also bound up with self-worth; he was acutely sensitive to the stresses and indignities of not having a job. Despite his "roaring boy" image, he found it difficult to rid himself of the guilt and self-reproach that often accompanies a deeply ingrained work ethic, or, again, what Max Weber described as the "iron cage": "the idea of duty in one's calling [that] prowls about in our lives like the ghost of dead religious beliefs" (12). His friend Slater Brown remembered the first time he met Crane in 1923: "[he] showed me, somewhat to my surprise, a large scrapbook in which he had pasted all the material an advertising agency or agencies in Cleveland had used of his own work. He seemed very proud of it though his enthusiasm may also have been caused by some misled hope that I could get him a job."[20] We are not so well acquainted with this side of Crane; of how his efforts to find employment and secure an income for himself were often as sustained and sincere as any effort he made to write poetry.

Once established in a particular job, though, he soon became frustrated that he was not dedicating enough time to his writing. This usually led

---

[18] Hart Crane to Sherwood Anderson, January 10, 1922, *Selected Letters*, 263.
[19] Hart Crane to Grace Hart Crane, September 8, 1923, Brom Weber Papers, Hart Crane Collection, Beinecke Library, Yale University, New Haven. Hereafter "Weber Papers."
[20] Slater Brown to John Baker, December 9, 1962, Baker Papers, Hart Crane Collection, Beinecke Library, Yale University, New Haven. Hereafter "Baker Papers."

him either to resign suddenly or force his employer to sack him. Stanley Patno, Crane's manager at the advertising firm NASP wrote that he "felt obliged to release him because his output was small and uneven." "Whilst working for me," he continued, "Hart showed not the slightest bit of creativity as far as ideas and headlines were concerned."[21] During his work on a campaign for The Pittsburgh Water Heater in December 1922, Crane complained to Bill Wright that he was

> growing bald trying to scratch up new ideas in housekeeping and personal hygiene—to tell people WHY they need more and quicker hot water [...] Last night I got drunk on some sherry. Even in that wild orgy my mind was still enchained by the hot water complex—and I sat down and reeled off the best lines written so far in my handling of the campaign. All of my poems in the future will attest this sterilising influence of HOT WATER![22]

Though Crane asserts here that writing ad copy puts his poetic efforts in "HOT WATER," in reality, the professional frustrations of these months coincided with one of his most important creative bursts: he completed his sequence "For the Marriage of Faustus and Helen" in January, the "Voyages" poems were now well under way, and his initial conception of *The Bridge* was first mentioned to Gorham Munson on February 6.[23] On January 14, excited by the energies he had started to channel, Crane wrote to Munson "The last three evenings! Have been wonderful for me! [...] A kind of ecstasy and power for WORK."[24] WORK in this instance meant poetry; he explained that his poem was "so packed with tangential slants [and] interwoven symbolisms" that he was "not sure whether it [would] be understood."[25] He was unable to see however (perhaps necessarily) that it was in this state of convulsive professional accord that he most successfully courted the muse.

Throughout this period, he relentlessly, prolifically traffics back and forth between irresolvable laboring impasses that leave him in professional limbo. Holding down a job and writing poetry seemed irreconcilable and yet his writing at this time exemplifies the ways in which they were necessarily intertwined. Indeed, his career-defining poem *The Bridge* emerged from precisely this moment of simultaneity; just two days after he sent the first draft of *The Bridge*, "Atlantis" to his friend Wilbur Underwood, he also sent examples of his advertising copy to Gorham Munson: "Thought you might like to see this stuff I wrote. Two

---

[21] Stanley Patno to John Baker, September 1962, Baker Papers.
[22] Hart Crane to William H. Wright, December 4, 1922, *Selected Letters*, 111.
[23] Hart Crane to Gorham Munson, February 6, 1923, *Selected Letters*, 123.
[24] Hart Crane to Gorham Munson, January 14, 1923, *Selected Letters*, 119.
[25] Hart Crane to Gorham Munson, January 14, 1923, *Selected Letters*, 118.

campaigns for the same company featuring two types of water heaters. It is so well illustrated and printed that it is really exemplary among direct advertising campaigns."[26] It is tempting to read these lines as the lament of the arch poet, dryly mocking the banality of the workaday world. But this letter is sincerely meant—an effort to recuperate the kind of work that he at some level knew was playing a foundational and animating role.

Crane's constant search for an exemplary, satisfying form of "WORK" did not correspond to any clear-cut conception of the impersonal poetic labor. Even as he contrived often generative professional compromises, he immediately flinched from them—getting bored with any routine, but also always thinking that he was falling short of some kind of optimal form of productivity. He tried out various fidgeting professional combinations but was never able to fully settle on an acceptable solution. This had the curious effect of imbuing his writing with the accreted and conflicting traits of the successive circumstances he negotiated for himself. As he shifted restlessly from position to position, his writing procedure began defining itself as an effort to paradoxically discard the latest effort and start afresh—all the while doggedly hanging on to the idea that had initiated the search in the first place. Started in 1923, *The Bridge* (by no means a particularly long "long poem") was eventually published in 1929. In the scores of drafts it took him to work up particular poems, such as "Atlantis" or "Cape Hattaras," he at once remained faithful to the initial synthesizing premise, but then industriously forced his successive efforts out of sight—searching for the final immaculate expression. It is unclear when he decided on the epigraph for *The Bridge* (possibly in late 1928), but it displays a curious, half-conscious prescience: "From going to and fro in the earth, | And from walking up and down in it—THE BOOK OF JOB." This is Satan's answer to God's question: "Whence comest thou?" To and fro, back and forth: little wonder that Crane wrote in terms of apocalyptic vortices and shaking suspension bridges; shadowing the symbology that characterizes the New York poetry of 1923 and 1924 is the restlessness of a man who continually dissolved the terrain upon which he wrote.

When he arrived back in the city in 1923, he was unemployed and spent weeks filling in applications and attending interviews whilst accepting the generosity of numerous friends and acquaintances: "J. Walter Thompson have had me on the string for three weeks, and a letter this morning tells me that within the next few days I must drag myself up there

---

[26] Hart Crane to Gorham Munson, February 8, 1923, Hart Crane Papers, *c.*1909–1937, Rare Book & Manuscript Library, Columbia University, New York City. Hereafter "Hart Crane Papers."

again for another interview with one more Thompson executive."[27] With
the help of Waldo Frank, he eventually secured a position at the firm's
head office on 244 Madison Avenue. Working at the biggest advertising
agency in the world transformed Crane's experience of the city: "I begin to
see N.Y. very much more intimately since I've been working. It makes
living here far more pleasant than ever before."[28] Up to that point, he had
always been an outsider in Manhattan, excluded from the daily patterns of
work; he now rode the subway to the office and socialized with artists and
poets who were also attempting to maintain variations on the divide
between work and writing.

It was not long however before the familiar impatience started setting
in. By October 1923, whilst at work on the 14th floor of the J. Walter
Thompson headquarters in midtown Manhattan, he wrote to Jean
Toomer on the reverse of a particular advertisement he was working on,
which extolled the virtues of "Naugahyde bags." The letterhead reads
"Editorial Department, J. Walter Thompson Company, New York."
Crane's letter begins: "The other side betrays my present whereabouts
and 'interests' (alas)."[29] The typed advertisement on the other side (his
own, rather comically uneven work) reads:[30]

> IF –
> you pry yourself loose from your fireside
> and step out into the big world on an average of
> two or three times a year—it doesn't make a great
> deal of difference what kind of a grip you carry.
>
> You may spend a week's salary on pig-skin and
> never live to regret it.
>
> BUT IF—
> you've got to have a bag that will
> stand the wear and tear of day in day out use—
> you'll want a Naugahyde.
>
> A Naugahyde bag wears longer than leather,
> stands harder treatment, and costs less. It is
> waterproof and dust-proof. It will not scratch as
> easily as leather, has no seams to come unstitched
> and is built with the best solid brass lock and
> catches made.

---

[27] Hart Crane to William Sommer, May 9, 1923, Weber Papers.
[28] Hart Crane to Grace Hart Crane, June 10, 1923, *Selected Letters*, 153.
[29] Hart Crane to Jean Toomer, October 2, 1923, *Selected Letters*, 165.
[30] It is likely to be Crane's copy because the date of the letter and the date of the copy
match—October 2, 1923. See Hart Crane to Grace Hart Crane, August 18, 1923, Weber
Papers.

It's good-looking not only on the first trip
out—but on the hundred and first. And a lot more
after that!

Railroad men, travelling men and sportsmen
everywhere are carrying Naugahyde bags today. If
your dealer cannot supply you, write direct to us.
Sizes and prices below.   (See Fig. 6.2)

The Naugahyde bag is the exemplary product for the dynamic, "day in day out" workingman. If you do not get out much, the advertisement claims, it does not really matter what kind of "grip" you carry around—the standard, parochial and expensive "pig-skin" will suit your (limited) needs. The substitution of "pig-skin" for leather is telling here—Crane's copy draws attention to hand-stitched leather as something slightly unpleasant and perishable: this is "skin," liable to come apart at the seams. By contrast, the cheaper, pristine Naugahyde bag is more durable—fitted (passive construction) with the "best solid brass lock and catches *made*".

At exactly this moment, he was also writing to his mother, informing her that his "work (poetry) was becoming known for its formal perfection and hard glowing polish." He allowed that "most of these qualities are due to a great deal of labor and patience on my part."[31] Not as ideologically averse to this seamless Naugahyde as you might expect—and always keen to accentuate his own work ethic—his poetry labored towards a synthetic seamlessness that radiated a paradoxical and feverish effort to conceal his own struggle. Looking over his drafts for particular poems, you can see this conflicted dynamic actually forming into the subject matter of particular poems. On October 2, 1923, whilst Crane worked on this ad copy, he was also in the process of drafting "Voyages II." The poem is widely regarded as one of Crane's finest achievements, an ecstatic address to his lover Emil Opffer. The following reading does not deny its power as a love poem, but rather provides a different account of how it achieves such intensity, and why its particular affective and imaginative range is inseparable from the complicitious and conflicted constitution of the work that Crane performs at this moment.[32] Crane's multiple drafts of the following stanza

---

[31] Hart Crane to Grace Hart Crane, November 16, 1924, *Selected Letters*, 198.

[32] This account of Crane's strategy of revision both extends and diverges a recent argument put forward by Hannah Sullivan in *The Work of Revision* (2013). Sullivan suggests that artistic perceptions of revision shifted in the modernist era towards their current associations with "good writing." In a nineteenth century guided by Romantic principles of artistic genius, revision was thought to blemish an organic and spontaneous act, whereas revision in the modernist era was increasingly practiced by writers anxious to justify their own "difficulty." Crane's revisions, I would suggest, are characterized by an entanglement with a self-confirming work-ethic dogma which strives towards the status of immaculate product, rather than "difficult" poem per se.

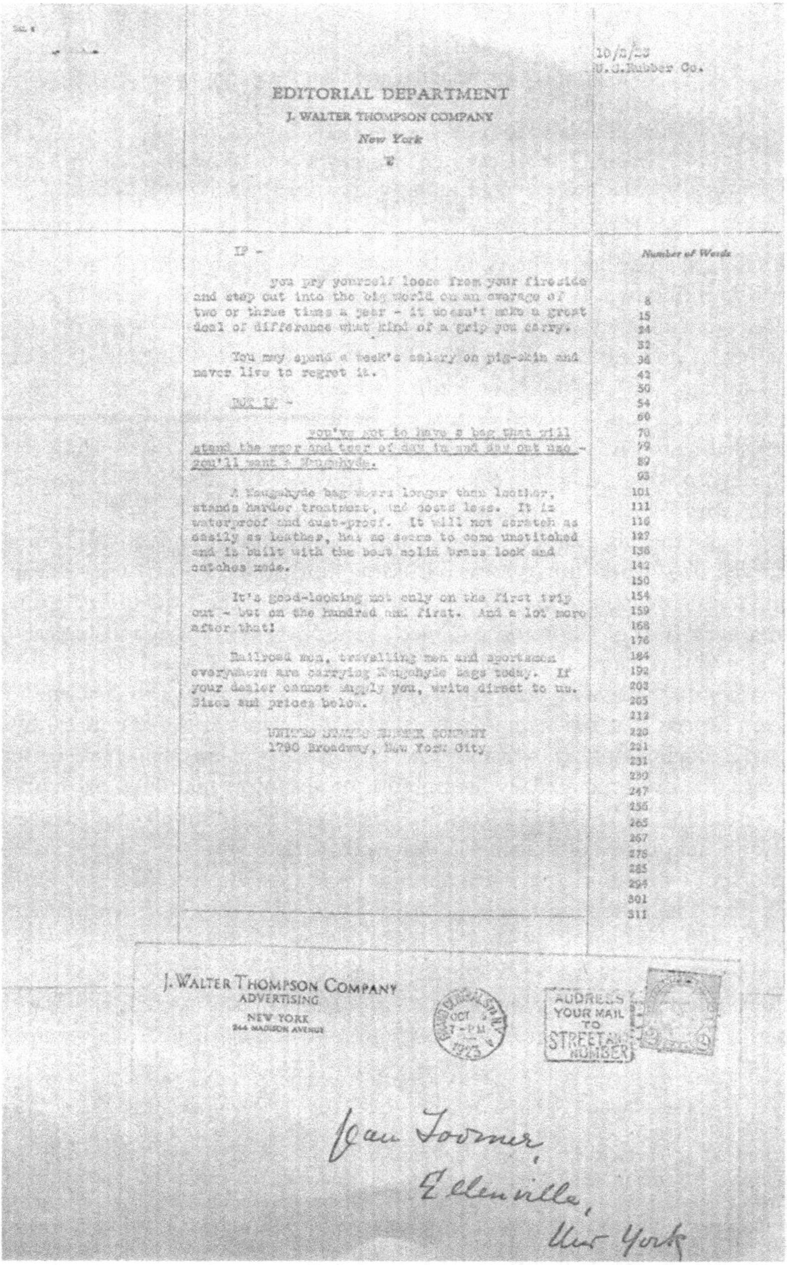

Fig. 6.2. Hart Crane's advertising copy on the back of a letter to Jean Toomer, Hart Crane Collection. Yale Collection of American Literature, Beinecke Rare Book & Manuscript Library.

relentlessly discarded and renewed every line—the following is just one verso side of countless attempts:

> vermiculate
> aureate
>
> Take this sea, then, veined and processioned,
> breathing the crocus lustres of the stars
> and set with silhouettes of sceptres roving
> —isle to isle—imaginary hands enlist us here.
>
> Take this sea, then; imaginary hands
>   enlist us . . . [-] circled by ~~their~~ scepters roving
>
> Take this sea, then: [for] imaginary hands
>   enlist us ~~circled by~~ [yet with] sceptres roving [wide]
>   ~~frondage of dark islands that breathe in~~
> the crocus lustres of the stars.
>
> [from inland frondages that breathe
> slowly the crocus lustres of the stars]
>
> [Take this sea, then; ~~for~~ imaginary hands
> enlist us, sea with sceptres roving wide
> from island frondages that breathe
>   slowly the crocus lustres of the stars]
>
> [enlist us ~~with~~ by what sceptres roving wide
> from isle to isle here churned to aureate breath
> already the crocus lustre of the stars]
>
> Take this sea, then. ~~Imaginary~~ [forboding] hands
> enlist us by what sceptres roving wide
> from isle to isle have <u>churned</u> to aureate breath
> already the crocus lustres of the stars.
>
>   [or, maybe, in the ~~T~~terror of its veins
>   ~~I find~~
>   ~~Aure~~ Entangled, ~~the~~ I find sessions][33]

As though caught in the endless feedback loop of a pushy sales pitch—"Take this"—Crane subsumes his concentrated labor within metaphoric churning water, increasingly obscured by oceanic currents that are themselves whipped up by the relentless effort to perfect the verse. Simply tracing the many reworkings of the verbs "breathe" and "churn" illustrates his feverish compositional process. First, Crane tries the participle "breathing the crocus lustres of the stars," before shifting to the transitive "frondage of dark islands that breathe in | the crocus lustres of the stars." He decides that the effect of this is too breathless and so qualifies

---

[33] Pencil markings are in square brackets—everything else is typed out by Crane. "Voyages II" (draft), Hart Crane Papers.

"breathe" with an adverb: "from inland frondages that breathe | slowly the crocus lustres of the stars." He then discards the verbal form "breathe" and churns it into a noun: "from isle to isle here churned to aureate breath." Still dissatisfied, he discards the adjective "aureate" and writes "what sceptres roving wide from isle to isle have churned to breath already the crocus lustres of the stars"—"to breath" now looks like the intransitive verb "to breathe", an ambiguity that bifurcates the referent of the adverb "already"—it now refers to "churned" but also looks as though it could qualify "breath". These workings are then all but discarded—in fact, "breath," "breathe," "churned," and "aureate" do not even make an appearance in the final draft of "Voyages II." Yet these versions provide us with a glimpse of the ways in which Crane searched for his sought-after veneer of perfection. "Churn" and "breathe" residually chime with later phrases in the poem such as "her *turning* shoulders" and "*Bequeath* us to no earthly shore." Half-submerged residues of the writing process—the flotsam and jetsam of discarded efforts—remain infused and scattered on the published poem's swirling surface: "sentence," "Scrolls," "en*list*." Tellingly, Crane does not know what to do with his "hands": they are transformed from "imaginary hands" to "forboding hands"—and in the final version to "lovers' hands." He eventually hands the poem over to the lovers whilst trying to keep his own labors well out of sight.

At the top of this draft, Crane writes "vermiculate/ aureate", which serves as an abbreviated self-reflexive commentary on his compositional procedure. Crane's drafts look vermiculated; they consume themselves until they take on an aureate or gilded sheen, as larvae clean a wound. The vermiculate writhings of an infestation—a hive of entangled meanings, allusions, and connotations—work to varnish this poem into its aureate state. The last equivocation of the draft—"Aure Entangled," the first syllable of which fittingly puns on pure-gold "ore" and transcendent "awe"—catches the poem in its attempt to knot itself into autonomy, ingesting its ties and transforming itself into a final immaculate form. This straining vermiculate text crushes together so many raw materials that it begins to swell, as though feeding on its own involutions. The penultimate stanza signals the beginnings of the final vortex:

> Mark how her turning shoulders wind the hours,
> And hasten while her penniless rich palms
> Pass superscription of bent foam and wave,—
> Hasten, while they are true,—sleep, death, desire,
> Close round one instant in one floating flower.   (*Complete*, 35)

The poem begins to twist in on itself as "her turning shoulders wind the hours." The speaker impels his lover to hasten while "her penniless rich palms | Pass superscription of bent foam and wave." The "superscription" or transcription of "bent foam and wave" onto the surface of the sea intensifies; her (the undine's) happily splashing "palms" (also palm trees) fan the ocean into a swirling undertow; the effort of hands—of churning palms—creates a current that drags the poem under. "Sleep, death, desire" inverts the sequence of sex; the passage of time upends as the poet spins the experience of love into a whirlpool of reordered time and space, revealing one last glimpse of the lovers just as they are sucked below: "Close round one instant in one floating flower." It is at this climactic moment that Leopold Bloom bobs up in the bath:

> He saw his trunk and limbs riprippled over and sustained, buoyed lightly upward, lemonyellow: his navel, bud of flesh: and saw the dark tangled curls of his bush floating, floating hair of the stream around the limp father of thousands, a languid floating flower.   (Joyce, 83)

Just as Crane started selling ad space for *The Little Review* in 1919, the magazine published the passage from *Ulysses* in which Leopold Bloom— also an advertising canvasser—attempts to strike a deal with the editor of the *Evening Telegraph*, Myles Crawford (Joyce, 49). Crane's tidal consummation throws up a dismembered allusion to this fictional colleague just before sucking him back into the maw:

> Bind us in time, O Seasons clear, and awe.
> O minstrel galleons of Carib fire,
> Bequeath us to no earthly shore until
> Is answered in the vortex of our grave
> The seal's wide spindrift gaze toward paradise.   (*Complete*, 35)

The lovers ask to remain in this ecstatic vortex of love, and request that the burning, singing rescue boat of tropical fire not bequeath them to an earthly shore. That is, "until | Is answered in the vortex of our grave, | The seal's wide spindrift gaze toward paradise." The last two lines articulate Crane's impossible bind: the more he gazes towards paradise and strains towards an aureate veneer of perfection, the more violently the poem drags itself under in a chaos of aquatic vermiculation. His work, incompatible with the synthetic finish it reaches out for, at once affirms and destroys itself—creating a semantic turmoil dispersed among symbolic oceanic gyrations that have been whipped up throughout the course of the production process.

Harold Bloom has memorably described the "Voyages" series in terms of a barely contained "impacted density" (*Anatomy*, 14); as though encapsulating a process of imminent internal rupture. One way,

I think, of fleshing out this suggestive formulation is to place it in dialogue with Adorno's conception of the modernist artwork as "absolute commodity." "Voyages II" maintains a state of suspension, which at once seems to approach—but then begins equivocating at—the threshold of Adorno's vision. In *Aesthetic Theory* (1970), Adorno presents his elegant defense of autonomous art, which, for him, offered the only form of resistance to the otherwise all-encompassing permutations of consumer capitalism. The poetry of Baudelaire he suggests—contra the various "sentimental" anti-capitalist stances of the "Romantics"—"neither railed against nor portrayed reification." Instead it syncopated *with* reification, thereby converging the characteristics of the absolute artwork with the characteristics of the absolute commodity. Adorno memorably defines reification as the capitalist commodity's tendency to "wipe out any human trace"; to conceal its own tangible relation, not only to human labor, but also to the specific way in which a particular commodity meets human needs (otherwise known as its "use value" [28]). In other words, Baudelaire's poetry (Adorno suggests) embodies, to the furthest extreme possible, the chief characteristic of the reified commodity: "exchange value." This matters because under the conditions of consumer capitalism, exchange value always forms an antagonistic relationship with a more socially orientated use value, threatening to disorientate the particularity of human use, and establish exchange as the ultimate, antisocial, value in and of itself.

As Marx makes clear though, the relationship between exchange and use values, though fundamentally at odds, can never be fully separated out. In order to be exchangeable, the commodity must retain, at however far a remove, a utility for someone—a product always needs a market:

> In order to become a commodity, the product must be transferred to the other person, for whom it serves as a use-value, through the medium of exchange [. . .] nothing can be a value without being an object of utility. If the thing is useless, so is the labor contained in it; the labor does not count as labor, and therefore creates no value. (*Capital*, 131)

For Adorno, a poem by Baudelaire becomes the abstract exemplar, or "cipher", of a pure exchange value that is completely detached from any necessary or identifiable use value ("a useless thing"). The poem thereby repeatedly invites continually frustrated questions regarding its own utility and meaning. As an absolutely reified commodity, it circulates without ever being reducible to a decipherable human trace or tangible use. Paradoxically then, the absolute artwork achieves its autonomy from the marketplace by becoming an exemplary marketplace—transforming exchange value into a value that exists for its own sake. The poem consequently confronts the reader-consumer with something completely disorientating: the full force of exchange-value's ultimately alienating power of non-utility.

"Voyages II" formalizes a process of poetic production that reaches vehemently towards Adorno's absolute commodity status but then also resists becoming something purely exchangeable. The poem hangs on to the last personal vestiges of use-value, as this value is subjected to the full force of exchange's violent impersonal disorientations. Rather than constituting a form of sentimental Romantic opposition (as Adorno would claim) to the processes that characterize capitalist production, the poem captures a freeze-frame representation of reification's violent transformation: "human traces" in the process of being warped and buckled into new forms and combinations under the dynamic force of exchange. Figured as a vortex, rather than the hurricane metaphor its Caribbean setting might suggest (a hurricane leaves a visible trail of destruction, whereas water soon reverts to surface calm), the poem glimpses a whirl of body parts, flowers, and allusions just as these new combinations are about to be sucked out of sight. No wonder that in his final stanza Crane fixates on the final lines of *Moby-Dick*. Fragments of the *Pequod* also toss among "awe," "vortex," and "spindrift": "And now, concentric circles seized the lone boat itself, and all its crew, and each floating *oar*, and every lancepole, and *spinning*, animate and inanimate, all round and round in one *vortex*, carried the smallest chip [. . .] out of sight" (499). The agitated nature of Crane's allusive text prevents the consummation of Melville's final "collapse," in which the "great shroud of the sea" rolls on "as it rolled five thousand years ago" (499). Refusing that reified timelessness of historical oblivion, the poem implies the hope embodied in the figure of Ishmael, holding out for something different amongst the wreckage. While Whitman's metaphors of adhesiveness and coagulation (explored in Part I of this book) focus on the imaginative possibilities inherent in provisionally arresting the process of commodification, Crane's poetry captures the imminence of the moment just before reification wipes out all human trace; just before the absolute commodity state renders the last personal vestiges of this deeply conflicted labor of love insensible.

*   *   *

After leaving J. Walter Thompson, Crane held a further two positions. During his two-week tenure at Pratt and Lindsay Co., he wrote a pamphlet on the merits of cheese (now unfortunately lost), after which he was made redundant because of over-staffing. He then found a position at Sweet's Catalogue Service, sharing an office with Malcolm Cowley from

April 1924 to June 1925. His former boss Stanley Patno was surprised to hear that Crane had started working at Sweet's: "I was quite amazed [...] If that isn't the nadir in creative writing I don't know what is."[34] Crane now had to write about industrial pipe-fittings, chimneys, and paint; Slater Brown remembered Crane helping to decorate his house one weekend in Pawling just after he had contributed a catalogue page on Dutch Boy White Lead Paint. Crane was full of mock-heroic praise for the product and brought several sample containers with him; Brown continues: "the house hadn't been painted for a generation at least and the boards and siding 'just drank the paint up'—a phrase which Hart and I repeated so often that my wife Sue Jenkins threatened to pack up and leave home if she heard either of us repeat the phrase more often than once an hour."[35] For a while, Crane treated his situation with good humour, no doubt measuring the contrast between his growing reputation as a poet and the need, on any given day, to praise paint. This relatively palatable compromise afforded Crane the opportunity to extend his "Voyages" suite to six poems, and work on his forthcoming collection *White Buildings*, a title that may well have occurred to him whilst painting Slater Brown's house.

By June 1925, Crane had once again refused his own relatively stable working arrangement. He quit Sweet's and faced all of the familiar instabilities and a consequent creative block. This time it was Allen Tate and Caroline Gordon who offered him a temporary refuge—an offer that coincided with the most improbable event in Crane's short and episodic life. Earlier that year, Crane had requested the patronage (speculatively at best) of one of the richest financiers in New York City. In June, he received a reply, and against all the odds, the millionaire Otto Kahn became Crane's patron in December 1925. All of a sudden, Crane was released from the predicament that—though personally burdensome—had helped forge his distinctive, experimental voice. The shock of Kahn's affirmation should not be underestimated; Crane, who had hustled and adapted to life strung out between Ohio and New York City, could at last dedicate all his time to poetry. The news was unexpected; Rainey refers to something that C. A. Crane was meant to have said when he found out Otto Kahn had given his son the grant: "I understand Harold (Hart) has a new Daddy" (6–7). After the news had sunk in and he had celebrated with his newly purchased African chief's costume, caviar, and a weeklong rampage in Manhattan, Crane turned to "Atlantis." What is sucked under in "Voyages II" now comes surging up out of the ocean:

---

[34] Stanley Patno to John Baker, date illegible, Baker Papers.
[35] Slater Brown to John Baker, September 9, 1963, Baker Papers.

Serenities, anathema to say,
O Bridge, synoptic foliate dome:
Always through blinding cables to our joy
—Of thy release, the square prime ecstasy.
Through the twined cable strands, upward
Veering with light, the flight of strings,
Kinetic choiring of white wings . . . ascends.[36]

Written between January and March 1926, in the excitement of just having been given a substantial amount of money, the drafts of "Atlantis" start deliriously rebounding. Crane speaks, "Of thy release, the square prime ecstasy," with "prime" playing on the language of Wall Street and its bullish "prime" market. Precariously conceived in one financial context, *The Bridge* now surges out and up into another. Kahn's money came with a price—it disturbed the precarious economic compromise upon which *The Bridge* and Crane's conflicted poetic labors had been founded. After the initial rush of "Atlantis" he wrote the dubious dedicatory poem "Ave Maria," which casts Kahn as Luis de San Angel to his questing Columbus: "O you who reigned my suit | Into the Queen's great heart that doubtful day,—I bring you back Cathay!"[37] In other words, his poetry lost its tightly wound provisional accord. This is the "The Mango Tree," written shortly after he decided to remove himself to the Caribbean Isle of Pines in 1926:

First-plucked before and since the Flood, old hypno-
tisms wrench the golden boughs. Leaves spatter dawn from
emerald cloud-sprockets. Fat final prophets with lean ban-
dits crouch: and dusk is close
                    under your noon,
                    you Sun-heap, whose
ripe apple-lanterns gush history, recondite lightnings, irised.
                                        (*Complete*, 115)

Now apparently protected from the arena that forged his early poetic achievements, Crane's writing is glutted with visual and auditory excess, from the "ripe apple-lanterns" that "gush history" to "leaves" that "spatter dawn from emerald cloud-sprockets." Compared to the modulating equivocations of his other fruit tree poem "Garden Abstract," "The Mango Tree" sags under its own verbosity and ripeness. The verse is unrestrained by the mediating context that had once been its sustaining force.

---

[36] "Atlantis" fragment, *c*.1926, Hart Crane Papers.
[37] See Miriam Fuchs's discussion of this relationship in "Poet and Patron: Hart Crane & Otto Kahn," *Book Forum: An International Transdisciplinary Quarterly* 6.1 (1982), 45–51.

Crane had gone to the Caribbean to work on *The Bridge*—and though he thought this geographic retreat would be productive—he initially struggled to write anything at all. As he complained to Wilbur Underwood: "I have not been able to write one line since I came here—the mind is completely befogged by the heat and besides there is a strange challenge and combat in the air—offered by 'Nature' so monstrously alive in the tropics which drains the psychic energies."[38] In this disorientated and pessimistic mood, the bridge now had "no more significance beyond an economical approach to shorter hours, quicker lunches, behaviourism and toothpicks."[39] *The Bridge* was suddenly drained of its symbolic potential; Crane now proclaimed that "Rimbaud was the last great poet that our civilisation will see—he let off all the great cannon crackers in Valhalla's parapets."[40] Crane had assumed that by exempting himself from New York—by removing himself from the distractions and energies of the city—he would finally sit down to "work." But when confronted by the blank page (that exceptional, now unencumbered zone of creativity) he wrote nothing.

Just a few days after writing this letter, however, having articulated the familiar distinction between Rimbaud's heavenly parapets and his bridge of merely "economic" significance—between poetry and commerce—he suddenly found a voice: "I feel an absolute music in the air again, and some tremendous rondure floating somewhere—perhaps my little dedication ['To Brooklyn Bridge'] is going to swing me back to San Christobal again [...] that little prelude, by the way, I think to be almost the best thing I've ever written, something steady and uncompromising about it."[41] The poem begins:

> How many dawns, chill from his rippling rest
> The seagull's wings shall dip and pivot him,
> Shedding white rings of tumult, building high
> Over the chained bay waters Liberty—
>
> Then, with inviolate curve, forsake our eyes
> As apparitional as sails that cross
> Some page of figures to be filed away;
> —Till elevators drop us from our day   (*Complete*, 43)

---

[38] Hart Crane to Wilbur Underwood, July 1, 1926, *Selected Letters*, 260–1.
[39] Hart Crane to Waldo Frank, June 20, 1926, *Selected Letters*, 259.
[40] Hart Crane to Waldo Frank, June 20, 1926, *Selected Letters*, 259.
[41] Hart Crane to Waldo Frank, July 20, 1926, *Selected Letters*, 263–4.

Compare this passage to the view Crane had from his position as copywriter in 1923:

> I'm up on the fourteenth floor now with a wonderful view out over the Murray Hill section and the East river right off the edge of my desk[42]

It seems that Crane, at this moment of writer's block, had to send himself back to work to start writing again—not only back to work but back to the same office in which he had written the advertisement for Naugahyde bags. He thought back to the sails and sales of the East River that once seemed to distractedly cross the papers on his desk as he wrote copy. The office that had helped produce such powerful poetic gyrations in his verse of 1923 becomes the panoptic point of departure for his epic poem; he imaginatively delivers himself back into the predicament that so many assume imprisoned him.[43]

This says something about the scope and implications of Hart Crane's contribution; he generated something new by tirelessly shifting the terrain under his feet, refusing to accept the carefully structured lives of his contemporaries:

> O harp and altar, of the fury fused,
> (How could mere toil align thy choiring strings!)
> Terrific threshold of the prophet's pledge,
> Prayer of pariah, and the lover's cry,—   (*Complete*, 44)

Here the poet's "mere toil," half submerged within brackets, momentarily reveals itself: fury-fused with harp and altar. How could "mere toil" align the choiring strings of his bridge? By continually trying to make ends meet. Notice that the line seemingly disparaging "toil" is not punctuated by the expected question mark: Crane's passionate commitment was to the promise of somehow redeeming his own "mere toil." In the continual dislocations from such an ideal, he measured the discordant straining of a life that agitated at the interstices of apparently discrete labors. Crane's convulsive symbolic order registers the promise of a "not yet"—a non-vocational imaginary that refuses to desert the possibility of another, better

---

[42] Hart Crane to Grace Hart Crane, August 18, 1923, Weber Papers.
[43] Paul Giles has pointed out that this poem is full of money: "How many," "Till," "page of figures," "apparitional" (parity), "sails." See "Capitalism" and "Capitalism and the Underworld" in Paul Giles, *Hart Crane: The Contexts of "The Bridge"* (1986), 29–56. In Malcolm Cowley's words, he "borrows a little punch and confidence from American business". Quoted in Giles, *Contexts*, 30.

future. His poetry is important because it inscribes at every turn the failure to carry out the injunctions of his contemporary cultural milieu, marking a convulsive threshold of resistance towards the latest instantiation of exceptional poetic calling. His shaking suspension bridges, all-consuming vortices, "whirling pillars, and lithe pediments" are simply traces of so many other possibilities for commitment and becoming.

Coda

Why I am not Talking about Frank O'Hara

Viewed from the performance-driven vantage-point of contemporary neo-liberal capitalism, the preoccupied labors examined throughout this book may seem particularly vulnerable to being incorporated by an increasingly pervasive ethos of efficiency and productivity.[1] Former Microsoft consultant Linda Stone's idea of "continuous partial attention" (CPA) is one of the recent affirmations of a partially distracted state of mind that might "optimize functionality": "we pay continuous partial attention in an effort NOT TO MISS ANYTHING. It is an always-on, anywhere, anytime, anyplace behavior that involves an artificial sense of constant crisis" (np). Paraphrasing Benjamin, Jonathan Crary has suggested that the history of late modernity or postmodernity has been characterized by anxieties surrounding the politics of attention: attention is both "a means by which an individual observer can transcend [...] subjective limitations" and "at the same time a means by which a perceiver becomes open to control and annexation by external agencies" (4). In other words, while vacillations between attention and distraction may still facilitate (in Benjamin's sense) various potential forms of subversion, distraction itself is now commonly aligned with disciplinary conceptions of the increasingly flexible liberal subject who is continually "called to consciousness, intentionality, and effective will" (Berlant, 779). Though it is well known that poet Frank O'Hara held down a day job, I didn't talk about his time at the Museum of Modern Art in New York precisely because I see his particular form of preoccupation as aligning more closely with current discourses of corporatized productivity than with the work of the other, historically resistant figures in this book.

The international division of the museum hired O'Hara fresh out of grad school, initially employing him on a temporary basis in January

---

[1] For a discussion of "overload" in relation to twentieth-century poetry, see Paul Stephens' *The Poetics of Information Overload: From Gertrude Stein to Conceptual Writing* (2015), 1–4.

of 1955 to help out on an exhibition they were organizing called "From David to Toulouse-Lautrec: French Masterpieces from American Collections" (Gooch, 257). O'Hara's ample abilities were rewarded in early April of that same year with a more permanent position as "Administrative Assistant" on the International Programme. He would go on to become a curator. MOMA employed O'Hara to be the glittering, erudite, anecdote-laden persona that is so recognizable in his verse. His career traded on an early form of Stone's CPA—attending parties, courting prospective artists and patrons, interviewing painters, writing brochures for exhibitions, traveling the world, and writing poetry during his lunch break. Even when "off" he was "on".

His archives at MOMA reveal how he functioned as a culture industry insider whose status as poet endeared him to patrons and artists alike. So, for example, one of his tasks was to persuade private owners to lend their works out to the various exhibitions he helped organize. While negotiating the loans of a Mark Rothko and Clyfford Still in 1958, O'Hara circulated a memo stating that of the five loans the museum was preparing to receive from collector and patron Ben Heller, "two must be unstretched to get them out of the apt at 280 Riverside Drive." "The Still" had "very thick pigment on its surface and Mr. Heller has requested that someone from the Museum be there to supervise the workmen when they are unstretch-ing and rolling it."[2] O'Hara became intimately acquainted with the paintings he helped display, knowing their addresses, their owners, how to care for them, and how to transport them.

If O'Hara was busily tuned in to the day-to-day details of the art world, he must also have been at least half-aware of the broader political implications of what he was doing. At the height of the Cold War, the American government was investing heavily in cultural propaganda, and O'Hara—who was later sent to Spain, France, Austria and Germany—soon became one of the international faces of American erudition. Russell Lynes, in her history of MOMA, claims that the International Programme was overtly designed to "let it be known, especially in Europe, that America was not the cultural backwater that the Russians were trying to demonstrate that it was" (384). At the head of the operation was the formidable Porter McCray, who has been described by historian Eva Cockcroft as "a particularly powerful and effective man in the history of cultural imperialism":

> both the CIA's undercover aid operations and MOMA's international
> programmes were similar and, in fact, mutually supportive. As director of

---

[2] Frank O'Hara Papers, 14b, The Museum of Modern Art Archives, New York.

MOMA's international activities throughout the 1950s, Porter A. McCray in effect carried out governmental functions. (Cockroft, 39)

The works of the abstract expressionists—particularly of Gorky, Hartigan, de Kooning, Kline, Motherwell, Pollock, and Rothko—were being exhibited around the world to demonstrate the "freedom of expression" offered to artists in an "open and free society" (Cockcroft, 40). McCray, as well as admiring O'Hara's social grace, organizational ability, and creative flair, also recognized in his writerly reputation an opportunity to get closer to the artists he was promoting. O'Hara was on intimate terms with the people who were worth knowing; he was McCray's man on the inside. Bill Berkson, somewhat tersely, has said that O'Hara acted as a conduit between corporate MOMA and the downtown artists; he eased the dialogue between painters, who were often suspicious of MOMA's motivations in promoting their work, and the museum's management.[3]

O'Hara's verse was, in part, a remit of his job; it garnered respect from the individuals the museum was attempting to court. Hazel Smith suggests that "O'Hara's poetry emerges from the intersection of the uptown and downtown milieu, and both participates in, and maintains some distance from, each" (Smith, 25). He was employed by McCray to be exactly who he was; if he wrote poetry during his lunch hour, then all the better as this reinforced his reputation as a brilliantly flexible, multi-talented dilettante. "Nerves" always "humming," O'Hara had to be everywhere at once and have every angle covered (*CP*, 210).

Figure C.1 shows a typical page from his work papers. The doodle, jotted down during a spare moment in the middle of work-related notes, is a representation of CPA or productive distractedness. What's particularly interesting about this page is that this apparently absent-minded doodle has become paradoxically and self-consciously aware of its own state of distraction. One eye stares back and out at us, and the other on some information regarding Franz Klein.

There is, I want to suggest, a qualitative difference here between this self-representation and the states of receptive distraction explored in this book. Whereas the formal innovations of a Whitman constitute a residuum of half-conscious preoccupation, O'Hara transforms such diversion into an endorsed-by-the-employer art of attentiveness. His labor is marked by a sanctioned, self-aware genial promiscuity. His poems are casually typed out during work breaks or at parties, and, yet, in this apparently side-tracked state, there is something distinctly premeditated.

---

[3] Bill Berkson speaking at MOMA on "Modern Poets: Frank O'Hara", November 30, 2006, http://www.moma.org/audio_file/audio_file/118/ModernPoets_113006.mp3.

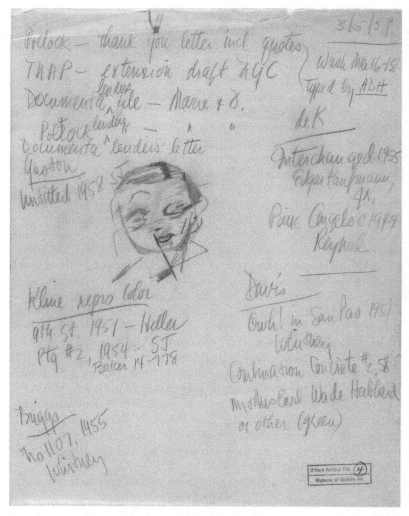

Fig. C.1. Worksheet and self-portrait. Frank O'Hara Papers, 4. The Museum of Modern Art Archives, New York. O'Hara, Frank (1926–1966): One page of handwritten notes on the (1)(A) exhibition "Documenta II" including a self portrait, n.d.. New York, Museum of Modern Art (MoMA). Pencil on paper, 11 8 3/8" (27.9 21.3 cm). Frank O'Hara Papers, 4. The Museum of Modern Art Archives, New York. Inv.: ARCH.1622. © 2018. Digital image, The Museum of Modern Art, New York/Scala, Florence.

O'Hara's job was to be distracted, a mandate evident in how his poetic voice manages to be so secure in its fleeting cleverness.

Unlike his distracted precursors, whose extra-literary labors were often incorporated into their poetic productions unconsciously, O'Hara's poems explicitly play with his office context. In a note included in the *Collected Poems*, Bill Berkson picks out a specific series, which he calls the "F.Y.I. works," a group of poems that had to do "with what [his and O'Hara's] lives in New York were like at the time (1960–61)." Berkson explains that "F.Y.I." comes from the typical heading for office memorandums—"For Your Information" (*CP*, 551). It was also the title of a gossip magazine circulated by the employees of *Newsweek*, a publication that Berkson had worked at a couple of years earlier. Both men were eagerly engaged with their work at the time, and the F.Y.I. poems were "supposed to form 'The Collected Memorandums of Angelicus & Fidelio Fobb'—2 brothers (Frank was Angelicus, [Berkson] was Fidelio) who wrote poems, letters, postcards (all memorandums) to each other." The speakers of these poems enjoy the connective pace at which their minds operate, finely attuned to the disorientations of the cityscape. While eminently likable, these voices are ironically distanced, continually referring back to their own self-awareness and behind-closed-doors knowledge. Instead of a Benjaminian reception in distraction, O'Hara's work displays a postmodern self-consciousness that collapses the distinction between attention and distraction altogether—transforming distraction into a marketable commodity in and of itself. Nothing slips past his notice, and he notices when it does.

Whitman and Crane (and perhaps to a lesser extent Melville) often missed things: they were thankfully denied the chance of ever becoming (mere) commentators or observers. They invert (and in Melville's case challenge) the idea that a poet requires a vocationally secure space or frame of mind in which to "create." The immediacy and simultaneity of their intersecting labors subsumed the very possibility of the poet's repose, and aided in diverting them from indulging in introspective platitudes. It was while muddling conventional divisions of labor that their poetry approximated something akin to the living sensuous activity Marx associates with redemptive, non-capitalist becoming. It turns out that it was their disrupted and disruptive working lives that aided in figuring the world as always susceptible to historical transformation—no matter how "realistic" the contemporary political and economic horizon might have seemed.

In this book, I have provided an account of the coeval labors of Whitman, Melville, and Crane to show how each refuses the terminal creative garret of exceptional vocational thinking. Instead of excluding other forms of supposedly lesser work, these quotidian labors were an integral part of their poetic contributions. Offering an alternative account of these often all too familiar careers, I hope to have provided a fundamental challenge to their status as vocational icons—offering up a rejoinder to the ways in which poets and their poetry continue to be conscripted into justifying the increasingly threadbare vocational promises offered up by contemporary capitalism.

One final note. Anyone currently working in the academy will, I think, recognize the further implicit correspondence this book has been more or less consistently gesturing towards. In invoking the specter of "contingent" labor in relation to the largely receding promises of vocation, I have been implying a historical analogy and a (perhaps sometimes unhelpful) slippage between the current dilemma faced by numerous members of the academic precariat and the careers of the poets under discussion. Most academic laborers are now familiar with the current trend: increasingly market-oriented institutions of Higher Education depend on attracting ever more graduate students to fulfill their unsustainable growth projections. Meanwhile, tenure-track positions available to degree-holders become ever more scarce as universities increasingly exploit contingent and zero-hour workers to secure their bottom line. And then there is the ongoing and seemingly steadfast allegiance to the academic calling—a remarkably durable allegiance that seems to encourage a wide-scale acceptance of these deteriorating conditions. Instead of wages, many are simply paid in vocational promissory notes. Even for those who are lucky enough to "win" the crap shoot of the academic job market, the academic calling continues to be wielded as an insidious immaterial compensation that justifies the supposedly necessary increase to workloads, cuts to benefits, and real-terms decreases to wages. At the current rate of erosion, many frankly do not know what their jobs will look like in eighteen months from now. As the old "rite of passage" narrative turns into a perverse hazing ritual without end for so many graduate students and temporary faculty, perhaps the time has come to begin questioning the complicities involved in maintaining this broken situation. An initial step might be to recognize that the vocational doctrines that once undergirded the academy have now largely been eroded. And instead of reacting to the sustained upward pressure of the job market by once again reaffirming the traditional sanctities of the exceptional academic career path, perhaps we should dare to imagine what the labor of thinking and writing might look like when it is no longer secured by the familiar promises; when there is no longer an exceptional vocational path to cling to.

Bibliography

Adorno, Theodor W. *Aesthetic Theory*. London: Bloomsbury, 2013.

Allen, Jane. "Population", in *The Encyclopedia of New York City*, ed. Kenneth T. Jackson. New Haven, CT: New York Historical Society and Yale University Press, 1995.

Allen, Theodore W. *The Invention of the White Race*, Vol. 1: *Racial Oppression and Social Control*. London: Verso, 1994.

Anderson, Benedict. *Imagined Communities: Reflections on the Origin and Spread of Nationalism*. London: Verso, 2006.

Anderson, Margaret. "The Chicago Grand Opera Invades New York." *The Little Review* 4.10 (February 1918): 61–3.

Anderson, Margaret. "Judicial Opinion (Our Suppressed October Issue)." *The Little Review* 4.8 (December 1917): 46–9.

Anderson, Margaret. "Marguerite D'Alvarez." *The Little Review* 7.3 (Fall 1920): 74.

Anon. *Annual Report of the Metropolitan Board of Health of the State of New York*. New York: Appleton and Co., 1867.

Anon. "Compulsory Retirement." *New York Times*. 30 December 1881.

Anon. "Crane's Mary Garden Chocolates" advertisement. *The Little Review* 6.1 (May 1919).

Anon. "Fall of a Building." *Brooklyn Eagle*. November 24, 1851.

Anon. "Fall of Building and Loss of Life." *Brooklyn Eagle*. March 29, 1852.

Anon. "Fall of a Building – Serious Accident." *Brooklyn Eagle*. July 1, 1852.

Anon. "May Day In New York." *Harper's New Monthly Magazine* (May 1856).

Anon. "Our Sanitary Condition." *New York Times*. June 19, 1865.

Anon. *Report of the Council of Hygiene and Public Health of the Citizens' Association of New York upon the Sanitary Condition of the City*. New York: D. Appleton and Co., 1865.

Anon. "The Coddled Author.' *New-York Tribune*. (New York [NY]), December 3, 1922.

Anon. "The Moving Season." *Brooklyn Daily Eagle*. March 15, 1854.

Anon. "The Steinert Piano, Back Advertisements." *The Little Review* 9.1 (Autumn 1922).

Anon. "A Visit to Walt Whitman: He Recalls the Years When He Lived in Brooklyn [. . .] Leaving the Carpenter's Work to Turn Poet. What Might Have Been Had He Continued to Build Houses—Where 'Leaves of Grass' First Saw the Light." *Brooklyn Eagle*. July 11, 1886.

Appadurai, Arjun. *Modernity at Large: Cultural Dimensions of Globalization*. Minneapolis, MN: University of Minneapolis Press, 1996.

Arac, Jonathan. "The Politics of *The Scarlet Letter*" in Sacvan Bercovitch and Myra Jehlen (eds), *Ideology and Classic American Literature*. Cambridge: Cambridge University Press, 1986.

Attridge, Derek. *Poetic Rhythm: An Introduction*. Cambridge: Cambridge University Press, 1995.

Attridge, Derek. *The Rhythms of English Poetry*. London: Longman, 1982.

Barthes. Roland. *Mythologies*, trans. Annette Lavers. London: Vintage, 2009.

Belasco, Susan, Ed Folsom, and Kenneth M. Price (eds). *Leaves of Grass: The Sesquicentennial Essays*. Lincoln, NE: University of Nebraska Press, 2007.

Benjamin, Walter. "The Work of Art in the Age of Its Technical Reproducibility: Second Version" [1936] and "Theory of Distraction" [1936] in *Selected Writings*, Vol. 3, trans. Edmund Jephcott, Howard Eiland, and others, ed. Howard Eiland and Michael W. Jennings. Cambridge, MA: Belknap Press, 2002.

Bercovitch, Sacvan. *The Rites of Assent: Transformations in the Symbolic Construction of America*. New York: Routledge, 1993.

Berkson, Bill. Speech at MoMA on "Modern Poets: Frank O'Hara," November 30, 2006, http://www.moma.org/audio_file/audio_file/118/ModernPoets_1130 6.mp3.

Berlant, Lauren. "Slow Death (Sovereignty, Obesity, Lateral Agency)," *Critical Enquiry* 33.4 (2007): 754–80.

Bezanson, Walter E. "Historical and Critical Note" in Herman Melville, *Clarel: A Poem and Pilgrimage in the Holy Land*, ed. Harrison Hayford, Alma A. MacDougall, Hershel Parker, and G. Thomas Tanselle. Evanston, IL: Northwestern University Press, 1991: 505–637.

Blackmar, Elizabeth. *Manhattan for Rent 1785–1850*. Ithaca, NY: Cornell University Press, 1989.

Bloom, Harold. *The Anatomy of Influence: Literature as a Way of Life*. New Haven, CT: Yale University Press, 2011.

Bloom, Harold. *Herman Melville's Moby-Dick*. New York: Bloom's Literary Criticism, 2007.

Bourdieu, Pierre. *Distinction: A Social Critique of the Judgement of Taste*, trans. Richard Nice. Cambridge, MA: Harvard University Press, 1984.

Braga, Ruy. "Sob a sombre do precariado," in Ermínia Maricato et al., *Cidades rebeldes*, São Paulo (2013): 82.

Brodtkorb, Paul, Jr. "The Definitive *Billy Budd*: 'But Aren't It All Sham?'" *PMLA* 82 (December 1967): 600–12.

Brunner, Edward. *Splendid Failure: Hart Crane and the Making of The Bridge* Urbana, IL: University of Illinois Press, 1985.

Bryant, John. *Melville and Repose: The Rhetoric of Humor in the American Renaissance*. New York: Oxford University Press, 1993.

Bucke, Richard. *Walt Whitman*. New York: Wilson and McCormick, 1884.

Bunce, James E., and Richard P. Harmond. *Long Island as America: A Documentary History to 1896*. London: Kennikat Press, 1977.

Burrows, Edwin G., and Mike Wallace. *Gotham: A History of New York City to 1898*. New York: Oxford University Press, 1999.

Burroughs, John. *Notes on Walt Whitman as Poet and Person*. New York: American News, 1867.

Busch, Frederick. *The Night Inspector*. New York: Random House, 1999.

Carlyle, Thomas. "On History" [1830] in *Critical and Miscellaneous Essays*. London: Chapman and Hall, 1869: 345–59.

Casarino, Cesare. *Modernity at Sea: Melville, Marx, Conrad in Crisis*. London: Minneapolis, University of Minnesota Press, 2002.

Certeau, Michel de. *The Practice of Everyday Life*, trans. Steven Rendall. Berkeley, CA: University of California Press, 1988.

Charvat, William. *Literary Publishing in America* 1790–1850. Amherst, MA: University of Massachusetts Press, 1959.

Cockcroft, Eva. "Abstract Expressionism, Weapon of the Cold War," *Artforum* 15.10 (June 1974): 39–41.

Cohen, Daniel. *Homo Economicus: The (Lost) Prophet of Modern Times*. New York: John Wiley & Sons, 2014.

Cohen, Matt. "Martin Tupper, Walt Whitman, and the Early Reviews of *Leaves of Grass*." *Walt Whitman Quarterly Review* 16.1 (1998): 23–31.

Cohen, Matt. "'To reach the workman direct': Horace Traubel and the Work of the 1855 Edition of *Leaves of Grass*" in Susan Belasco, Ed Folsom, and Kenneth M. Price (eds), *Leaves of Grass: The Sesquicentennial Essays*. Lincoln, NE: University of Nebraska Press, 2007: 299–320.

Coviello, Peter. *Tomorrow's Parties: Sex and the Untimely in Nineteenth-Century America*. New York: New York University Press, 2013.

Cowen, Walker. *Melville's Marginalia in Two Volumes*. Vol. 1. New York: Garland Publishing, 1987.

Crane, Hart. *Complete Poems and Selected Letters*, ed. Langdon Hammer. New York: Library of America, 2006.

Crane, Hart. *Complete Poems of Hart Crane*, ed. Marc Simon, intr. Harold Bloom. New York: Liveright, 2001.

Crane, Hart. "Discussion: A Note on Minns." *The Little Review* 7.3 (Fall 1920): 60.

Crane, Hart. "Garden Abstract." *The Little Review* 7.3 (Fall 1920): 78.

Crane, Hart. "Joyce and Ethics." *The Little Review* 5.3 (July 1918): 65.

Crane, Hart. *Letters of Hart Crane and His Family*, ed. Thomas S.W. Lewis. New York: Columbia University Press, 1974.

Crane, Hart. *O My Land, My Friends: The Selected Letters of Hart Crane*, foreword by Paul Bowles, ed. Langdon Hammer and Brom Weber. New York: Four Walls Eight Windows, 1997.

Crary, Jonathan. *Suspensions of Perception: Attention, Spectacle, and Modern Culture*. Cambridge, MA: MIT Press, 2000.

Crawford, Robert. *The Modern Poet: Poetry, Academia, and Knowledge since the 1750s*. Oxford: Oxford University Press, 2001.

D'Appollonia, Ariane Chebe. *Frontiers of Fear: Immigration and Insecurity in the United States and Europe*. Ithaca, NY: Cornell University Press, 2012.

Douglass, Frederick. *Narrative of the Life of Frederick Douglass, an American Slave. Written by Himself*. Boston: Anti Slavery Office, 1849.

Delbanco, Andrew. *Melville: His World and Work*. London: Picador, 2005.

Deleuze, Gilles. "What is a Dispositif?" in *Michel Foucault, Philosopher*, trans. Timothy J Armstrong. London: Routledge, 1992.

Deleuze, Gilles, and Félix Guattari. *A Thousand Plateaus*, trans. and foreword by Brian Massumi. London: Continuum, 2004.

Dennis, Helen Bishop. "The Reader Critic: The Modest Woman." *The Little Review* 7.1 (May/June 1920): 73–4.

Dimock, Wai Chee. *Empire for Liberty: Melville and the Poetics of Individualism*. Princeton, NJ: Princeton University Press, 1977.

Douglas, Ann. *The Feminization of American Culture*. New York: Knopf, 1977.

Dowling, David. *Capital Letters: Authorship in the Antebellum Literary Market*. Iowa City, IA: University of Iowa Press, 2009.

Dublin, Thomas. *Transforming Woman's Work: New England Lives in the Industrial Revolution*. Ithaca, NY: Cornell University Press, 1995.

Eagleton, Terry. *Literary Theory: An Introduction*. London: Wiley, 2008.

Eaton, Dorman Bridgeman. *The "Spoils System" and Civil Service Reform in the Custom-House and Post-Office at New York*. Publication of the Civil Service Reform Association. New York: G.P. Putnam's Sons, 1881.

Eckel, Leslie. *Atlantic Citizens: Nineteenth-Century American Writers at Work in the World*. Edinburgh: Edinburgh University Press, 2013.

Edelman, Lee. *No Future: Queer Theory and the Death Drive*. Durham, NC: Duke University Press, 2004.

Edelman, Lee. *Transmemberment of Song: Hart Crane's Anatomies of Rhetoric and Desire*. Stanford, CA: Stanford University Press, 1987.

Eliot, T. S. *Selected Essays*. London: Faber & Faber, 1932.

Eliot, T. S. *The Letters of T. S. Eliot,*: Vol. 1: *1898–1922*. London: Faber & Faber, 2001.

Eliot, T. S. "Tradition and the Individual Talent" [1919] in *Points of View*. London: Faber & Faber, 1941.

Emerson, Ralph Waldo. *Nature and Selected Essays*, ed. Larzer Ziff. New York: Penguin, 2003.

Filreis, Alan. *Modernism from Right to Left: Wallace Stevens, the Thirties, & Literary Radicalism*. Cambridge: Cambridge University Press, 1994.

Filreis, Alan. *Wallace Stevens and the Actual World*. Princeton, NJ: Princeton University Press, 1991.

Fineman, Martha, and Terence Dougherty (eds), *Feminism Confronts Homo Economicus: Gender, Law, and Society*. Ithaca, NY: Cornell University Press, 2005.

Fisher, Clive. *Hart Crane: A Life*. New Haven, CT: Yale University Press, 2002.

Fisher, Mark. *Capitalist Realism: Is There No Alternative?* Ropley: O Books, 2008.

Folsom, Ed. "What We're Still Learning about the 1855 *Leaves of Grass* 150 Years Later," in Susan Belasco, Ed Folsom, and Kenneth M. Price (eds), *Leaves of Grass: The Sesquicentennial Essays*. Lincoln, NE: University of Nebraska Press, 2007.

Folsom, Ed. *Whitman Making Books/Books Making Whitman: A Catalog and Commentary*. Iowa City, IA: University of Iowa Obermann Center for Advanced Studies, 2005.

Foner, Eric. *Free Soil, Free Labor, Free Men: The Ideology of the Republican Party Before the Civil War*. New York: Oxford University Press, 1995.

Foss, Rachel. Qt. Alison Flood, "T.S. Eliot rejected Bloomsbury group's 'cursed fund' to work in bank." *Guardian*, September 2, 2009.

Frankenberg, Ruth. *White Women, Race Matters*. Minneapolis, MN: University of Minnesota Press, 1993.

Franco, James (dir.). *The Broken Tower*. RabbitBandini Productions, 2011.

Freedman, Audrey. "How the 1980's have Changed Industrial Relations." *Monthly Labor Review* (May 1988): 35–8.

Friedman, Susan Stanford. "Definitional Excursions: The Meanings of Modern/ Modernity/Modernism." *Modernism/Modernity* 8.3 (2001): 493–513.

Frost, Robert. *Collected Poems, Prose, and Plays*, ed. Richard Poirier and Mark Richardson. New York: Library of America, 1995.

Fuchs, Miriam. "Poet and Patron: Hart Crane & Otto Kahn," *Book Forum: An International Transdisciplinary Quarterly* 6.1 (1982): 45–51.

Gallup, Donald Clifford (ed.). *T. S. Eliot & Ezra Pound: Collaborators in Letters*. London: H. W. Wenning/C. A. Stonehill, 1970.

Garman, Bryan K. " 'Heroic Spiritual Grandfather': Whitman, Sexuality, and the American Left, 1890–1940." *American Quarterly* 52 (2000): 90–126.

Garner, Stanton. *The Civil War World of Herman Melville*. Kansas City, KS: University Press of Kansas, 1993.

Garner, Stanton. "Herman Melville and the Customs Service" in John Bryant and Robert Milder (eds), *Melville's Evermoving Dawn: Centennial Essays*. Kent, OH: Kent State University Press, 1997: 276–93.

Garner, Stanton. "Surviving the Gilded Age: Herman Melville in the Customs Service." *Essays in Arts and Sciences* 15 (1986): 1–13.

Genoways, Ted. " 'One Goodshaped and Wellhung Man': Accentuated Sexuality and the Uncertain Authorship of the Frontispiece to the 1855 Edition of *Leaves of Grass*", in Susan Belasco, Ed Folsom, and Kenneth M. Price (eds), *Leaves of Grass: The Sesquicentennial Essays*. Lincoln, NE: University of Nebraska Press, 2007.

Gibson-Graham, J. K. *The End of Capitalism (As We Know It): A Feminist Critique of Political Economy*. Minneapolis, MN: University of Minnesota Press, 2006.

Giles, Paul. *Hart Crane: The Contexts of "The Bridge"*. Cambridge: Cambridge University Press, 1986.

Gilroy, Paul. *The Black Atlantic: Modernity and Double Consciousness*. London: Verso, 1993.

Gooch, Brad. *City Poet: The Life and Times of Frank O'Hara*. New York: Alfred A. Knopf, 1993.

Graebner, William. *A History of Retirement: The Meaning and Function of An American Institution, 1885–1978*. New Haven, CT: Yale University Press, 1980.

Greenspan, Ezra, "Some Remarks on the Poetics of 'Participle-Loving Whitman' " in Ezra Greenspan (ed.), *The Cambridge Companion to Walt Whitman*. Cambridge: Cambridge University Press, 1995: 92–109.

Grossman, Mark. *Political Corruption in America: An Encyclopedia of Scandals, Power, and Greed*. Santa Barbara, CA: ABC-CLIO, 2003.

Hagar, Christopher, and Cody Marrs. "Against 1865: Reperiodizing the Nineteenth Century." *J19: The Journal of Nineteenth Century Americanists* 1.2 (2013): 259–84.

Halberstam, Judith. *The Queer Art of Failure*. Durham, NC: Duke University Press, 2011.

Hammer, Langdon. *Hart Crane and Allen Tate: Janus-Faced Modernism*. Princeton, NJ: Princeton University Press, 1993.

Harris, K. A. "The 'Labor Prophet?': Representations of Walt Whitman in the British Nineteenth-Century Socialist Press." *Walt Whitman Quarterly Review* 30 (2013): 115–37.

Hawthorne, Nathaniel. *The Centenary Edition of the Works of Nathaniel Hawthorne: The Letters, 1843–1853*, ed. William Charvat. Columbus, OH: Ohio State University Press, 1985.

Hawthorne, Nathaniel. *Life of Franklin Pierce*. Boston, MA: Ticknor, Reed and Fields, 1852.

Hawthorne, Nathaniel. *The Scarlet Letter*, ed. Brian Harding. Oxford: Oxford University Press, 1990.

Hawthorne, Nathaniel. *Tales and Sketches*. New York: Library of America, 1982.

Hayford, Harrison. "Unnecessary Duplicates: A Key to the Writing of *Moby-Dick*" in Faith Pullin (ed.), *New Perspectives on Melville*. Edinburgh: Edinburgh University Press, 1978: 128–61.

Heap, Jane. "A Letter." *The Little Review* 4.10 (February 1918): 63–5.

Hollander, John. *Vision and Resonance: Two Senses of Poetic Form*. New Haven, CT: Yale University Press, 1985.

Hollander, John. *The Work of Poetry*. New York: Columbia University Press, 1997.

Hulme, T. E. *The Collected Writings of T. E. Hulme*. Oxford: Clarendon Press, 1994.

Huxley, Aldous. *Letters of Aldous Huxley*, ed. Grover Smith. London: Chatto & Windus, 1969.

Huyssen, Andreas. *After the Great Divide: Modernism, Mass Culture, Postmodernism*. Bloomington, IN: Indiana University Press, 1986.

Jackson, Virginia. *Dickinson's Misery: A Theory of Lyric Reading*. Princeton, NJ: Princeton University Press, 2005.

James, Henry. *The Portable Henry James*, ed. John Auchard. London: Penguin, 2003.

Jameson, Fredric. *The Antinomies of Realism*. London: Verso, 2013.

Jameson, Fredric. "The Case for George Lukács". *Salmagundi* 13 (Summer 1970): 3–35.

Jameson, Fredric. *The Political Unconscious: Narrative as a Socially Symbolic Act*. London; New York: Oxford University Press, 2002.

Jamison, Anne. *Poetics en Passant: Redefining the Relationship between Victorian and Modern Poetry*. London: Palgrave, 2009.

Johnson, Barbara. "Melville's Fist: The Execution of *Billy Budd*." *Studies in Romanticism* 18 (Winter 1979): 567–99.

Jonik, Michael. *Herman Melville and the Politics of the Inhuman*. Cambridge: Cambridge University Press, 2018.

Josephson. Matthew. *Life Among the Surrealists: A Memoir*. New York: Holt, Rinehart & Winston, 1962.

Joyce, James. *Ulysses*. Paris: Shakespeare and Company, 1922.

Judson, E. Z. C. *The Mysteries and Miseries of New York: A Story of Real Life*. New York: Berford and Co., 1848.

Kaplan, Justin. *Walt Whitman: A Life*. New York: Simon and Schuster, 1980.

Kelley, Wyn. *Herman Melville, An Introduction*. Oxford: Blackwell, 2008.

Kelley, Wyn. *Melville's City: Literary and Urban Form in Nineteenth Century New York*. Cambridge: Cambridge University Press, 1996.

Kelley, Wyn. "Writ in Water: The Books of Melville's Moby-Dick" in Alfred Bendixen (ed.). *A Companion to the American Novel*. London: Wiley, 2014: 394–407.

Kenny, Vincent. *Herman Melville's Clarel: A Spiritual Autobiography*. Hamden, Connecticut: Archon Books, 1973.

Knapp, Joseph G. *Tortured Synthesis: The Meaning of Melville's Clarel*. New York: Philosophical Library, 1971.

Kovarik, Bill. *Revolutions in Communication: Media History from Gutenberg to the Digital Age*. New York: Bloomsbury Publishing USA, 2015.

Kracauer, Siegfried. "Kult der Zerstreuung: Über die Berliner Lichtspielhäuser" in *Das Ornament der Masse: Essays Mit einem Nachwort von Karsten Witte*. Berlin: Suhrkamp, 1963: 311–17.

Krasznahorkai, László, and Ornan Rotem. *The Manhattan Project*. London: Sylph Editions, 2017.

Kristeva, Julia. *Powers of Horror: An Essay on Abjection*, trans. Leon S. Roudiez. New York: Columbia University Press, 1982.

Latour, Bruno. *Reassembling the Social: An Introduction to Actor-Network Theory*. Oxford: Oxford University Press, 2005.

Lawrence, D. H. *Studies in Classic American Literature*. London: M Secker, 1924.

Lawson, Andrew. *Walt Whitman and The Class Struggle*. Iowa City, IA: University of Iowa Press, 2006.

Leiby, James. *Carroll Wright and Labor Reform: The Origin of Labor Statistics*. Cambridge, MA: Harvard University Press, 1960.

Leyda, Jay. *The Melville Log: A Documentary Life of Herman Melville, 1819–1891*, Vol. 2. New York: Harcourt, Brace, 1951.

Lindberg, Gary H. *The Confidence Man in American Literature*. New York: Oxford University Press, 1982.

Lippard, George. *New York: Its Upper Ten and Lower Million*. Cincinatti, OH: H. M. Rulinson, Queen City Publishing House, 1853.

Logan, William. "Hart Crane's Bridge to Nowhere: 'Review of *Hart Crane: Complete Poems and Selected Letters.*'" *New York Times*, January 28, 2007.

Longenbach, James. *Wallace Stevens, The Plain Sense of Things*. New York: Oxford University Press, 1991.

Lott, Eric. *Love and Theft: Blackface Minstrelsy and the American Working Class.* New York: Oxford University Press, 1993.

Luciano, Dana. and Ivy G. Wilson (eds). *Unsettled States: Nineteenth Century Literary Studies.* New York: New York University Press, 2014.

Lukács, György. "The Ideology of Modernism" in *The Lukács Reader*, ed. Arpad Kadarkay. Oxford: Blackwell, 1995.

Lynes, Russell. *Good Old Modern: An Intimate Portrait of the Museum of Modern Art.* New York: Atheneum, 1973.

Mariani, Paul. *The Broken Tower: A Life of Hart Crane.* New York: W. W. Norton, 1999.

Marrs, Cody. *Nineteenth-Century American Literature and the Long Civil War.* Cambridge: Cambridge University Press, 2015.

Marrs, Cody. "Introduction: Late Melvilles," *Leviathan: A Journal of Melville Studies* 18.3 (2016): 1–10.

Marx, Karl. *Economic and Philosophic Manuscripts of 1844*, trans. Martin Milligan. New York: Dover Publications, 2007.

Marx, Karl. *The German Ideology*, Part One, with selection from Parts Two and Three, together with Marx's "Introduction to a Critique of Political Economy". Edited and with Introduction by C. J. Arthur. New York: International Publishers, 1972.

Marx, Karl and Friedrich Engels. *Capital, A Critique of Political Economy*, Vol. 1. Introduction by Ernest Mandel, trans. Ben Fowkes. London: Penguin, 1976.

Matthiessen, F. O. *American Renaissance: Art and Expression in the Age of Emerson and Whitman.* London: Oxford University Press, 1941.

McGill, Meredith L. *American Literature and the Culture of Reprinting 1834–1853.* Philadelphia, PA: University of Pennsylvania Press, 2003.

McLaughlin, Joseph. *Writing the Urban Jungle: Reading Empire in London from Doyle to Eliot.* Charlottesville, VA: University of Virginia Press, 2000.

Melville, Herman. *Billy Budd, Sailor (An Inside Narrative).* Reading Text and Genetic Text. Edited from the Manuscript with Introduction and Notes by Harrison Hayford and Merton M. Sealts, Jr. Chicago: University of Chicago Press, 1962.

Melville, Herman. *Clarel: A Poem and Pilgrimage in the Holy Land.* Edited by Harrison Hayford, Alma A. MacDougall, Hershel Parker, and G. Thomas Tanselle. Evanston, IL: Northwestern University Press, 1991.

Melville, Herman. *The Confidence Man; his Masquerade*, ed. Harrison Hayford, G. Thomas Tanselle, and Hershel Parker. Evanston, IL: Northwestern University Press, 1984.

Melville, Herman. *Correspondence*, ed. Lynn Horth. Evanston, IL: Northwestern University Press, 1993.

Melville, Herman. *John Marr and Other Sailors with Some Sea-Pieces.* A facsimile edition edited by Douglas Robillard. Kent, OH: Kent State University Press, 2006.

Melville, Herman. *Journals*, ed. Howard C. Horsford with Lynn Horth. Evanston, IL: Northwestern University Press, 1989.

Melville, Herman. *Moby-Dick.* Longman Critical Edition. Edited by John Bryant and Haskell Springer. London: Pearson, 2007.

Melville, Herman. *Piazza Tales and Other Prose Pieces, 1839–1860,* ed. Harrison Hayford, Alma A. MacDougal, and G. Thomas Tanselle. Evanston, IL: Northwestern University Press, 1987.

Melville, Herman. *Published Poems: Battle-Pieces, John Marr, Timoleon,* ed. Hershel Parker, Robert C. Ryan, Harrison Hayford, G. Thomas Tanselle, and Alma A. MacDougall. Evanston, IL: Northwestern University Press, 2009.

Melville, Herman. *The Works of Herman Melville: Poems, Containing Battle-pieces, John Marr and Other Sailors, Timoleon, and Miscellaneous Poems.* New York: Russell & Russell, 1963.

Michaels, Walter Benn. *The Gold Standard and the Logic of Naturalism: American Literature at the Turn of the Century.* Berkeley, CA: University of California Press, 1987.

Michaels, Walter Benn. *Our America: Nativism, Modernism, and Pluralism.* Durham, NC: Duke University Press, 1995.

Milder, Robert. *Exiled Royalties: Melville and the Life We Imagine.* New York: Oxford University Press, 2006.

Miller, James E. *T. S. Eliot: The Making of an American Poet 1888–1922.* University Park, PA: Pennsylvania State University Press, 2005.

Miller, Matt. *Collage of Myself: Walt Whitman and the Making of "Leaves of Grass."* Lincoln, NE: University of Nebraska Press, 2010.

Miller, Matt. "The Cover of the First Edition of *Leaves of Grass*". *Walt Whitman Quarterly Review* 24 (Fall 2006): 85–97.

Monroe, Niall. *Hart Crane's Queer Modernist Aesthetic.* New York: Palgrave, 2015.

Moon, Michael. *Disseminating Whitman: Revision and Corporeality in* Leaves of Grass. Cambridge, MA: Harvard University Press, 1991.

Morris, Roy, Jr. *The Better Angel: Walt Whitman in the Civil War.* Oxford: Oxford University Press, 2000.

Morse, Dean. "The Peripheral Worker" [1969] in Kathleen Barker and Kathleen Christensen, *Contingent Work: American Employment Relations in Transition.* Ithaca, NY: Cornell University Press, 1998.

Muñoz, José Esteban. *Cruising Utopia: The Then and There of Queer Futurity.* New York: New York University Press, 2009.

Nelson, Dana. *National Manhood: Capitalist Citizenship and the Imagined Fraternity of White Men.* Durham, NC: Duke University Press, 1998.

Newcomb, John Timberman. *Would Poetry Disappear? American Verse and the Crisis of Modernity.* Cleveland, OH: Ohio State University Press, 2004.

O'Connor, William Douglas. "The Carpenter: A Christmas Story." *Putnam's Monthly Magazine* (January 1867): 55–90.

O'Connor, William Douglas. *The Good Gray Poet: A Vindication.* New York: Bunce and Huntington, 1866.

O'Hara, Frank. *The Collected Poems of Frank O'Hara,* ed. Donald Allen. Introduction by John Ashbery. Berkeley, CA: University of California Press, 1995.

Otter, Samuel. *Melville's Anatomies*. Berkeley, CA: University of California Press, 1999.

Otter, Samuel. "The American Renaissance and Us." *J19: The Journal of Nineteenth-Century Americanists* 3.2 (2015): 228–35.

Parker, Hershel. "Damned by Dollars: 'Moby-Dick' and the Price of Genius" in *Moby-Dick*. Edited by Hershel Parker and Harrison Hayford. New York: W.W. Norton and Company, 2002: 713–24.

Parker, Hershel. *Herman Melville: A Biography*, Vol. 1, *1819–1851*. Baltimore, MD: Johns Hopkins University Press, 1996.

Parker, Hershel. *Herman Melville: A Biography*, Vol. 2, *1851–1891*. Baltimore, MD: Johns Hopkins University Press, 2002.

Parker, Hershel. *Melville: The Making of the Poet*. Evanston, IL: Northwestern University Press, 2008.

Pascal, Richard. "'Dimes on the Eyes': Walt Whitman and the Pursuit of Wealth in America." *Nineteenth Century Literature* 44.2 (September 1989): 141–72.

Pease, Donald E. "Melville and Cultural Persuasion" in Sacvan Bercovitch and Myra Jehlen (eds). *Ideology and Classic American Literature*. Cambridge: Cambridge University Press, 1986.

Poirier, Richard. *The Renewal of Literature: Emersonian Reflections*. New York: Random House, 1987.

Pratt, Lloyd. *Archives of American Time: Literature and Modernity in the Nineteenth Century*. Philadelphia, PA: University of Pennsylvania Press, 2010.

Pratt, Lloyd. "Historical Totality and the African American Archive" in Dana Luciano and Ivy Wilson (eds), *Unsettled States: Nineteenth-Century American Literary Studies*. New York: New York University Press, 2014: 134–6.

Rainey, Lawrence. *Institutions of Modernism: Literary Elites and Public Culture*. New Haven, CT: Yale University Press, 1998.

Rancière, Jacques. *The Politics of Aesthetics: The Distribution of the Sensible*. Translated by Gabriel Rockhill. London: Bloomsbury, 2014.

Rancière, Jacques. *Proletarian Nights: The Workers' Dream in Nineteenth-Century France*, trans. John Drury. With an Introduction by Donald Reid. London: Verso, 2012.

Rancière, Jacques. *Staging the People: The Proletarian and his Double*. Translated by David Fernbach. London: Verso, 2011.

Reynolds, David S. *Walt Whitman's America: A Cultural Biography*. New York: Alfred A. Knopf, 1996.

Reynolds, Larry J. "Billy Budd and American Labour Unrest: The Case for Striking Back" in Donald Yannella (ed.), *New Essays on "Billy Budd."* Cambridge: Cambridge University Press, 2002.

Richards, I. A. "On TSE" in Allen Tate (ed.), *T.S. Eliot: The Man and His Work: Critical Evaluation by Twenty-six Distinguished Writers*. New York: Delacort Press, 1966.

Robertson, Michael. *Worshipping Walt: The Whitman Disciples*. Princeton, NJ: Princeton University Press, 2010.

Rodgers, Cleveland. "The Good Gray House Builder." *Walt Whitman Review* 5 (December 1959): 63–9.

Roediger, David R. *The Wages of Whiteness: Race and the Making of the American Working Class.* New York: Verso, 1999.

Ruben, Joseph Jay. *The Historic Whitman.* University Park, PA: Pennsylvania State University Press, 1973.

Ryan, Robert Charles. "*Weeds and Wildings Chiefly: With a Rose or Two by Herman Melville.* Reading Text and Genetic Text. Edited from the Manuscripts, with Introduction and Notes." Unpublished doctoral dissertation. Northwestern University, 1967.

Saxton, Alexander. *The Rise and Fall of the White Republic: Class Politics and Mass Culture in Nineteenth-Century America.* London: Verso, 2003.

Schmidgall, Gary. "1855: A Stop-Press Revision." *Walt Whitman Quarterly Review* 18 (Summer/Fall 2000): 74–6.

Shakespeare, William. *The Merchant of Venice* in *The Complete Works*, 2nd edn, ed. Stanley Wells, Gary Taylor, John Jowett, and William Montgomery. Oxford: Clarendon Press, 2005.

Shell, Marc. *Money, Language, and Thought: Literary and Philosophical Economies from the Medieval to the Modern Era.* Berkeley, CA: University of California Press, 1982.

Sidoti, Francesca. "Untangling the Narratives of Precarious Work: An Auto Ethnography." *Social Alternatives* 34.4 (2015): 43–9.

Simmel, George. "The Metropolis and Mental Life" in *On Individuality and Social Forms*, ed. Donald Levine, trans. Edward Shils. Chicago: University of Chicago Press, 1971: 324–39.

Singer, André. "Rebellion in Brazil: Social and Political Complexion of the June Events." *New Left Review* 85 (2014): 19–37.

Smith, Hazel. *Hyperscapes in the Poetry of Frank O'Hara: Difference/Homosexuality/Topography.* Liverpool: Liverpool University Press, 2000.

Smith, Matthew Hale. *Sunshine and Shadow in New York.* Hartford, CT: J. B. Burr and Company, 1868.

Snediker, Michael D. "Hart Crane's Smile." *Modernism/Modernity* 12.4 (2005): 629–58.

Spanos, William V. *The Exceptionalist State and the State of Exception: Herman Melville's "Billy Budd, Sailor."* Baltimore, MD: Johns Hopkins University Press, 2011.

Spanos, William V. *Herman Melville and the American Calling: The Fiction after Moby-Dick, 1851–1857.* New York: State University of New York Press, 2009.

Spann, Edward K. *The New Metropolis: New York City, 1840–1857.* New York: Columbia University Press, 1981.

Standing, Guy. *The Precariat: The New Dangerous Class.* London: Bloomsbury, 2011.

Stein, William Bysshe. *The Poetry of Melville's Late Years: Time, History, Myth, and Religion.* Albany, NY: State University of New York Press, 1970.

Stephens, Paul. *The Poetics of Information Overload: From Gertrude Stein to Conceptual Writing*. Minneapolis, MN: University of Minnesota Press, 2015.

Stevens, Wallace. *Letters of Wallace Stevens*, ed. Holly Stevens. Berkeley, CA: University of California Press, 1996.

Stevens, Wallace. "The Noble Rider and the Sound of Words" in *The Necessary Angel: Essays on Reality and the Imagination*. London: Vintage Books, 1951.

Stone, Linda. "Continuous Partial Attention," 2017. https://lindastone.net/qa/continuous%20partial-attention.

Sullivan. Hannah. *The Work of Revision*. Cambridge, MA: Harvard University Press, 2013.

Sutherland, Keston. "Marx in Jargon." *World Picture 1* (2008).

Tate, Allen. *T. S. Eliot: The Man and His Work: Critical Evaluation by Twenty-six Distinguished Writers*. New York: Delacort Press, 1966.

Terry, Richard Runciman. *The Way of the Ship: Sailors, Shanties, and Shantimen*. Tuscon, AZ: Fireship Press, 2009.

Thomas, M. Wynn. *The Lunar Light of Whitman's Poetry*. Cambridge, MA: Harvard University Press, 1987.

Thomas, M. Wynn. "Whitman and the Dreams of Labor" in *Walt Whitman: The Centennial Essays*. Edited by Ed Folsom. Iowa City, IA: University of Iowa Press, 1994: 133–52.

Thompson, E. P., *Poverty of Theory: or an Orrery of Errors*. London: Merlin Press, 1995.

Thompson, Graham. "'Through consumptive pallors of this blank, raggy life': Melville's Not Quite White Working Bodies," *Leviathan: A Journal of Melville Studies* 14.2 (2012): 25–43.

Thoreau, Henry David. *The Writings of Henry David Thoreau*, Vol. 11, ed. Franklin Benjamin Sanborn. Boston, MA: Houghton Mifflin and Co., 1894.

Trachtenberg, Alan. "Hart Crane's Legend" in *Hart Crane: A Collection of Critical Essays*. Englewood Cliffs, NJ: Prentice-Hall, 1982.

Trachtenberg, Alan. "The Politics of Labor and the Poet's Work: A Reading of 'A Song for Occupations'" in *Walt Whitman: The Centennial Essays*, ed. Ed Folsom. Iowa City, IA: University of Iowa Press, 1994: 120–32.

Trask, Michael. *Cruising Modernism: Class and Sexuality in American Literature and Social Thought*. Ithaca, NY: Cornell University Press, 2003.

Turner, Catherine. *Marketing Modernism between the Two World Wars*. Amherst, MA: University of Massachusetts Press, 2003.

Turpin, Zachary. "Introduction to Walt Whitman's *Life and Adventures of Jack Engle*." *Walt Whitman Quarterly Review* 34 (2017): 225–61.

Unterecker, John. *Voyager: A Life of Hart Crane*. Plymouth: Clarke, Doble & Brendon 1970.

Weber, Brom. *Hart Crane: A Biographical and Critical Study*. New York: The Bodley Press, 1948.

Weber, Brom. *The Letters of Hart Crane 1916–1932*. New York: Hermitage House, 1952.

Weber, Max. *The Protestant Ethic and the Spirit of Capitalism*, trans. Talcott Parsons, with an introduction by Anthony Giddens. London: Routledge, 2005.

Weeks, Kathi. *The Problem With Work: Feminism, Marxism, Antiwork Politics, and Postwork Imaginaries*. Durham, NC: Duke University Press, 2011.

Weinstein, Cindy. *The Literature of Labor and the Labors of Literature: Allegory in Nineteenth-Century American Fiction*. Cambridge: Cambridge University Press, 1995.

Wenke, John. "Melville's Indirection: *Billy Budd*, the Genetic Text, and 'The Deadly Space Between'" in Donald Yannella (ed.), *New Essays on "Billy Budd."* Cambridge: Cambridge University Press, 2002.

Whitman, Walt. *Complete Poetry and Collected Prose*, ed. Justin Kaplan. New York: Library of America, 1982.

Whitman, Walt. *The Correspondence*, Vol. V: *1890–1892*, ed. Edwin Haviland Miller. New York: New York University Press, 1969.

Whitman, Walt. *Notebooks and Unpublished Prose Manuscripts*, Vol. 1: *Family Notes and Autobiography, Brooklyn and New York*, ed. Edward F. Grier. New York: New York University Press, 1984.

Whitman, Walt. "How to Avoid Dangerous Fires." *Brooklyn Eagle*. October 10, 1845.

Whitman, Walt. *Leaves of Grass*. Brooklyn: 1855.

Whitman, Walt. *Leaves of Grass*. Brooklyn: Fowler and Wells, 1856.

Whitman, Walt. *Leaves of Grass*. Boston, MA: Thayer and Eldridge, 1860.

Whitman, Walt. *Leaves of Grass*. New York: 1867.

Whitman, Walt. *Leaves of Grass*. Philadelphia: David McKay, 1891.

Whitman, Walt. "Tear Down and Build Over Again." *The American Review: A Whig Journal of Politics, Literature, Art and Science* 2.5 (November 1845): 536–8.

Williams, Raymond "Base and Superstructure in Marxist Cultural Theory," *New Left Review* I/82 (November–December 1973): 4.

Wilson, Christopher P. *The Labor of Words: Literary Professionalism in the Progressive Era*. Atlanta, GA: University of Georgia Press, 2010.

Wimsatt, W. K., Jr, and M. C. Beardsley."The Intentional Fallacy," *The Sewanee Review* 54.3 (1946): 468–88.

Wineapple, Brenda. *Hawthorne: A Life*. London: Random House, 2004.

Winters, Yvor. "The Progress of Hart Crane" (1930) in *Hart Crane: A Collection of Critical Essays*. Englewood Cliffs, NJ: Prentice-Hall, 1982.

Winton, J. R. *Lloyds Bank 1918–1969*. Oxford: Oxford University Press, 1982.

Yingling, Thomas E. *Hart Crane and the Homosexual Text: New Threshold, New Anatomies*. Chicago: University of Chicago Press, 1990.

Yothers, Brian. *Melville's Mirrors: Literary Criticism and America's Most Elusive Author*. Rochester; NY: Camden House, 2011.

Yuval-Davis, Nira. "Intersectionality and Feminist Politics." *European Journal of Women's Studies* 13 (2006): 193–209.

Zuba, Jesse. *The First Book: Twentieth-Century Poetic Careers in America*. Princeton, NJ: Princeton University Press, 2015.

Index